THE BIBLE AND POPULAR CULTURE IN AMERICA

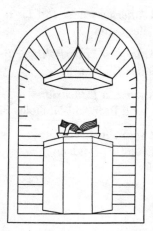

SOCIETY OF BIBLICAL LITERATURE

The Bible in American Culture

General Editors:

Edwin S. Gaustad
Professor of History
University of California, Riverside

Walter Harrelson
Distinguished Professor of Old Testament
Vanderbilt University

1. *The Bible and Bibles in America*
   Edited by Ernest S. Frerichs

2. *The Bible and Popular Culture in America*
   Edited by Allene S. Phy

3. *The Bible and American Arts and Letters*
   Edited by Giles Gunn

4. *The Bible in American Law, Politics, and Rhetoric*
   Edited by James T. Johnson

5. *The Bible in American Education*
   Edited by David Barr and Nicholas Piediscalzi

6. *The Bible and Social Reform*
   Edited by Ernest R. Sandeen

THE BIBLE AND POPULAR CULTURE
IN AMERICA

edited by

ALLENE STUART PHY

FORTRESS PRESS
Philadelphia, Pennsylvania

SCHOLARS PRESS
Chico, California

SOCIETY OF BIBLICAL LITERATURE

CENTENNIAL PUBLICATIONS

Editorial Board

Library of Congress Cataloging in Publication Data
Main entry under title:

The Bible and popular culture in America.

(The Bible in American culture ; 2) Centennial publications / Society of Biblical literature)
   Bibliography: p.
   Includes index.
   1. Bible—Influence. 2. United States—Popular Culture.
I. Phy, Allene Stuart. II. Series. III. Series: Centennial publications (Society of Biblical Literature)
BS538.7.B537 1984   261.1'0973   83-11548
ISBN 0-89130-640-4 (Scholars Press)
ISBN 0-8006-0735-X (Fortress Press)

K976K84   Printed in the United States of America   1–735

This book is dedicated to
the memory of Helen Stuart
Phy, to whom I owe my
love for the Bible.

A. S. P.

CONTENTS

Editor and Contributors ix

Preface to the Series xi

Preface to the Volume xiii

   I.   The Bible in American Popular Culture:
       An Overview and Introduction
       Allene Stuart Phy 1

  II.   The Bible and American Popular Humor
       G. Frank Burns 25

 III.   Retelling the Greatest Story Ever Told:
       Jesus in Popular Fiction
       Allene Stuart Phy 41

 IV.   Bible Country: The Good Book in Country Music
       Charles Wolfe 85

  V.   The Electronic Church
       Perry C. Cotham 103

 VI.   The Traveling Bible Salesman:
       The Good Buck from the Good Book
       Ralph W. Hyde 137

 VII.   The Bible as Literature for American Children
       Allene Stuart Phy 165

VIII.   Popular American Biblical Imagery:
       Sources and Manifestations
       Ljubica D. Popovich 193

Selected Bibliography 235

Index 239

Editor and Contributors

G. FRANK BURNS, a former journalist and editor of the *Lebanon Democrat*, is regarded as one of the South's master university teachers. For twenty years he has also been a writer of feature articles and a regular reviewer of books on all subjects for the Nashville *Tennessean*. To write his essay on humor and the Bible, he took time from his work on two books, a biography of a legendary Tennessee congressman, Joe E. Evans, and a study of the friendship and literary relationship between Allen Tate and T. S. Eliot. With his wife, Dr. Johnny Burns, he has done extensive research and writing in England as well as in the United States. He is a professor of English at Tennessee Technological University.

PERRY C. COTHAM is a former college professor of political science and communications and the author of numerous articles and reviews, which have appeared in a variety of religious journals and magazines. He has written two books on mass communication, politics, and American Christianity and has edited a volume on Christian social ethics. Dr. Cotham, who is in demand nationally as a speaker, is the only practicing member of the clergy among the contributors to this volume; he is currently pulpit minister of the historic Otter Creek Church of Christ in Nashville, Tennessee.

RALPH W. HYDE is a fiction writer, folklorist, and retired professor of English of Middle Tennessee State University. For many years, as editor of the *Tennessee Folklore Society Bulletin*, he extensively explored the rich lore of his region and its different (sometimes obscure) ethnic groups. Today Dr. Hyde devotes his time chiefly to free-lance writing and world travel.

ALLENE STUART PHY has taught in Africa and has worked as a Peace Corps consultant for programs in language and literature for Zaire, Kenya, and Liberia. For several years she taught courses in biblical heritage, comparative religion, world literature, and children's literature at George Peabody College. The author of many articles and translations, she has also been a staff book reviewer for a variety of academic and popular journals and newspapers. Currently Professor of English at Alabama State University, she is collaborating with Frederick B. Olsen on a book about religion in science fiction.

LJUBICA D. POPOVICH is one of the nation's leading authorities on early Christian and Byzantine art. She delivers papers at conferences throughout the world, teaches her specialty at Vanderbilt University, and is currently at work on a comprehensive study of the iconography of the Hebrew prophets. Her scholarly interests and topics of publication are many and varied, including Byzantine jewelry, the iconography of female saints, Ethiopian folk art, Tutankhamen, and now popular American religious illustration.

CHARLES WOLFE has been a pioneer in the academic study of popular culture and is known throughout the English-speaking world for his writings on country and western music. He is the author, coauthor, or editor of many acclaimed books published by both university presses and commercial houses, and his *Grand Ole Opry: Early Years, 1925–35* (London: Old Time Music Press, 1975) is regarded as definitive. Dr. Wolfe has served as Associate Producer for the Public Broadcasting System (PBS) television series "Southbound" and was Associate Producer for the Emmy-award-winning documentary *Uncle Dave Macon*. As a producer of folk and country music recordings, he was nominated for a Grammy award in 1981. Not only is Dr. Wolfe currently serving as Chief Consultant for the Time-Life Books Country and Western Classic record series, but he is also working on a comprehensive study of Gospel music. He is on the English faculty at Middle Tennessee State University.

Preface to the Series

To what extent are Americans a "people of the book"? To what degree is the history of their nation intermixt with the theology and story and imagery of the Bible? These and other questions are addressed in the several volumes of our series, The Bible in American Culture.

Initially conceived as part of the 1980 centennial celebration of the Society of Biblical Literature, this series explores the biblical influence—for good or ill—in the arts, music, literature, politics, law, education, ethnicity and many other facets of American civilization in general. It is the task of other series to examine biblical scholarship per se; these books, in contrast, search out the way in which the Bible permeates, subtly or powerfully, the very fabric of life within the United States.

The undersigned heartily commend the individual editors of each volume. They have persisted and pursued until all authors finally entered the fold. We also gladly acknowledge the wise counsel of Samuel Sandmel in an earlier stage of our planning, regretting only that he is not with us at the end.

Finally, we express our deep appreciation to the Lilly Endowment for its generous assistance in bringing this entire series to publication and wider dissemination.

EDWIN S. GAUSTAD
WALTER HARRELSON

Preface to the Volume

This volume, we hope, will contribute to an understanding of the ways Americans have used—and misused—the Bible. It is intended not as a comprehensive reference work but as a book to be read and enjoyed. A ludicrous discrepancy will sometimes be seen between the ancient wisdom of the scriptures and the vulgarities of American popular culture. Yet some genuine insights will also emerge; the American masses have sometimes discovered profound ways in which the holy books of the Jewish and Christian religions relate to their lives.

Among the contributors to this volume will be found scholars from several disciplines, representing a variety of religious persuasions from Eastern Orthodoxy and evangelical Christianity to agnosticism. These contributors do not and need not always agree among themselves; they include conservative Bible students, liberal interpreters of the Bible, and others for whom the Bible is a book of wisdom somewhat richer but roughly comparable to the Qur'an or the Tao Te Ching.

Despite their diverse origins and attitudes and the fact that most have lived and worked in many parts of the United States and abroad, the contributors have in common their current professional practice and residence in the southern United States. The southern Bible Belt, with Nashville, Tennessee, as its buckle, is the place from which much of the Bible-based popular culture emanates, reaching out to the rest of the country and the world through the mass media; therefore, it does not seem inappropriate to spotlight this region.

From the many possible topics for investigation in popular culture, we have chosen the biblical relationship to North American art, music, fiction, humor, the electronic church, children's literature, and Bible marketing. Little has previously been written on some of these topics, and academic consideration of them is still something of a novelty outside limited special-interest circles. The contributors have cast aside their professional jargons and the elaborate cross-referencing and documentation that makes so much professorial writing formidable in order to address the informed reader of a broader audience. We hope this reader will find these essays informative, enjoyable, and stimulating to further investigation and discussion.

ALLENE STUART PHY

I

The Bible and American Popular Culture:
An Overview and Introduction

Allene Stuart Phy

It is customary to speak of popular or "pop" culture as distinguished, sometimes too radically, from the high culture which transmits traditions of refinement and discrimination and the fast-dying folk cultures which in the past have arisen, half-consciously, from the masses. Popular art is generally not the self-expression of sensitive and gifted individuals who think of themselves as practicing a vocation. It differs from folk art in that it does not emerge from the people as an expression of universal experience and longing. The "pop" songs, advertisements and posters, motion pictures, television programs, and novels are, rather, beamed at the people by commercial purveyors who make it their business to supply entertainment and satisfy the emotional needs of the populace. Those who produce popular artifacts frequently obscure their own personalities and shun stylistic subtlety, stateliness of language, and complexity of thought. Popular culture at its worst is cliché-ridden and elicits stock responses. But at its best, popular culture can demonstrate interesting diversity, richness, and vitality. It always reveals, sometimes innocently, the preoccupations of the people who consume it.

Today it is in the American South that the Bible and American popular culture often seem to experience their closest union, and Nashville, Tennessee, has become a sort of Vatican of North American "pop" religion. Here one will find a high concentration of Gospel radio shows, denominational schools, Bible publishing houses, and a quantity of evangelists to rival Tulsa or Virginia Beach. Nashville is also the center of a popular music industry, long known for its pious platitudes, that now extends its influence throughout the land. Recent Gallup polls have confirmed that the South is the nation's most intensely religious region. The "Word" holds the supreme place of honor as more than an ancient book of wisdom, a spiritual guide, or even a manual of salvation. For millions of southern people the Bible is an account of origins, a history, and a record of God's continued wrestling with humanity, inerrant in its every jot and tittle. It provides all one wishes to know or needs to know about life in this world and in the world to come.

New York politicians, as everyone knows, must eat pizza, praise Israel, and wear green on St. Patrick's Day. Bible Belt politicians must quote the Bible, and it is better yet if they, like Frank (How Long, Oh Lord, How Long) Clement, a former governor of Tennessee, are Methodist Sunday school teachers or, like Alabama's Senator Jeremiah Denton, a Roman Catholic, conduct morality crusades.

The religious denominations of the South have established elementary schools, high schools, and colleges with a vengeance. A quick look at the mixed racial composition of some of these schools clearly reveals that they are not all mere "segregation academies." A major purpose of these institutions has been a shielding of the young of the region from the "ungodly, secular influences" abroad in the land. The metropolitan centers of the nation in the North and the West are often viewed with horror: New York, headquarters of the "Godless media," is Babylon, while San Francisco is Sodom.

Religious language even permeates what passes for secular culture in the area. On the Grand Ole Opry it is often difficult to separate the sacred selections from those dealing with home, mother, "that silver-haired Daddy of mine," battle in foreign lands and the exotic girlfriends found there, so filled are they all with Bible echoes. The blues songs of the black people have been replete with biblically phrased longings. "If I had wings like Norah's dove," wistfully croons the lady blues singer, "I'd fly across the river to the man I love."

The American South as "a land of the Book" has been compared to remote Islamic areas, where it is possible to travel truly "among the believers." According to the historian John B. Boles, the southern mind in its biblicism, derived largely from the great revival that swept the region in the 1790s, had already by the time of the Civil War become insular, imbued with a religious orthodoxy that "barricaded itself against change." Religious thinking became entrenched dogma, taking its toll on the lives of the two great races of people living in the South. Since foreign immigration was almost nonexistent in the area and for a long time urbanization and industrialization were slight, the South could ignore the insights of several generations of Jewish and Christian scholars, learned commentators, and all the "higher criticism" of the Bible. All too often, the status quo of society too was unfortunately reinforced by the institutional churches, which reigned as a dominant influence. Historians have repeatedly observed that, without any indigenous movement of critical thinking or the influx of ideas from either the North or Europe, the South entered the Civil War as one of the few remaining thoroughly religious societies in the Western world, comparable at the time to czarist Russia and that "priest-ridden province" of Quebec to the north.

Despite the evils of prewar slavery and the racism that continued to taint society long after hostilities ended, the pietism that resulted from the biblical literalism that dominated the South brought a measure of leveling in what was otherwise almost a caste society. There was little disagreement between the fundamental beliefs of the lower and the upper classes; though worship styles might have differed, blacks and whites alike accepted a conservative faith, a common orthodoxy that told them—whether they liked it or not—that they were brothers, and they both responded to basically the same pious formulas.

The religiously conservative South, which would be known as the Bible Belt after H. L. Mencken coined the phrase, moved into the twentieth century with changes coming only slowly and painfully. Even in public schools, until the increased vigilance of groups like the American Civil Liberties Union put an end to such practices, student arguments were often settled by appeals to the scriptures. In Kentucky in the early decades of the present century, elementary teachers were sometimes known to "save" as well as instruct their students. Many southern religious societies stressed an appeal to scripture alone, rejecting all pious traditions and postbiblical writings, which they referred to as "the creeds of men." Replacing formulated creeds were mottos such as "We speak where the Scriptures speak and are silent where the Scriptures are silent. We call Bible things by Bible names. We do Bible things in Bible ways." This attitude sometimes resulted in a stifling biblical literalism or even a "Pharisaic legalism," as well as considerable confusion. With each person, regardless of the level of understanding, knowledge, and insight, free to interpret the scriptures, the denominations flourishing in the South were subject to constant schism and yet were probably among the few fully democratic religious institutions in the world, where every man—and later on every woman—could be his or her own priest.

The regional distinctiveness of the South can be viewed in terms of its racial attitudes or its provincialism, but it is perhaps most fruitfully examined in the light of its religious conservatism, as John B. Boles and other scholars have observed. Along with problems, the Bible-based culture brought certain reassurances and benefits. People had a sense of identity and destiny. In a nation where today the name of Archie Bunker is recognized more readily than that of Jeremiah or Esther, college students from the South are still more likely than others to understand the many biblical allusions that are sprinkled throughout the secular literature of earlier ages. When they later visit Europe, the art work of the splendid cathedrals and galleries presents no arcane mysteries. No alienation is experienced in the presence of the greatest glories of Western civilization.

Entering the Bible Belt used to be as definable an experience as moving from one European country across the border into another. Ralph Hyde has fittingly observed:

> In the fall of 1979 I toured New England and returned to the South by way of Washington, Richmond, and the North Carolina coast, and at Elizabeth City, North Carolina, turned westward to my home in Tennessee. Washington is often referred to as a half-Southern city. Richmond has the aura of a Southern city, what with its history as capital of the Confederacy and its great statues of Confederate heroes in prominent view. But it was not until I left Elizabeth City and saw, a few miles out on Highway 17, a roadside sign with the words in great block letters "Try God" that I knew I was home./1/

The fundamentalist South used to show itself most characteristically in those old roadside signs, often situated on hairpin curves and at ominously narrow bridges: "Prepare to Meet God!" "The End Draweth Near!" and "Jesus Saves the Lost!" Mostly bypassed now by the interstates, which do not generally allow pious admonitions (though "Jesus Christ is King" recently turned up outside Montgomery, Alabama), these texts are still to be found on state highways and secondary roads, crudely lettered and fading, attesting that some zealous if unskilled text-painter once passed this way.

When H. L. Mencken scornfully referred to the particular style of religion that characterized the South as belonging to the "Bible Belt," he was probably thinking chiefly of the legacy of Scottish-Irish Calvinism. The piety he had in mind expressed itself in congregational churches by earnest praying, folk hymn singing, proselytizing, and above all by Bible study. Yet in the South the broader influence of this piety could be seen everywhere; even Episcopalians and Roman Catholics have been known to be touched by this contagion of Bible reading, scripture quoting, and hymn singing. Episcopalian clergymen frequently dared not refer to themselves as "Father," preferring to be called "Preacher." It was not unknown for Episcopalian congregations, after observing their stately liturgy and eucharistic feast, to adjourn to their parish hall to sing "What a Friend We Have in Jesus," "Amazing Grace," "Blessed Assurance," "In the Garden," and the other hymns loved by Protestants throughout the South. After the innovations of Vatican II, some of the more experimental Roman Catholic congregations started singing these hymns as well.

The air waves throughout the region are even today filled with the cadence of the evangelists, when these stations are not playing their staple program of Nashville country and western music, in which the sacred, as has been mentioned, is hardly distinguishable from the secular. On automobile radios up and down I–65 between Louisville and Mobile, the Nashville troubadour admonishes: "It takes more than Ivory soap to wash your sins away. Get down, Brother, on your knees and pray." European travelers have sometimes commented that south of the Mason-Dixon line the pace of modern secular activity slows as "Jesus starts saving."

Today television with all its gore as well as its piety has replaced the Bible as the central influence even in many southern homes. Yet far from disappearing in the latter half of the twentieth century, the Bible Belt, according to many native and foreign observers, has expanded and is no longer merely a regional phenomenon. In 1974 a Nashville journalist, John Egerton, published an interesting if impressionistic and inconclusive book, *The Americanization of Dixie*, subtitled *The Southernization of America*. His thesis was that homogenization is far advanced; there is accelerated cultural exchange between North and South, with gains and losses to both regions. With the great migrations from the South and the increased diffusion of southern music and folkways, the Bible Belt, generally thought of as defining the fundamentalistic South, has expanded to become the Bible Belt defining—some would say confining—the nation. Don Butler, executive director of the Gospel Music Association, confirms this observation, pointing out that Gospel singers, once limited to performing in rural southern circuits or the "hillbilly" enclaves of cities such as Detroit, now have national—even international—careers (Anderson and North: 12).

Though the expansion of southern attitudes has not made the entire nation students of the scriptures, southern ideas have permeated popular culture, and evangelical religion, often promoted in the media by southern evangelists, has in the last two decades gained at the expense of traditional "mainline" denominations, though there is now some indication this trend is slowly reversing. If the thesis of Egerton and others is correct, much of the rest of the country has been southernized by the black and white migrations, by the ghettos that both races have established in major cities, by the California exodus, by the spread of southern country and western music, by Billy Graham evangelism, and by the flowering within Protestantism of an evangelical emphasis that is actually an urbanization of the older Fundamentalism. The popularity of politicians like George Wallace and America's brief but significant romance with Jimmy Carter—who was initially viewed as a pious romantic, a Rousseauistic innocent, a saint discovered in a peanut field— can be understood.

All over the country many of the same Americans who watched Neil

Armstrong walk on the moon continue to express themselves in the language of Bible Belt religiosity, now as sometimes modified by Tulsa or
Virginia Beach. John B. Boles has perceptively observed:

> The rapid growth of cities and industry after the Second World War
> has brought surprisingly little accommodation on the part of religion.
> Skyscrapers have sprung up in Atlanta, Memphis, Houston, and Dal-
> las, and a sophisticated space-age industrial complex has developed
> along the Texas and Florida coasts, but still emotional, personal
> revivalism resounds from most pulpits. In "Space City, U.S.A.," as
> Houston calls itself, one can still hear ministers fighting the century-
> old battle against science and evolution. Population and technological
> change, John Ezell and Francis B. Simkins have noted, only aid old-
> time religion. The people comprising the booming urban populations
> are still basically rural people, and they prefer a rural religion. The
> concentration of people only makes larger crowds possible, and radio
> and television mean that the evangelical message can span the region
> every Sunday and any weeknight. (201)

The old-time religion, now frequently the prime-time religion, has
found innovative, if not always tasteful ways of communicating in the
age of technology. One form of self-expression to emerge in recent years
is the T-shirt message and the bumper-sticker exhortation, and evangelistic groups have made abundant use of these opportunities for further
proclaiming their message. A Sunday inspection of the parking lot of one
of the more enthusiastic churches will reveal an assortment of interesting
bumper stickers from "I found it" (parodied by an opposing group as "I
lost it"), "The Rapture, the Only Way to Fly," to the notorious "Honk if
you love Jesus." (The less reverent response, now also seen on the highways, is "Drive safely if you love Jesus; any stupid bastard can honk.")
Even such a dignified, if schismatic, group as the American Anglican
Church widely displays a bumper sticker that officially announces "The
1928 Prayer Book is Alive and Well in the American Anglican Church."

In every possible way Bible-loving Americans have tried to share
their good news. From the drive-in churches, established several decades
ago, to the television electronic churches, which reach millions in one
prime-time slot, the Gospel goes forth to people wherever they may be
found. The U.S. Postal Service is mobilized and Uncle Sam himself is
made an evangelist, with a constant stream of "personalized" letters
pouring out to persons on selected and often valuable mailing lists. Competition for followers and contributions is said to be very keen among
the leading media evangelists. Though members of the Jewish faith have
usually been more restrained, Jews for Jesus and cult competition have
forced some into the streets trying to retrieve Jewish youth with "mitzva
mobiles" and other forms of street ministry, evident in eastern cities. In

the revival of Jewish evangelism, it will be interesting to observe to what extent Jewish preachers will be tempted to adopt methods that Christians have found successful in reaching the masses./2/

When preachers borrow from the techniques of the comedians and talk-show hosts of secular television and compete with the superstars for ratings, they necessarily subject themselves to the same sort of critical scrutiny that Johnny Carson, Tom Snyder, Merv Griffin, Phil Donahue, and others must endure every day. They also become appropriate targets for witticisms in the Carson opening monologues, which they have learned so well to imitate. Guest comedians on "The Tonight Show," usually attired in the familiar bouffant wigs, have given painfully pointed imitations of celebrity evangelists, capturing the unmistakable cadence and body language. Johnny Carson has even proposed a restructuring of the Emmy award categories, with a new competition for "the best toupee worn by an evangelist on Sunday night television."

In answer to their critics, who feel that the vulgarities of Gospel television imitate too readily the gaudiness of Las Vegas, that this instant salvation—marketed like a McDonald's hamburger—is unworthy of the Christian Gospel message, the advocates of Gospel programs point out that mass communication is the key to the universal spread of the message. Christianity was born in "the fullness of time," they like to remind their critics, when the Roman roads and Greek language had opened channels of communication throughout the ancient world. Defenders see a parallel situation today. The First Advent came when the world was ready for communication and when social-political conditions made a universal religion possible, and defenders of television evangelism feel that in the same way the Bible promises the Second Advent when "the Gospel shall be preached to all lands." Only now, with satellite communications and the omnipresence of "the tube," is this becoming possible. Ben Armstrong, probably the most forceful advocate of television as the most efficient medium for spreading the Word, has even suggested that it may be through this means that "every eye will behold Him; every ear will hear," when Jesus comes again in glory, according to scriptural prediction! If this sounds like a scenario from a more imaginative science fiction novel, with Jesus appearing on prime time, Armstrong and his colleagues might well respond that they are our true moderns in their full acceptance of current technology as a means of spreading the age-old faith (167–68).

Television preachers have emerged from a number of different Christian persuasions, yet their appeal is largely nondenominational. Loyalty appears to be to the personality of the evangelist rather than to any religious society. "Did Rex Humbard die for you?" the critics ask the faithful. Jerry Falwell has a substantial Roman Catholic following, numbers of whom send him generous contributions, disillusioned and disheartened as some of them are by reforms within their own tradition brought about by Vatican II. Falwell also claims to have Jewish sympathizers who support his social programs and moral crusade, and he has been publicly honored by the Israeli government. As yet there has appeared no comparable figure advocating a media version of the Jewish faith to the entire nation, though "Hebrew Christians," those claiming to be "Completed Jews," can be frequently seen on television.

Each evangelist, whatever his denominational background or present affiliation, tends to promote his own style, often with an original gimmick, and builds what amounts to his own denomination. The flock become "The Falwell Ministry," or "The Copeland Ministry," or "The Bakker Ministry," and, despite their show of brotherhood, there is said to be great rivalry among the television superstar preachers.

The feminine presence in television evangelism is also significantly increasing. In the Christian Foundation of Tony and Susan Alamo, Mrs. Alamo, who is now deceased, was the preacher, while her husband, Tony, was generally relegated to second place as a sidekick or a hymn singer. Ruth Carter Stapleton was another highly publicized evangelist, chiefly because she was the sister of a U.S. president. Other women with regional followings hope to initiate national ministries within the next months or years. Kay Arthur of Chattanooga, Tennessee, has already started warning cable television audiences of international conspiracies that employ demonic numerology. The male evangelist is still almost always the star of the show and is often accompanied by a glamorous wife, who sings, testifies, or peddles the books, tapes, or other devotional aids sold by the ministry. An assortment of musicians and visiting celebrities complete the roster of the typical show.

Christian coffee houses provide more personal and immediate forums and entertainment arenas for the "baptized" show business acts. Christian clowns, following the biblical directive to become fools for Christ, perform over selected territories and hold national conventions. Comparable to the Association of Gospel Clowns of America (*Time*: 52–53) is the Fellowship of Christian Magicians, who use magic to emphasize Bible messages. The magicians organized twenty years ago in San Francisco to provide for the exchange of ideas on the use of magic for object lessons in Sunday schools and churches. In addition to performing, the organization presents workshops to assist others in learning Gospel through magic. Christian jugglers are also in demand, teaching Bible lessons with their art. One explains how she uses her juggling balls to illustrate a basic Bible message:

I use the blue ball to represent God. In fact, I start out just by showing them the blue ball, and then I introduce the red ball, which is
Jesus Christ. The color red reminds me of the Blood of Christ, and I
just juggle the two. Then the white ball is introduced, which is God's
Purity, the Holy Spirit. In the Bible there's the Trinity of God, and
you're juggling the three of them at this time: you're juggling the
three balls and you throw the blue one up higher and when you say
God the Father, it falls down. Then you throw the red one up and
say God the Son and you throw the white one up, it's sort of like an
exclamation mark it emphasizes what you're saying. (Whitman: 55)

Trucks, vans, and luxury buses carrying traveling Christian musical
acts, comedians, and evangelists, complete with their paraphernalia,
move across the land proudly proclaiming in lettering on the sides of the
conveyances "God is Love" and "For God So Loved the World That He
Gave His Only Begotten Son."

Some performers, such as Pat Boone (who had secular superstar
status in the late fifties and has since maintained a constant exposure in
various phases of show business), have been professing Christians from
the beginning and have waged constant and highly publicized struggles
to maintain a precarious marriage between Evangelical Christianity and
show business. There seems no reason to doubt Boone's commitment
when he speaks of his singing career and his Christian vocation, though
it is possible sometimes to be critical of his judgment and taste.

Boone, an industrious author as well as performer, acknowledges in
his book *A New Song* that the Bible is central to his thought; in fact, he
states that he believes in Jesus because the Bible witnesses to him, which
would appear to give the book priority over the man. Boone's career, in
following where he has felt the Bible directed, has been fraught with
painful conflicts. Boone was reared in a God-fearing family and initially
was educated at Bible-oriented schools, but understanding of the escha-
tological and charismatic teachings of the Bible led to his break with the
church of his youth. In recent years his interpretation of the Bible has
led to his espousal of an ardent political Zionism, and he, despite his
origins, appears now to regard himself as a Christian Jew. Though show
business comedians may refer to Boone as "Pat Bland," he is confident in
his show business ministry. With members of his immediate family, he
continues to provide what he regards as rare and much-needed family-
style entertainment. His books equate material success and high ratings
with God's blessing, and he is proud to be able to baptize sinners in his
luxurious Belle Aire swimming pool.

Through his many Hollywood tribulations, Boone has remained,
sometimes uneasily, a professing Christian as well as a popular entertainer. If in his personal life he did not go the pathetic way of Elvis

Presley, neither did he ever become the quasi divinity that Elvis was in the minds of his public by the end of his life. Elvis (who like Tallulah Bankhead became known the world over simply by his given name), also a southern boy, appears to have been deeply and sincerely religious, if at times muddled and misguided. According to former employees, he loved nothing more in his free moments than to gather together any musicians who happened to be hanging out at Graceland, his Memphis mansion, and sing Gospel songs around the piano. The Bible, first heard in Holiness churches and associated in his mind with his beloved mother, haunted his consciousness, even in those last drug-hounded days when the gaudy Las Vegas style seemed more evident than the piety of his native Mississippi or of Memphis. His paraphrase of the Sermon on the Mount, reported in *What Happened?* (West: 168–69), was ludicrous, pathetic, even curiously moving.

The names of the superstars of Gospel show business are well known. They range from immensely talented, truly great interpreters of sacred music such as George Beverly Shea and the late Mahalia Jackson, innovative composers such as André Crouch, and skilled pianists such as Dino Kartsonakis, who studied in France under Arthur Rubinstein, to performers who are less talented and can be embarrassingly vulgar, as they sometimes appear to peddle the Gospel along with their tapes and records. The Presleyesque gyrations of male Gospel singers and the honky-tonk mannerisms of their female counterparts do not greatly differ from the stage styles of other popular performers, even rock singers. Marjoe, the former child evangelist who later renounced his Gospel career in favor of an acting one, admitted patterning his pulpit performance after the frenetic stage movements of British rock star Mick Jagger. It has become increasingly difficult to distinguish the more blatantly commercial among Gospel performers from secular musicians; both have high fees, staffs of attendants, promotional personnel, managers, and record advertisements. They appear on the "PTL Club," the "700 Club," and elsewhere on the Gospel circuit, calling attention to their books and recordings. They perform on Oral Roberts television specials and Christmas travelogues from the Holy Land, in which they dance in sequined tuxedos to Gospel jigs. Answering their critics, they point out the thousands, possibly millions, of people they reach with their version of the Gospel. They further observe that the Bible teaches all to use their unique talents for the glory of the kingdom. These performers are simply bringing their diverse gifts to the altar, much like the medieval juggler of Our Lady, and, besides, what is wrong with combining entertainment with a Gospel message and even earning some money in the process?

Many, perhaps most, Gospel singers are fulfilling childhood ambitions in answer to prayers of Christian parents. But another recent, highly publicized phenomenon has been the conversion of superstars from non-Christian and secular backgrounds. Cynics, such as Gore Vidal, have suggested that a number of show business personalities past their prime have found lucrative second careers on the Gospel circuit. A more objective scrutiny of the careers of the most celebrated superstar converts suggests otherwise, that the convert may in fact be very sincere and may have made substantial financial sacrifice with his "born again" career reorientation.

Bob Dylan was perhaps the most famous example of the superstar convert, though he seems now to have returned to Jewish practice. Cynics suggested that Dylan's conversion to Christianity came at an opportune moment, when his former career as protest guru and minstrel of the counterculture was practically at an end. Yet those close to Dylan affirmed his conversion to be sincere, and reports indicated that the sale of his records considerably declined after he switched from castigating the "ministers of war" to affirming the love of Jesus. Dylan's family background was Jewish midwestern, and he was much a part of the youth movements of the sixties. By the early seventies his songs hinted that real changes were taking place in his thought and style. His lyrics had always revealed a keen social conscience, probably both the expression of an individual creative voice and a response to the demands of his sixties constituency, yet Dylan's perceptions deepened as he matured. Family problems too may have played a part in his spiritual crisis and subsequent conversion. Certainly his recordings started speaking in a new voice as he approached middle age, acquiring distinct Gospel affirmations. The early imagistic style was gone; he seemed no longer musically a disciple of Woody Guthrie. Dylan's weaknesses did not disappear; the monotony characteristic of folk-rock and his own repetitiveness were still evident in his work, but now the new lyrics and tunes, performed with his long-celebrated vitality, echoed southern Gospel and black soul. Dylan sang of being "Saved," of meeting a "Covenant Woman," of "Pressing On" and of gaining "Saving Grace." On recent discs he sings of a Second Coming, though how soon Dylan expects this to be is not revealed. "Do Right to Me Baby" is his version of "Do unto others as you would have them do unto you." "Men Gave Names to all the Animals" presents his interpretation of a part of the Genesis story, which might—in its simplicity and easily recalled lyrics, even in its whimsical twists—have been composed for Sunday school children. To use the language of Gospel promotion, "for Bob Dylan Solid Rock has now been replaced by the Rock of Ages."

The musical superstar himself, which Dylan certainly was at one time, has taken on biblical associations and Jungian dimensions in the public mind. If Jesus is thought of in counterculture art as a betrayed charismatic superstar done in by the Establishment, he also becomes the prototype of all the other sad performers, the Janis Joplins and the Elvises, hounded and destroyed by public adulation and envy. Indeed the pop entertainer has become the contemporary embodiment of the Jungian savior-hero, and it appears that this modern Orpheus is now sometimes even required to die for his fans. The macabre cult that emerged at the death of Elvis Presley illustrates the myth-making process going on in the public mind. Even during the last days of his life, Elvis could only travel by night, surrounded by his disciple-bodyguards, for fear of the adoring multitudes of his fans. Elvis's long-deceased mother came to be viewed by his admirers as a madonna figure, while Vernon Presley, the father who survived his son by a few years, in a memorial recording marketed shortly after Elvis's "dormition," was compared to God the Father, since each gave "his only begotten son" to the public. Icons of Elvis—in his last days a pathetic, bloated, half-blind demigod—materialized in every flea market and curio shop in the land. No sooner was Elvis in his grave than plans, foiled by the Memphis police, were afoot to steal his body from its tomb. Despite subsequent revelations of drug addiction and accusations of moral turpitude, the apotheosis of Elvis continues unabated.

Perhaps the strangest and most suspicious conversion to Christianity from the secular branch of media entertainment was that of Larry Flynt, publisher of *Hustler*, who under the influence of President Jimmy Carter's evangelistic sister, Ruth Carter Stapleton, says he was "born again." Flynt and his wife (Mrs. Flynt did not claim to have had the conversion experience) talked, almost unbelievably, of a journal, a revised *Hustler*, which they seemed to believe could combine pornographic titillation and "born-again" Christianity. Perhaps they envisioned a magazine designed to touch many bases, somewhat on the order of that old hypothetical super-best-selling book, *Lincoln's Doctor's Dog*. These plans were, however, hampered by an assassination attempt which disabled Flynt.

While so-called Christian pornography has not caught on, manuals of Christian sexuality definitely have. With the proliferation of evangelical bookstores and "born-again" books on almost every conceivable subject, some rather startling publications have appeared. If all scripture is given for edification, ingenious uses have certainly been found for previously neglected portions of the Bible. The Song of Solomon, generally a bewilderment to a literalistic age incapable of understanding allegorical or anagogical uses of any literature, has been rediscovered by Christian marriage couselors. There has to be some practical use for that book, the consensus seems to be! Though King Solomon, the traditionally designated author, is hardly a role model today for the Jewish or Christian monogamous husband, he was, the Bible declares, the wisest of men, and so his wisdom, recorded in sacred scripture, must still be of assistance to us. *Solomon on Sex*, by Joseph C. Dillow, is a manual of erotic instruction for the Christian and must surely be one of the more imaginative exegetical exercises on the market. Other "biblically-based" sex manuals which seem to believe the Bible offers more on the subject than merely the Mosaic and Pauline prohibitions include Charles and Martha Shedd's *Celebration in the Bedroom*, which recommends reading the Song of Solomon for erotic arousal, and Lewis B. Smede's *Sex for Christians*. The books generally take what might be called a Lutheran rather than a Calvinistic approach to the scriptures, applying to sexuality the principle that only those acts prohibited by the Bible are taboo. Otherwise, the authors advise Christian couples to be experimental and enjoy themselves (Woodward and Salholz: 71)!

That the Bible and sexuality are a terrific combination was discovered years ago by the motion picture industry. Biblical films, from the days of the silent cinema on, have enjoyed great popularity. These films have included trivial and embarrassing examples of the exploitation of religious sentiment and vehicles for eccentric stars, as well as genuine efforts to produce serious and even devout artistic statements. Probably the most daring subject of all for film presentation has always been Jesus himself, yet the history of the cinema reveals a substantial number of attempts to film either a full life of Jesus, episodes from his life, or historical scenarios in which he appears. While European film makers paved the way, it was, fittingly enough, the American Cecil B. De Mille who is best remembered for the genre. In a series of films over the years, he gave his public not only Jesus on screen but Samson, Delilah, Moses, and other personalities from Holy Writ. De Mille was a lay reader in the Episcopal Church and appears to have regarded himself as a religious man as well as a show business professional alert to the tastes of mass audiences. His 1927 *The King of Kings*, filmed on full budget and released with characteristic Hollywood fanfare, may be the most interesting of all the films he directed. H. B. Warner played a spiritually glowing, if slightly effeminate, Savior. The role was so acclaimed that years later people were still telling the then aging actor how, after having seen the film in childhood, they still envisioned his face when they thought of Jesus. The film's popularity, however, almost ruined Warner's acting career, for after his success as the Christ nobody wanted to employ him for merely mortal roles!

The circumstances surrounding the making of De Mille's spectacular were, not coincidentally, a press agent's dream. Clergy from America's leading religious denominations were constantly present on the set as advisers, thus establishing a precedent that continues today on television and radio when biblical subjects are presented. Steps were taken to insure what De Mille regarded as suitable reverence while scenes were being filmed. H. B. Warner was driven to the set in a closed car and was allowed to speak only to his director while in costume. The very first day of shooting for the film started with prayers offered by representatives of Protestant, Catholic, Jewish, Buddhist, and Muslim faiths. Prayers were again offered before the filming of the crucifixion, which De Mille insisted should occur on Christmas Eve (Butler: 38–39).

Less commercially successful was George Stevens's 1965 film, *The Greatest Story Ever Told*, memorable for the interesting performance of the distinguished actor Max von Sydow as Jesus. Von Sydow was both sensitive and virile and brought to the role the added charm of humor, all too frequently absent from these films, which have generally portrayed Jesus as melancholy and unsmiling. Other well-known actors, playing lesser cameo roles with varying degrees of success, distracted rather than enhanced the film's narrative. The motion picture became too much a game of "spot the star."

Most of the other American-made films about Jesus have been unmitigated embarrassments. Harry and Michael Medved's *The Golden Turkey Awards* presents four nominees for "The Worst Performance by an Actor as Jesus Christ." Robert Elfstrom both directed and acted the role of Jesus in Johnny Cash's *The Gospel Road*, providing viewers a glimpse of the Savior as "a big-boned, clumsy, flat-footed Swede who looks horribly uncomfortable in his long robe and sandals," according to the Medveds (127). Jeffrey Hunter's performance in the 1961 *King of Kings*, directed by Nicholas Ray, was the result of a truly grotesque bit of miscasting. In a review of the film on the occasion of its release, *Time* observed that Christianity has survived many persecutions and disasters and would also probably survive this film, though individual Christians who saw it might wish to receive Extreme Unction. The film did not advance the acting career of Hunter, a perennial juvenile who, before this role, had been notable for his portrayal of drunken fraternity boys. Hunter died not many years after the film's release, with no other major roles to his credit.

The other remarkable atrocity in Jesus-casting was that of the otherwise fine actor Donald Sutherland in *Johnny Got His Gun* (1971). Although Jesus appeared only briefly in this film, he was introduced in such a maladroit fashion that he is not easily forgotten. According to the Medveds, "we see Christ as a hip, blissed-out child of the sixties, and once again this Middle Eastern Messiah is inexplicably graced with flowing blond hair. Sutherland's performance is full of shrugs and grunts which are apparently meant to prove that Jesus is a mellow, modern guy who is acquainted with the techniques of method acting" (130–31).

Despite such formidable competition for the honor, the Medveds bestowed their Golden Turkey Award itself on Ted Neeley, who had been chosen above Mick Jagger, David Cassidy, and John Lennon for the title role in the film version of *Jesus Christ Superstar*. Neeley's formal preparation for the coveted role of Savior of Mankind had included performances in Los Angeles supper clubs and sessions with Grand Ole Opry warm-up bands. His subsequent film performance was so generally regarded as hysterical that *Newsweek* compared him to Charles Manson, while *Playboy*, noted for its pretentious excursions into theology as well as art, called him "the Screaming Jesus" (Medved and Medved: 130). Nevertheless, the film, directed by Norman Jewison, was at least an interesting curiosity and became one of the most financially successful musicals ever made.

Jesus Christ Superstar, certainly some sort of definitive "pop" statement, was a major cultural phenomenon in the United States throughout the 1970s. Though the rock opera was imported from England, the American film version, the stage play, and the original cast recordings of both, which enjoyed vast sales, made *Superstar* American at least by adoption. The central song, "Jesus Christ, Superstar," saturated the air waves, was recorded by a number of famous performers, and even turned up as theme music when celebrity evangelists were introduced on the secular television talk shows. *Jesus Christ Superstar* had been initially a hit record, composed and designed as a rock oratorio. So popular was the recording that a stage presentation emerged, followed by Jewison's cinema adaptation, filmed in the Holy Land, with implied parallels between the political intrigues in the time of Jesus and the turmoil in the present Middle East.

When the stage production first opened in New York in the fall of 1971, to both great fanfare and angry protests—which, as always, only increased the excitement surrounding the premiere—almost all major religious groups in the country found something that offended them. Mayor John Lindsay was met at the opening night performance by Roman Catholic pickets, outraged at the hippy interpretation of Jesus. Officials of the music department of Bob Jones University condemned the production on musical as well as theological grounds when it opened in South Carolina, and Jewish groups were offended by the scenario's suggestion that Jewish priests were those most responsible for the crucifixion of Jesus. It is curious that black groups did not fully share in the protest, despite the fact that the role of Judas was effectively played by the highly talented actor Ben Vereen, who appears to have a predilection for roles some members of his race find offensive, and the black Judas quickly became a convention of major productions of *Superstar*.

Though less epic in its sweep, certainly less spectacular, and even less controversial, another rock musical, *Godspell*, opened at Cherry Lane Theatre in New York the same fall as *Jesus Christ Superstar*. Sometimes labeled "the muscial comedy version of the Gospel According to Saint Matthew," *Godspell* was a suprisingly attractive pop adaptation of Gospel narrative, with a lively, youthful cast of clowns representing the central Bible personalities and a stylized crucifixion scene near the end, backed by electronic rock music. The portrayal of the Last Supper, in which the audience was invited on stage with the performers, provided a moving example of participatory theater, quite close to church ritual.

These two popular Jesus-rock musicals are projections of the vivid image of "Jesus Our Contemporary" that has been evident in the informal Christianity of the last couple of decades. Hippy culture and the youth movement broadly have stressed Jesus as an itinerant teacher, plucking grain for his meals where and when he found it, making wine without a license, and socializing with a motley crew. The alleged communal life of the apostles and early Christians has been emphasized. A strong strain of pastoralism, reinforced by this interpretation of Jesus' life and a selective reading of the pastoral passages of the Bible, expressed itself in the desire of many youth of the seventies to get back to the earth and live off the land. This new romanticism also manifested itself among older and more conventional people, as has been observed, in the national demand to be rid of what came to be regarded as the corruptions of big-city Washingtonian government and to establish a wholesome, honest, "born-again" president as leader of "an America as good as the American people."

Popular piety exerts a constant influence on staid conventional and academic religion alike. One such influence from contemporary popular Christianity has been the increased attention given to the Third Person of the Trinity, previously relegated to mysterious allusions in scripture and ambiguous creedal references as far as most American Christians were concerned. The Pentecostal churches, in whose arcane ceremonies the Holy Spirit had always been celebrated, had long been regarded as fringe sects; now they were dignified by the designation "classical Pentecostals." Roman Catholics, Episcopalians, and groups within almost every other major denomination opened themselves to "The Spirit," many becoming ardent in their devotion to the Third Person, suddenly revealed as the most immanent rather than the most hidden member of the Holy Trinity. Among the "gifts of the spirit," glossolalia, a charismatic exercise that exists in some form in all great religions, received the most attention. Scientific linguistic investigations have appeared to establish that ecstatic speakers use the phonemes of their native language, though there may be strong suggestions of a "biblical sound," reminiscent of Hebraic utterances such as "alleluia." The interpretation of tongues in the language of the hearers, regarded as another charismatic gift, usually delivers a message closely paraphrasing a favorite Bible passage, though further commentary by the interpreter may be provided in quasi-biblical jargon. There are reports of persons who have spoken in languages, ancient or modern, unknown to them in their conscious state, but the "tongue" is almost always described as "angelic" by a believer or as "gibberish" by a skeptic. Some persons, in fact, habitually use their tongue as a "prayer language," an instrument of praise very close to musical improvisation or certain ecstatic Chassidic chants.

Jewish groups have not been untouched by the recent burst of charismatic enthusiasm. A revival of Chassidic mysticism, interest in the Cabala, and a stronger emphasis on the more cryptic passages of the Hebrew scriptures are all reported. This exuberance and this joy in worship are also being more visibly expressed in holy dancing. Celebrating like David, who "danced before the Lord," modern Jewish groups can be observed during their holidays in the streets of cities such as New York and Montreal.

Where the older ecumenism of mainline denominations of Christianity has fallen upon troubled days, a new charismatic fellowship has grown up which totally transcends not only denominational lines but has even been known to break down the barrier between Jew and Christian. Those on whom "gifts" have been bestowed, whether Chassidic, Holiness, Catholic, or Lutheran, generally find they have more to discuss with each other than with the more rationalistic and restrained members of their own denominations. Eastern Orthodox Christianity, for whom mysticism has been a consistently honored tradition, views the new ecstatics with fraternal concern. This new ecumenism, if it is not merely faddish, may be more lastingly successful than the old—at least its advocates hope—perhaps because it appears, in their judgment, to be more spiritual than social in origin.

The healing ministry, whatever may have been its practice and significance in the time of Jesus, is highly visible today in popular American religion. Christian Science and related religious philosophies have always made healing central to their version of the Gospel. Now in countless sermons of the television evangelists the healing passages from the scriptures, both Old and New Testaments, receive particular stress. Though Oral Roberts, once the best-known American faith healer, has polished his image, joined the Methodists, and channeled his concern for the ill into the establishment of a first-class hospital practicing orthodox medicine, and though Kathryn Kuhlman is dead, others continue the healing ministry. The most flamboyant healer today is probably television preacher Ernest Angley, noted for his individualistic speaking cadences and his habit of "zapping" his followers as they are healed. Angley and his aides claim extraordinary miracles, cures for everything from annoying discomforts such as sties and coughs to major illnesses and handicaps including cancer and deafness. Ernest Angley in fact has both a straight following and a "camp" audience at colleges and universities around the country. Studying and socializing often come to a halt when the Angley show appears on television, and some informal campus reports suggest that Angley is as popular as Johnny Carson in certain localities. From their lounges and dormitory rooms students hoot ¬oar, and yell encouragement to the evangelist-healer.

In these days of less rationalistic, more experiential religion for the masses, the biblical books of prophecy are often receiving disproportionate attention. Not only are Daniel, Ezekiel, and the Apocalypse (Revelation) avidly read to discern "the signs," but the cults, charismatics, and—even a little surprising—secular youth devour these books and the art work inspired by them. Media evangelists provide elaborate interpretations of current events, relating these events to prophetic utterances from scripture by means of mysterious numerology and ingenious calculations. Survivalism is of course a secular preoccupation, and the apocalyptic note is sounded also in the literature of the broader society, which fears destruction by the Bomb or the smothering cloud of pollution.

In recent years North America has witnessed a proliferation of cults beyond anything the region, always relatively hospitable to such groups, has known in the past. The Jonestown tragedy and scandals involving other groups—the Moonies, followers of Krishna, practitioners of Scientology—seem not to have fatally damaged the cult movement. Even Oriental cult leaders are fond of using the Bible for their own ends, isolating passages they claim support their various stands, sometimes playing upon the general ignorance of the Bible among the young. A leader may shrewdly suggest that prophetic passages of the Bible apply to him personally, his present movement, and the fate of the select few who are his followers in "these end times." Referred to as "Bible Benders" by their critics (Sire), the cult leaders have made abundant use of the Bible and have demonstrated anew the authority and potency of the Bible, even with rebellious youth who have rarely bothered to study it.

Less than two decades ago Protestants, Catholics, and Jews alike were trying, sometimes frantically, to make themselves pertinent to the times, contemporary, and socially conscious, in part by revising ancient liturgies and translating religious texts into the vernacular. Their jovial theologians were enthusiastically "doing theology" in new keys, praising the secular city and all forms of avant-garde art. Major denominations have subsequently experienced either steep decline in membership or charismatic renewal (though, as mentioned earlier, this trend may now be slowly reversing as the mainline churches accommodate themselves to the new demands of their faithful), while Evangelical churches, Pentecostal bodies, and cults have experienced great growth. Any student of the history of religions should have been able to warn the well-meaning modernizers that the vast majority of people look to religion more for mystery, myth, symbol, and poetry than for "relevance" and intellectual stimulation. A relative neglect of the Bible now also appears to have been a chief mistake made during the search for a Christianity applicable to a "world come of age." The popularity of the Bible as the supreme witness to the Jewish and Christian faiths has been reaffirmed, and the groups that have flourished in recent years have tended to be precisely those, "relevant" or not, which have at least given lip service to the Bible as the central guide to faith and life. Those groups that have a holy tradition as supplement to biblical authority—Roman Catholics, Eastern Orthodox, Episcopalians, and others—have nevertheless started offering more Bible classes and discussion groups. Charismatics, of course, have their direct channels, but even they often take pains to establish biblical authority for their practices.

Some Christians, even those allied with the growing popular movements, still prefer intellectual to charismatic stimulation. It is slightly ironic that the germinal thinker for much of the revived Evangelical movement in North America is C. S. Lewis, a brilliant Oxford and Cambridge lecturer in medieval and Renaissance literature, who never regarded himself as a professional theologian but who published, in addition to his learned discussions of literary problems, a series of satires and meditations affirming the doctrines of classical Christianity. Lewis, an Anglican layman, was an individual of urbane wit and immense culture. This can scarcely be said of Francis A. Schaeffer, who directed the Schaeffer family ministry and publishing industry from the comfortable Swiss retreat of L'Abri. The Schaeffer Seminar was extravagantly produced in various parts of the United States a few years ago. Tickets sold for as much as good seats for a secular theater performance, and vendors hawked the Schaeffer books, tapes, and other materials during the intermissions of a long program. (Schaeffer's habit of constantly footnoting himself makes a purchase of his complete works essential to any serious student of his approach to the Bible and Western civilization.) The Schaeffer films, slickly and professionally produced, appeared to be attempting a Christian version of "Civilization," Sir Kenneth Clarke's own embarrassingly superficial television series. With all the skill and care that went into their production, it is surprising that the Schaeffer films were so dull. During the seminar, between the showing of different segments of the film, Dr. Schaeffer himself, a diminutive figure in beard and Tyrolean costume, appeared on stage to expound his humorless Christian perspective on world civilization and contemporary culture.

Schaeffer may bore, but he gratifies his admirers, even those who admit that they find his books unreadable. Working in disciplines where learning is too frequently compartmentalized, he may sound impressive because he has read Albert Camus and Jean Paul Sartre; yet he can also quote St. Paul and John Calvin. Nevertheless, his superficiality is clear; for example, his hasty dismissal of the Christian art of Michelangelo in only a few pages of largely irrelevant observations can only distress serious readers of his magnum opus, *How Shall We Then Live?*

When one considers that the Bible is mentioned on every stage, screen, and television set, that Christian outdoor summer pageants are given in more and more locations, and that reconstructions to scale of biblical places and landscapes—Holy Disneylands, as it were—are in elaborate planning stages, one wonders if the book itself is still read or is obscured by all the talk and activity surrounding it. As the publishing industry discovered years ago, a successful dramatization of a classic always leads to increased demand for the book. It is not surprising that Bible selling remains big business, though the market for secular books has grown as well. Whether they read them or not, most Americans possess Bibles. The Bible remains the volume most frequently sold in bookstores and stolen from public libraries in North America, still somewhat ahead of Gothic novels, Silhouette romances, and science fiction stories. For the first time, however, the King James Version of the Bible, for years almost the only translation acceptable in popular religion, appears to have lost ground. A number of vernacular Bibles have presented some challenge to the KJV, in all its seventeenth-century glory. The Cotton Patch Bible, hardly a serious competitor, is a curiosity, with its folksy Dixie rhetoric. The Good News Bible, a more serious alternative, has been widely accepted by the young of the Jesus movement.

A specialized edition of the KJV that merits attention is the Black Heritage Bible, sold by the Southwestern Company of Franklin, Tennessee. Though awkwardly compiled, with hastily assembled features designed to appeal to black Americans, this edition has been successful because it has met a need and has been sold door-to-door by energetic, appealing college students. The Black Heritage Bible highlights in print and illustrations Bible characters of "the darker color," designating, among others, the Queen of Sheba, who according to tradition was "black and beautiful," the wife of Moses, the Ethiopian eunuch, and Joseph of Arimathea, who had the honor of carrying Jesus' cross. The edition's preliminary commentary stresses the contribution of the world's darker peoples to the biblical saga, and testimonials from distinguished black Americans, who tell what the Bible has meant in their lives, are featured. Why the scriptural text should also be prefaced by a Tennyson poem, out of harmony with both the theme of the edition and the KJV's own golden rhetoric, defies explanation. If a modern poet deserved inclusion within the edition's covers—a questionable notion at best—why was not one of the excellent black poets chosen? Nevertheless, the Black Heritage Bible, despite its many gaucheries, has met a real demand and is an example of creative marketing, if not of commendable editing.

The verbal imagery of black preachers, who have ranked among the nation's finest folk artists, has contributed substantially to the American understanding of the Bible. Black religion has, in fact, been one of the most vital forces in American Christianity in this century, having a freshness, vitality, and originality often lacking in the mainline, predominantly white Protestant denominations. Toni Morrison, fictional chronicler of black American life, has observed a grimmer side of this Christianity, commenting that black folk have tended to believe that "the only way to avoid the Hand of God is to get in it" (56). Yet despite its vivid preoccupation with sin, black Christianity has been a living religion, a celebration, and an affirmation of the joy of salvation. The typical greeting in a black church is "feel free to clap your hands, stamp your feet, and make a joyful noise unto the Lord." Black Christianity has further demonstrated that social action and effective protests against injustice need not exclude deep personal spirituality and biblical commitment. Black Christians have not felt pressured to choose between social and personal Gospels; they have, at the best moments of their religious history, been provided both simultaneously. When historians of American religion lament the absence of social conscience and creative thought in Bible Belt religion, they are forgetting Martin Luther King, Jr., and the Bible-based doctrines of nonviolent social reform that have influenced people all over the world, even persons outside Christendom.

What the world knows as "Negro Spirituals" are more properly categorized as "art songs," made famous on world tours by classically trained artists such as the Fisk Jubilee Singers, Roland Hayes, and Marian Anderson. Today they are sung—complete with their marvelous echoes of both Old and New Testaments—in every Christian denomination and belong among the artistic treasures of American Christianity. But equally interesting, if less artistically appealing, is the popular soul singing and playing of the black churches, which has influenced both religious and secular music for the masses. White pop singers in both the United States and

Great Britain often try to "sound black," and part of sounding black is adopting a scriptural cadence and sprinkling one's speech with the biblical allusions that are part of the Bible Belt vernacular.

Americans remain, according to the latest Gallup polls, among the most religious people in the world. The majority of U.S. citizens, and Canadians too, also claim to be devoted to the Bible, even though many actually know very little of the scriptures and would indeed be shocked to discover some of the assertions contained therein. Though they vociferously affirm their total faith in the Bible when questioned by the pollsters, many North Americans would surely disagree with certain particular Bible precepts if they really took the time to read them. When the Bible is actually read, the reading is selective. Perhaps this has always been true. Here is the ultimate paradox. The culture echoes the Bible at every level, yet actual knowledge of the scriptures is slight and declining even in the Bible-thumping American South. The Bible itself is studied less than ever before, and it may be that it reaches Americans today, for better or worse, largely as it is filtered through the popular culture.

NOTES

/1/   This comment was taken from an unpublished communication from Ralph Hyde, noted Tennessee folklorist and contributor to this volume.

/2/   The new Jewish evangelism seeks, according to official statements, to provide a message for those with none and will not try to "sheepsteal" from the Christians or convert the already committed.

WORKS CONSULTED

Anderson, Robert, and Gail North
    1979   *Gospel Music Encyclopedia*. New York: Sterling Publishing
                            Company.

Armstrong, Ben
    1979   *The Electronic Church*. Nashville: Thomas Nelson.

Boles, John B.
    1972   *The Great Revival, 1787–1805: The Origins of the Southern
                            Evangelical Mind*. Lexington: University of Kentucky Press.

Boone, Pat
    1972   *A New Song*. Carol Stream, IL: Creation House.

Butler, Ivan
    1969   *Religion in the Cinema*. London: A. Zwemmer.

Dillow, Joseph C.
1971   *Solomon on Sex*. Nashville: Thomas Nelson.

Egerton, John
1974   *The Americanization of Dixie: The Southernization of America*. New York: Harper's Magazine Press.

Medved, Harry, and Michael Medved
1981   *The Golden Turkey Awards*. New York: Berkeley.

Morrison, Toni
1975   *Sula*. New York: Bantam Books.

Sire, James W.
1980   *Scripture Twisting: 20 Ways the Cults Misread the Bible*. Downers Grove, IL: Intervarsity Press.

Time
1980   "Becoming Fools for Christ." 116: 52–53.

West, Red, Sonny West, Dave Hebler, and Steve Dunleavy
1977   *Elvis What Happened?* New York: Ballantine Books.

Whitman, Alan
1978   *Christian Occasions*. Garden City: Doubleday.

Woodward, Kenneth L., and Eloise Salholz
1982   "The Bible in the Bedroom." *Newsweek* 99: 71.

II

The Bible in American Popular Humor

G. Frank Burns

There is much joy in the King James Version of the Bible, but little laughter. There is a promise that in the new heaven and the new earth there will be neither sorrow nor crying (Rev 21:4), but there is no mention of laughter there. The righteous laugh (Ps 52:6), and God laughs also, once with scorn rather than merriment (Job 12:4) and again at the wicked (Ps 37:13), while Bildad assures Job that God will fill the mouth of a perfect man with laughter (Job 8:21). In spite of the rarity of the word "laughter" in the Bible, however, in American popular humor the Bible is one of the most frequently used sources, even in the society of the last quarter of the twentieth century, a society that, although secular, still is so dependent upon the religious tradition that signs in shopping malls warn shoplifters "Thou shalt not steal."

Various techniques are used to adapt the biblical material to popular humor. The most direct method is verbatim quotation from the scriptures by a comic character; next is the analogue—the placement of specific biblical situations in a modern setting. Neither of these methods requires much familiarity on the part of the audience with biblical material or scripture texts. Nevertheless, these two methods are less frequently used in popular humor than other, more indirect methods.

Misquotation of scripture or the use of malapropisms is a method used more often in spoken comedy than in written, perhaps because its effect is most immediately felt by the ear, while the eye must translate the misuse into the proper form before the comic intent is comprehended. More subtle is the misapplication of scripture, in which the words are correctly quoted but are wrongly applied or are applied in an inappropriate situation, as in Clarence Day's widely quoted misapplication of Genesis, "Adam created two beings, Jehovah and Satan—yea, in his own image created he them." This is close to the fifth method, inversion, in which the plain meaning of a scriptural text or situation is turned upside down. For example, "Train up a child in the way he should go. When he's big enough, there he goes."

The biblical pun is relatively easy to devise and is found with moderate frequency; for example, "If all flesh is grass, then Adam was the fodder of mankind." It is understandable that most puns are anonymous. Authors of parody, however, have much pride and usually identify themselves. These include Robert Benchley, who parodied the distinctive cadences of the King James Version on more than one occasion, and William Faulkner. It is the distinctive seventeenth-century cadence and sonority that make biblical parody so frequent in American popular humor, sometimes at second hand in parodies of frontier preachers who found the King James rhetoric and rhythm irresistible in delivering their own original exhortations.

Finally, the eighth method is the unexpected twist. A well-known example is by W. R. Inge: "As Adam said to Eve when he led her out of Paradise, 'My dear, we live in an age of transition.'" Here is a perfect example of the periodic jest—not until the very last word is it a jest at all. Another example is anonymous: "The hardest thing to believe in the Bible is that when Noah had loaded the ark there were only two jackasses."

In discussing the Bible as found in American popular humor, it is necessary to keep in mind at all times that it is the Bible that is the object of analysis and not religion or the clergy, or ethnic groups, particularly the people of the Bible, the Jews. Jokes about Jews (and these are most often told by Jewish comedians) are not necessarily a humorous use of the Bible, even when the joke depends upon Judaism for its point. The same is true of jokes about the clergy, whether priest, vicar, rabbi, Baptist preacher, or Methodist parson. Scottish jokes, once so popular during the heyday of Sir Harry Lauder, may be jokes about Presbyterianism but they need not involve the Bible.

Joey Adams, in his *Encyclopedia of Humor*, listing popular jokes of the 1960s, illustrates this necessity to distinguish between ethnic humor, religious humor, and biblical humor. There are twenty-five pages of jokes involving Jewishness, including the only two pages set aside for jokes that directly refer to the Bible. There is one Baptist joke—and it is nonbiblical—and one nonbiblical Quaker joke. Of the ten Roman Catholic jokes, six also involve Jews and none is biblical. The nineteen jokes that make direct allusion to the Bible include seven that are distinctively Jewish, and most of them refer to Moses and the exodus, a favorite allusion in American popular humor.

Bennett Cerf, the publisher-raconteur, compiled a similar collection, *An Encyclopedia of American Humor*, but it is not indexed and it contains no one-liners or short jokes. Cerf is interested in longer humorous pieces, and most of these are neither heavily ethnic nor more than tangentially biblical. However, the editor himself took charge of the chapter of his book called "A Texas Sampler." This is a collection of the short anecdotes that Cerf himself told so well, and one of these is biblical: "A Texas dowager presented herself at the Pearly Gates, and when St. Peter asked for her credentials, proudly presented a membership card to the Symphony, receipted bills from Neiman-Marcus and the Shamrock Hotel, and a picture of herself shaking hands with Ted Dealey of the *Dallas News*. Saint Peter, duly impressed, remarked: 'Come in, Madam, by all means—but I don't think you'll like it'" (386).

Cerf also included one of the best-known twentieth-century American humorous works based on the scriptures, a section of Roark Bradford's *Ol' Man Adam and His Chillun*, a retelling in Bradford's version of southern black dialect of three Old Testament episodes, "Eve and That Snake," "Sin," and "The Wisdom of King Solomon" (239–50). Bradford's book, published in 1928 with great success in the marketplace, retold the Old Testament as he felt a semiliterate black preacher might have told it to his congregation. Good-humoredly ethnic, the book was adapted for the stage by Marc Connelly under the title, *The Green Pastures*. Connelly's version won a Pulitzer Prize for drama. As a motion picture it was also very successful. Not until the civil rights movement of the 1960s were there second thoughts about the appropriateness of the well-intended stereotypes of black people. Perhaps the most memorable scene of both film and play was the creation of the world by "De Lawd" at a fish fry in heaven. Cerf included this in his excerpts from the Bradford book, showing the earth being needed as a place to drain off the excess of firmament created for the boiled custard when Gabriel's jug runs dry. "When I say let hit be some firmament, I mean let hit be a whole heap of firmament," declares De Lawd, firmly.

The prose style of the King James Version lends itself well to parody. Ernest Hemingway, demonstrating the ease with which his own style yielded, once tossed off a virtuoso parody of *Across the River and into the Trees*, observing that only a recognizable, idiosyncratic style of the highest quality could be effectively parodied. (That this is not necessarily true is demonstrated by Mark Twain's well-known parody, "The Death of Stephen Dowling Botts," a travesty of a midwestern contemporary's trite sentimentality.) Most often appearing in parody form are the twenty-third psalm ("Roosevelt is my shepherd, I shall not want"), the Lord's Prayer, the Sermon on the Mount ("Blessed are the cheesemakers"), and the Ten Commandments. The cadences of the seventeenth-century English prose of the King James Version lend themselves to improprieties intoned in solemn measure. Two examples will illustrate the comic misuse of the Lord's Prayer. In one, a small boy named Howard inquires of his mother if he were named for God because they had prayed in Sunday school, "Our

Father who art in Heaven, Howard be thy name." The second was used by the late Lord Mountbatten when in command of a battered, obsolete destroyer, the Wishart. He told his men to be very proud of the name of their ship for the entire fleet prayed every morning, "Our Father Wishart in Heaven . . . ."

Robert Benchley, in his sketch "The Chinese Situation" (Lowrey: 33–35) explains that his protagonist, Whang the Gong, "had read enough of the Gospels to know the value of short words and the effectiveness of the use of the word 'and.'" He illustrates this by telling his wife, Rum Blossom, "Today you have a girl which is bitterness upon my head and the taste of aloes in my mouth." Hugh Kingsmill parodies the style of Lytton Strachey in *Eminent Victorians* with a mock biblical biography. Here, instead of a modern biography being rendered into biblical prose, the Old Testament story of Joseph and Potiphar's wife is put into Strachey's impeccable Edwardian sentences (Lowrey: 139–44).

Naturally, parodies of writers who themselves used biblical allusions generously will contain biblical allusions, and the tone will change from serious to humorous. T. S. Eliot provides a good example. His "The Waste Land" has become one of the most frequently parodied works of modern poetry, and Eliot himself was heard to observe, "Most parodies of one's own work strike one as very poor. In fact one is apt to think one could parody oneself much better. (As a matter of fact, some critics have said that I have done so.)" In Dwight Macdonald's *Parodies—An Anthology from Chaucer to Beerbohm, and After*, there is a parody of Eliot by a Cambridge University don who uses the pseudonym Myra Buttle. Biblical allusions abound, from the opening "Sunday is the dullest day, treating laughter as a profane sound, mixing worship and despair" to the words of Jesus and others at the end:

> "Love thy neighbor as thyself,"
> "Couldn't you bring better weather with
>   you?" and
> *Above all,*
> "Please adjust your dress before leaving."

Each of these lines is appropriately and laboriously explained in an Eliotine footnote (219, 222–23).

In the same collection, Wolcott Gibbs's parody of Hemingway's *Death in the Afternoon*, called "Death in the Rumble Seat," includes a story of God and Adam and the naming of the animals, told by the unnamed narrator to an uncomprehending cook in terse Hemingwayese. "It is a very strange story, sir," comments the cook, who is then told that "it is a strange world, and if a man and a woman love each other, that is strange too, and what is more, it always turns out badly" (249–50).

Parody is essentially literary. Because it is carefully wrought, it rarely incorporates the unexpected denouement. Oral folk humor, because it is essentially spontaneous, often depends for its humor upon just this kind of unexpected twist. A number of anecdotes and one-line quips involving the Bible must therefore be classified as folk humor, because, although they are familiar, they cannot be found in any formal collection of humor, probably because all are authentic spontaneous witticisms.

For example, apparently generated spontaneously upon publication of the Revised Standard Version more than twenty years ago was the assertion "If the King James Version was good enough for Jesus Christ, it's good enough for me." This has been traced authentically to two sources, an elderly Texas woman and a middle Tennessee evangelistic preacher. There are at least two variations, one referring only to "Jesus" and the other adding the typical courthouse square emphasis, "for Jesus Christ, by God, it's good enough for me." The Texas woman also figured later in another anecdote. After her death, her body was sent to another city by plane for funeral and burial. "My, my," exclaimed her daughter, "if Mama had known she was going to fly, she'd have just died."

An elderly Louisiana woman reminded her long-haired, bearded grandson, disapprovingly, "You look just like Jesus Christ, and you know what they did to Him."

She also said to another person, "What you say isn't the Gospel just because your mouth opens and shuts like a prayer book."

And about another man, "He reminds me of Moses. When he opens his mouth the bull rushes out."

Upon meeting a woman named Aquila, a Tennessee minister said, "You have an unusual name." She responded, "Well, you must meet my twin brother, Priscilla."

Confronted by a congregation of women with the then popular teased hair style, a minister in the early 1960s said he would preach on the text, "Top knot come down." Challenged to give chapter and verse, he pointed to Matt 24:17—"Let him which is on the housetop not come down."

Twentieth-century America has produced its share of satirists, many of whom use biblical allusions. Stan Freberg, a performer who hates the Las Vegas pleasure palaces, referred to that city as "Lost Voraces" in a bitter satire that he often used, a routine about two fiercely competitive night clubs, El Sodom and the Rancho Gomorrah (Adams: 16). Joey Adams was fond of satirizing his rival stand-up comics and once said that Henny Youngman was the King of the One-Liners although "I wouldn't exactly compare them to the ones Moses carried on the Tablet" (Adams: 10).

Satire is one of the chief weapons of the intellectual wit. It was popular in eighteenth-century England because the prose writers of the Augustan Age were brilliant social critics and it was for virtually the first time an age of literacy. In a singular way television, which has inflicted serious wounds on the basic concept of receiving information through reading the printed word, has produced an influential corps of intellectual writers whose scripts contain the most sharply cutting blades of wit since Pope, Rochester, Gay, Addison, and Lady Mary Wortley Montagu. The audience contains in increasing proportion a generation that combines a higher level of education with lifelong familiarity with television, and writers have shifted toward an increasing level of sophistication in humor, exactly the kind of shift required to restore satire to its earlier status as an effective weapon of social reproof and correction.

The first to use biblical material in satirical humor on television was a nightclub comic, Brother Dave Gardner. Of southern American origin, like many others who were to follow the pattern, Brother Dave consciously imitated the revival preachers of his native Jackson, Tennessee, filling his routines with parodies of Gospel sermons and allusions to biblical situations and characters. Jerry Clower, whose native Amite County, Mississippi, is about as Deep South as possible, conceals a witty sophistication beneath a rustic accent. He too relies heavily upon biblical allusion. The black comedian Flip Wilson invented a female character to share his comic dialogues, and it is Geraldine who says brightly when caught in some compromising situation, "The devil made me do it." It is Wilson who tells the story of David and Goliath as situation comedy, resorting to Geraldine's feminine tones to depict the ladies of King Saul's court urging, "Li'l David, play on yo' harp!"

But it was a program produced by the formidable Norman Lear that each week brought God and the Bible into American homes in the unlikely person of Archie Bunker. Two books written by Spencer Marsh, *God, Man, and Archie Bunker* and *Edith the Good*, first made a systematic analysis of the weekly television program. "All in the Family" persisted as America's most watched television show for season after season. Marsh sees Archie as the Adam figure; Edith is not Eve but the archetype of humanity itself, combining also the qualities of counselor and comforter, as she at times even becomes the Christ figure. On one show, the sophisticated writers on Lear's team (Marsh names twenty-two who worked on the program over a period of years) put these words into Archie's usually maladroit mouth: "He made everyone the same religion—Christian. Which He named after His son, Christian . . . or Christ for short. And that's how it was for years. One religion. Until they started splitting 'em up to all them other denumerations. But there's still only one religion. His up there." (Singularly, in his commentary Marsh moves away from the heart of this quotation from the script and notes a crucial point. Archie, even though unwittingly, is maturing, moving from a biased position to truth—that it is God's religion, not humanity's. Marsh uses the quotation to support a proposition that Archie, as Adam, has made a humanity-centered religion. But what the assertion by Archie Bunker really says finally is that religion and faith are God-centered. Reading Deut 6:4, 5 and Matt 22:37–40, it is hard to reach any other conclusion.)

On the American stage of 1979, the Bible does not appear in a humorous context, because traditional comedy almost disappeared from Broadway in the 1960s. Sister Bessie, the woman preacher of *Tobacco Road*, De Lawd of *The Green Pastures*, Mr. Antrobus in *The Skin of Our Teeth* are missing from the contemporary theater, as comedy becomes either absurd or black, except for such musical exceptions as *Fiddler on the Roof* and *Jesus Christ, Superstar*, both serious but with comic characters. In the first, Tevye brings into his humor strong biblical elements. In the other, Herod is both satirical and genuinely funny. This provides a curious link to the medieval European drama, the mystery plays, where Herod was always presented in broadly comic terms, as were Noah's wife, occasionally the devil, and always the devil's wife, who bears a remarkable similarity to Judy of the later Punch and Judy shows. In *Jesus Christ, Superstar* it is Herod whose posturing and extravagant mincing produce laughter in a stage production that depends for its impact on a melodious score, spectacular costumes and sets, and the initial shock of its basic premise, which is of course anything but comic.

Biblical allusions undergird the entire structure of Thornton Wilder's 1942 comedy, *The Skin of Our Teeth*. Antrobus is an Adam figure without much concealment. His story is the story of humanity, told simultaneously on three levels—in modern times, in biblical times, and in geological times. It is the world between the two great wars of the twentieth century, the world of Adam and Eve, Noah, Moses, and Homer, and at the same time the world of the approaching Ice Age. Wilder gives himself ample opportunity for topical jokes, most of them dependent on the audience's familiarity with the Old Testament. In Act I, Gladys recites Genesis 1. In Act II, a convention is reminiscent of Sodom and Gomorrah. As befits a comedy, the play is affirmative in its ending. Human beings, sustained by God, survive "by the skin of our teeth." Wilder is of course a playwright whose work reflects an optimistic outlook, and his comic protagonist is usually a winner, unlike the central characters of the theater of the absurd, who are almost always victims.

In the motion pictures, religious humor has frequently occurred, but usually it has been in the form of the jolly cleric. It has rarely been biblical. The year 1979, however, did produce two films opposite in tone but with equally obvious biblical premises. The first was the George Burns and John Denver comedy *Oh God!* This picture follows the traditional Old Testament premise that God appears to humans and walks and talks intimately with them. The biblical instances are numerous—Adam, Noah, Abraham, Moses, Samuel. In this film God appears in human guise as a little old man, beardless, with baseball cap, tennis shoes, and thick glasses. The dialogue is appropriate to the situation in the screenplay, and beneath its humor is a message that is both serious and deeply reverent. The second film, *The Life of Brian*, with the zany British comic troupe, Monty Python, is a ruthless attack on religion. It is also an attack on almost every other politicized institution of twentieth-century society, but its audiences, predominantly adolescent or postadolescent, have generally missed the thrusts at political radicalism, fanaticism, and terrorism. They leave the theaters clearly convinced that *The Life of Brian* is a savage satirical assault on Jews, Christians, and Christianity. Jesus Christ is satirized through the device of viewing the birth, life, career, and death of a contemporary of Jesus whose whole experience is one mistake and one misunderstanding after another. It is worthy of note that the Monty Python attempt to burlesque the crucifixion as the film ends generally leaves even immature audiences embarrassed.

Meanwhile an example of gentle humor whose point was made ever so subtly was seen on public television on 12 December 1979, when the Public Broadcasting System (PBS) showed "Simple Gifts," a program produced by station WNET (National Educational Television). Six episodes related to Christmas. In episode VI, "No Room at the Inn," with continuity and art by R. O. Blechman, the Bethlehem story from Luke was told, blending the historically authentic setting with modern times, melding a Judean town crowded with visitors come to obey the decree of Caesar Augustus with one that has become a tourist resort. As the journey into Egypt begins, Mary, on a mule with the child, and Joseph pass a sign, "You Are Now Leaving Bethlehem." A short distance beyond they pass a second sign, "Thank You. Please Come Again." As the implicit meaning dawns on the viewer, the subtle reminder of Rev 22:20 ("Even so, come, Lord Jesus") that lies beneath the familiar words of a small-town Chamber of Commerce possesses an impact more powerful than the more direct statement could have had, yet it preserves the quietly humorous tone of the piece.

The comic strip is the preeminent form of popular humor in America in the twentieth century. Many major cartoon strips rely heavily on allusions to the Bible. Others make occasional use of biblical materials or references. Although one, "Boner's Ark," by Addison, uses the Old Testament story of Noah and the flood as its basic structure, there are seldom any direct references in this strip to its biblical analogue. Probably the most popular strip of the 1970s, "Peanuts," by Charles Schulz, contains the most frequent and most consistent references to the Bible. It is also the most consistent in presenting an affirmative view of life.

That "Peanuts" is theological has been widely recognized, and on one occasion Schulz himself acknowledged this in a daily sequence. This was on 13 April 1965. Lucy and Linus are standing in the window of their home. It is raining. Lucy wonders whether the whole world will be flooded. Her brother reassures her by quoting Genesis 9 and God's promise to Noah. Lucy says, "You've taken a great load off my mind." Linus turns to her and observes that sound theology has a way of doing that. This sequence appeared the year after Robert L. Short's book, *The Gospel According to Peanuts*, was published. This book is generally conceded to have been the first to see theological implications in American comic strip art. Since 1958 Short had been lecturing to various audiences on the theological implications of the Schulz strip. He had effectively demonstrated that Shulz was delivering parables for our time. Any reader of "Peanuts" knows that direct quotation from the scriptures is frequent and is observed not only at Christmas time, the season when many cartoon artists make reference to the Bethlehem story. On at least one occasion Charlie Brown quotes part of John 16:33—"Be of good cheer"—to lift Snoopy's morale, although he omits the significant part of the text ("I have overcome the world"), and his assurance to Snoopy is in fact unjustified, for Snoopy is literally cold, shivering in the snow, and would have appreciated a blanket or even a warm hug more than empty reassurance. This of course is the point Schulz is making beneath his gentle humor.

Linus refers to the Old Testament in the strip of 21 March 1979, when he and Lucy are playing a board game using dice. "In the twenty-eighth chapter of Exodus, it tells of 'Urim and Thummim'. . . Some scholars say these were small stones like dice. These dice were used to obtain the will of God when decisions had to be made, . . ." Lucy, impatient at this erudition, screams "ROLL THE DICE!" Linus mildly murmurs, "That's a good decision."

Linus and Lucy are the participants in most of the biblical dialogues in "Peanuts." On 25 December 1977, Lucy exasperates her brother by wondering whether Jesus had not been born in a log cabin, and as he shows her pictures in a book, *Bible Lands*, he points out the Garden of Gethsemane, the Mount of Olives, the Sea of Galilee, and Bethlehem.

Insisting on a log cabin, Lucy replies to the question "You don't know anything about Christmas, do you?" with the calm declaration "I know I got my share of the loot."

Maintaining consistently her role of the scornful big sister, Lucy assumes the role of interpreter of scripture on 5 November 1977. Poring over her Bible, she tells Linus, "I'm looking up all the Scriptures that warn us about false prophets. I think you're off the hook. . . . I'm almost to the end, and I haven't come across your name."

But it is Snoopy who utters a memorable biblical observation on Father's Day, 19 June 1977. Reminiscing about his dad, who never chased rabbits but would invite them over to play cards, Snoopy says, "Those were good days. I remember the time a preacher came around telling about how the wolf and the lamb will lie down together and the leopards and the goats will be at peace. Cows will graze among bears. My Dad stood up and shouted, 'How about the beagles and the bunnies?' It broke up the meeting."

Obviously, none of these is in Short's book of thirteen years earlier, but they demonstrate that Schulz is not about to shift away from the use of the Bible in his distinctive brand of popular humor. Short does use what may well be the most often quoted "Peanuts" sequence. Linus and Lucy are present and Charlie Brown is also there, and it is Charlie who provides the famous punch line. The three are lying on a hillside looking at the clouds. Linus sees all sorts of things in cloud shapes, one group reminding him of the stoning of Stephen. "I can see the Apostle Paul standing there to one side," he declares. Lucy asks Charlie Brown what he sees. "Well," he says, "I was going to say I saw a ducky and a horsie, but I changed my mind!"

Most of the comic strips selected for the present discussion were taken from a controlled period—the year 1977. Fifteen separate strips were found to contain direct or indirect biblical references in one or more daily sequences. Others, particularly "Andy Capp," contained frequent references to religion or to the clergy, but unless there was a direct or indirect biblical allusion examples such as these have not been considered.

One exception to the controlled time period is a book that did appear on the racks in 1977 but that contains sequences first published earlier—Johnny Hart's *Back to B.C.* In this book Hart's testimonials include an admiring preface by Al Capp (who seldom used biblical material in his own strip, "Li'l Abner") and an apocryphal tribute from *The Caveman Quarterly*—"A prime evil collection of prehistoric nonsense . . . highly aboriginal." In two successive sequences Hart uses the Eden story. Two cave men are leaning on a rock in the first of these. A snake walks by on two legs. Says one man, "The world is younger than I thought." In the next, a man and a woman pass a fruit tree. Says the woman, "Oh look, apples. Want a bite?" Replies the man, "Who am I to defy the course of history?" Later, in a daily sequence, 6 October 1977, a cave man who is conducting a "trivia test" asks another, "What were the last words uttered by Lot's wife?" The other answers, "The heck with your fanatical beliefs. I'm going to take one last look!"

Another collection that appeared in 1977 was *Dennis and the Bible Kids: The Girls*. One of a series of six, this collection drawn by Hank Ketchum, creator of "Dennis the Menace," consists of cartoons not previously published in newspapers, although copyright is held by Field Newspaper Syndicate, which distributes the newspaper strip. Dennis Mitchell, the terrible little kid, hears his friend Margaret explain all about the outstanding women of the Bible. Although the material is serious and directly from the Bible, the tone is identical to that of "Dennis the Menace."

"Pogo," the much-loved strip by Walt Kelly, had disappeared by 1977, and its satirical method, derived from Joel Chandler Harris's *Tales of Uncle Remus* and through that work from African folklore, had not been duplicated on the comic page, but Craig Leggett's "Zoonies" (distributed by Newspaper Enterprise Association, NEA) uses the same device of the talking animal effectively. Ringo the Raccoon makes an Old Testament allusion in one sequence: "Speaking of strength," he says to the bear, "Samson could never have toppled that huge structure if it weren't for his hair." The bear scoffs, "You're pullin' my leg, Ringo! Who ever heard of a muscle-bound bunny rabbit?" Walt Kelly would not have used that kind of pun! Double talk, like Churchy La Femme's famous rendition of the Christmas carol, "Deck us all with Boston Charley," was Kelly's style. Parody of the style of the King James Version was also occasionally found in "Pogo." Such parody is also found on 26 June 1977, in Tom K. Ryan's "Tumbleweeds." Judge Frump presides over his ramshackle western court and thunders, "Woe to you! For the sword of justice shall smote asunder the corrupt! . . . The righteous shall prevail o'er the depraved!" The point of the episode is that the judge is piling up treasures on earth in the form of a series of exorbitant fines because, as one victim says, "his annual blackmail payment must be due." Judge Frump is again the speaker on 25 December 1977, but it is his own natural pompous style that is used, not parody, as he compares himself to the Magi. "Ring out, ye joyous Christmas bells! In emulation of my predecessors, the three wise men, it's time to dispense my Yuletide gifts to the folk of my belov'd district! 'Tis the season of Helpful generosity." His gifts are balloons imprinted "Frump for Senator."

The unrighteous witch of the strip "Broom-Hilda," by Russell Myers, was chomping her cigar on 7 August 1977, while her friend, Gaylord the Raven, paraphrased Ps 28:3, telling Irwin the Troll that innocent-looking people carry deep within their bosoms an evil beast which lurks beneath the surface. "Do we all have that beast inside us?" asks Irwin. "Well, not all," says Gaylord, looking at Broom-Hilda, "some of us keep it on the outside."

Tom Wilson's "Ziggy" is occasionally, like Noah, in direct communication with God, who on 31 July 1977 reminded Ziggy of his mortality. It was his birthday and a series of mishaps had befallen him—burst toothpaste tube, burned cake, spilled garbage, banana peel, an indignity committed by a passing bird, a bee sting suffered while sniffing a fragrant flower. Ziggy plaintively addresses God, "But it's my birthday!!" A voice thunders from above, "And one to grow on." An apple falls from a tree onto Ziggy's head. In a similar vein on 28 August 1977, Ziggy calls Dial-a-Prayer and is told "IT'S LATER THAN YOU THINK!" Pondering this for two frames, he then dials the time.

The Dial-a-Prayer service is frustrating to Art Sansom's Thornapple in "The Born Loser" of 24 June 1977. Thornapple, whose name may possess biblical symbolic significance indicating that he is an Adam figure, holds the telephone interminably after calling Dial-a-Prayer, finally gasping, "They hung up on me."

Like Ziggy, Mel Lazarus's "Momma" is often in direct touch with God, but it is she who speaks in prayer, either kneeling at her bedside or saying grace before meat. On 22 July 1977, Momma kneels and addresses God, "And also bless my beloved daughter-in-law who's just as close to my heart as a flesh and blood relation." Three panels then pass with no dialogue at all. Momma resumes, "In case you've forgotten, I'm referring to Tina, that woman my son Thomas saw fit to marry. Amen." On 27 June 1977, Momma is at table with Tina and Thomas and is saying grace. "Lord, we thank you for giving us this day our daily bread," she says, following the injunction of Matt 6:11, "Amen. Her tranches de jambon morvandelle we'll talk about later."

Likewise Andy Capp, Smythe's English working-class reprobate, is in touch with God, the Bible, and the church, but at a distance. Andy never addresses the deity, but he often addresses the vicar. A typical sequence occurred on 8 August 1977, when Andy meets the vicar and a friend on the street. The vicar invites Andy to hear his sermon on Sunday and Andy gives a noncommittal response. Passing on, the vicar's friend, also a clergyman, notes that he has one or two parishioners who fall asleep during his sermons. Asks Andy's vicar, "Have you got one that heckles?" The sequence of 18 July 1977 refers to a sermon also, but this time it is

Andy's wife who is about to deliver one on the subject of staying out late. Andy has learned that it is later than he thinks by looking at the clock in the steeple of the parish church. The wife's "sermon" confirms this bit of symbolism. The vicar and Andy have another exchange on 28 August 1977. This time Andy is passing the church door on his way to some worldly recreation—football, pigeon racing, or pub. "If you'd like to try something different this Sunday morning, I don't think you've ever heard me preach," the vicar calls after him. "I've never 'eard you do anythin' else, pal," Andy rejoinders. The vicar thinks, "He's sharp as a tack—wish I had a hammer!" Then, "Tch! Tch! What's happening to me? I never used to say things like that . . . !" Numerous scriptural texts come to mind, including one from Proverbs: "A soft answer turneth away wrath, but grievous words stir up anger."

Howie Schneider's "Eek and Meek," distributed by Newspaper Enterprise Association (NEA), on 14 June 1977 illustrated the technique of altering a biblical quotation slightly for humorous effect. In this sequence Eek philosophizes, "Basically there are only two types of people in this world, the doers . . . and the done to." This paraphrases Luke 6:31, the Golden Rule, and also changes the emphasis of the text. A Walt Kelly "Pogo" sequence from an earlier year did the same sort of thing with Matt 5:44, as Albert Alligator explains to Pogo why he has been fighting with ol' Beauregard, who is one of his best friends in the Okefenokee Swamp. "Man," exclaims Albert, "You go 'round fightin' with your enemies, you's liable to get yo' block knocked off!"

More biblical in situation than in quotation is the sequence of 31 July 1977 of an offbeat comic strip, "Howard the Duck," created by Steve Gerber and Gene Colan. A rowdy satire designed to appeal to the fundamentally incompatible audiences of Disney cartoons, science fiction, and the postadolescent agnostic critic of existing institutions, "Howard the Duck" normally operated by techniques of inversion, parody, and comic juxtaposition. Young veterans of classes in introduction to literary analysis insist that Howard is an Adam figure and point to the strip's subtitle, "Trapped in a World He Never Made." In the sequence of 31 July that is being examined, Howard is in a fast food restaurant when the door crashes open and a muscular female figure, wielding a staff, thunders through, uttering jeremiads. Like Jeremiah, this prophet warns nd admonishes, "Fools! Cast asunder your greasy foods, tobacco, and low morals!! For sake of your kidneys and your children's kidneys." The neo-Jeremiah then attacks the "cartel of food producers, tobacco growers, politicians, and fast women."

In a more reverent mood, Fearing's "Rooftop O'Toole" (United Features Syndicate) early the following year (5 April 1978) contemplated the cosmos. Rooftop looks up at the stars with his dog Rufus. "Imagine, Rufus," he says, "God created all this. He made the moon, the sun—space and all the stars and planets in it." Fearing brings this into a modern economic framework more gently than Gerber and Colan, as Rufus thinks, "Huh—sounds more like the work of a conglomerate."

The human dilemma is encountered by Broom-Hilda on 26 June 1977, and she discusses it in a dialogue with Gaylord. "Last night I dreamed I died," she says. "An angel appeared and said I had a choice of goin' to Heaven or the other place. He said in Heaven everything is beautiful and perfect, but in the other place they had everything I'd liked all my life." When Gaylord asks her what her choice was, she muses that she would like to commute.

"Doonesbury," the popular comic strip by Gary Trudeau, is political in its overall message and hardly ever utilizes biblical allusions, although for several years, and occasionally in isolated sequences, a campus chaplain—based, it is said, on William Sloane Coffin of Yale and Riverside Church—did appear. But on 5 December 1979, there is a reference to Jesus Christ in satirical context. Planning a 1970s nostalgia party for New Year's, Zonker Harris and Doonesbury are chatting at the breakfast table. "I can see you've given this party a great deal of thought, Michael," says Zonker. "Well," replies Doonesbury, "When you've made it through a decade like the Seventies, Zonk, some celebration is in order. It's also a grand opportunity to pay costumed tribute to the thousands of superstars who graced the era." Zonker interrupts, "Ah, yes, the 'Superstars.' Who was the first to get tagged with that, anyway?" Says Mike, "I believe it was Jesus Christ." The allusion may have been to the stage production, but through that it points to a solidly biblical source. Mike is, however, incorrect; strictly speaking it was the use of the term "superstar" by music promoters and the media that inspired the authors of *Jesus Christ, Superstar.*

The last appearance of the chaplain of "Doonesbury," now retired not only from the campus but, as it develops, from all the brave causes of the 1960s, is on 25 September 1977. The Reverend Scott and Doonesbury are talking in earnest reminiscence on the beach near Provincetown when the minister leads the conversation awkwardly to the insurance coverage on Walden, the old house where the young commune had flourished. "Uh-oh," thinks Mike, possibly thinking of Matthew 6.

Addison's "Boner's Ark" presents a Noah who has forgotten to bring any charts and who has absent-mindedly loaded aboard only one of a kind. Long after the strip began, feminist pressure brought Boner's wife, Bubbles, onto the Ark. A very unattractive scold, she is as shrewish as tradition suggests the biblical Noah's wife was. Apart from this, there have been no obvious allusions to the Old Testament story, after borrowing its central situation.

Just as the wise and witty sayings of the popular culture of Solomon's kingdom found their way into the Bible as the collection called Proverbs, the Bible has now contributed to the humorous elements of American popular culture. A. N. Whitehead was not correct when he observed, "The total absence of humor from the Bible is one of the most singular things in all literature" (Esar: 75). Humor is in the Bible and the Bible is to be found in popular humor. Wit and wisdom interweave, as in Proverbs, to reveal the tragicomic vision of life. Just as nothing in human life is too sacred for laughter, so laughter is not so secular as to avoid using sacred material. William Blake, Mark Twain, and Ambrose Bierce compiled their own dark books of proverbs: without the Old Testament pattern, their audiences would not have comprehended what they had done. And perhaps it was Martin Luther who said it best, "If you're not allowed to laugh in heaven, I don't want to go there."

WORKS CONSULTED

Adams, Joey
> 1968   *Encyclopedia of Humor*. New York: Bonanza.

Cerf, Bennett
> 1954   *An Encyclopedia of American Humor*. New York: Random House.

Esar, Evan
> 1968   *20,000 Quips and Quotes*. Garden City: Doubleday.

Hart, Johnny
> 1977   *Back to B.C.* London: Coronet Books.

Ketchum, Hank
> 1977   *Dennis and the Bible Kids: The Girls*. Waco: Word Books.

Lowrey, Burling, ed.
> 1960   *Twentieth Century Parody*. New York: Harcourt Brace.

Macdonald, Dwight
> 1960   *Parodies: An Anthology from Chaucer to Beerbohm*. New York: Random House.

Marsh, Spencer
> 1975   *God, Man, and Archie Bunker*. New York: Harper and Row.
> 1977   *Edith the Good*. San Francisco: Harper and Row.

Short, Robert L.
> 1964   *The Gospel According to Peanuts*. Richmond: John Knox.
> 1968   *The Parables of Peanuts*. Greenwich: Fawcett Publications.

III

Retelling the Greatest Story Ever Told: Jesus in Popular Fiction

Allene Stuart Phy

Popular American Fiction and Piety

A child growing up in North America does not usually absorb the images and lore of his religion from the paintings of the old masters, from the stained glass windows of majestic cathedrals, or even from the Bible itself. Cecil B. De Mille and the popular novelists may be more influential in determining the way Bible personalities and events **are** perceived. On a continent known for its flourishing branches of Judaism, its denominational variations of Christianity, and even its proliferation of cults, it is rather amazing to discover how much agreement can be reached when the mass audience adopts some popular cinematic or fictional interpretation of a favorite biblical character, be it Samson, David, Moses, or Jesus himself.

The reading public has been responsibly studied by a number of scholars, most notably James D. Hart, Alice P. Hackett, and Frank Luther Mott./1/ These studies, as well as other observations by sociologists (Lerner; Schneider and Dornbusch), have tended to demonstrate that North Americans buy books that confirm their opinions and reinforce their preferences, articulate their unexpressed attitudes, or provide consolation for them in their problems. Rarely if at all are books purchased and read by large numbers of people to correct the heresies of authors, debate facts and theories with them, carry on disputes in the margins of their books, or receive a genuine intellectual stimulation or expansion of understanding through dialogue with them. Popular religious books, therefore, become revealing documents. While many of these books have been purchased by active church members, there is also indication that these publications have helped provide many of the non-churched with a partial substitute for organized religion, even years before the television evangelists started addressing such audiences.

Biblical themes and "Christ figures" have been effectively employed by serious men and women of letters since the beginnings of American literature. Like their European counterparts, North American writers have freely borrowed from the poetic and numinous richness of Judaism and Christianity. Popular authors write from different motivations, according to different conventions. They tend to think of themselves as commercial craftsmen rather than as visionaries and artists. They do not employ "Christ figures," though they sometimes present Jesus as a personality in their fiction. Popular writers may be either skilled or maladroit, expressing personal views with conviction or merely producing a slick commercial product according to audience demand. But primarily they have written to entertain the masses. Writing novels is their trade; it may or may not be their calling.

In order to achieve full financial success, a work of religious fiction must reach an interdenominational public in North America. Though popular writing rarely claims for itself the intuitive wisdom and insight of the literary masterpiece, it does mirror the preoccupations of the society that consumes it. Yet it must always be remembered that there is not merely one best seller market. Lloyd C. Douglas's readers may be unmoved, even repelled, by a novel by Frank Yerby. In examining popular fiction, one observes several markets rather than only one.

Best sellers continue to run their successful course, often despite very bad reviews from the professional critics and the expressed disdain of academicians. Any analysis, even a superficial one, of a best seller list reveals the diversity of the materials that always appear there. Religion has been a constant preoccupation in frequently purchased books from the colonial period to the present. The clergy have been, at least until recent years, more frequently represented on best seller lists than members of any other profession. It would almost appear that being either a member of the clergy or a medical doctor would be an added qualification for a successful writing career in the popular field.

Fictional adaptations of biblical personalities and episodes, quite apart from treatises on pious living and positive thinking, have been among the most popular books ever published in America. Many have been all-time favorites, while others, which may not have reached sales of 1 percent of the total population of the continental United States for the decade in which they were published (which is Mott's arbitrary figure for determining a best seller), have nevertheless enjoyed substantial and sustained sales. These books of pious proclamation have taken their place on North American bookshelves along with worn copies of *The Sheik*, which permits the reader the vicarious thrill of being abducted by a desert chieftain; *The Garden of Allah*, in which the reader savors the delights of a priest's forbidden love in the North African desert; and *Three Weeks*, known informally as "three weeks of sin, on a tiger skin, with Elinor Glynn." Religious subjects have competed in popularity with the salacious accounts of escape from Brigham Young's Utah harem and the convent-brothels alleged to have existed in Montreal, the jungle adventures of Tarzan, the courtroom thrills of Erle Stanley Gardner, exciting romances in mythical principalities such as Graustark, and lessons in self-improvement by Amy Vanderbilt and Dale Carnegie.

Though many lurid and shallow books have reached the American mass audience, even today a suspicion, inherited from the nation's Puritan past, lingers over the novel in the minds of many. While American literature was born at seemingly an opportune moment, when the powerful resources of the English language had recently been so magnificently explored by the literary geniuses of the Elizabethan Age, the pressure of everyday concerns—clearing the wilderness, combating a new climate, establishing security in a hostile environment, not to mention promoting uncompromising ethical and religious themes—prevented the immediate flowering of belles-lettres on the part of our colonial ancestors, the gifted and courageous cousins of the English Elizabethans.

Even poetry was considered frivolous, and Puritan divines, alone in their closets, were sometimes forced to conceal the irrepressible vice of writing verse, but the novel, after it came to birth, was regarded as even more disreputable. If Plato said that the poets lie, how much more do the novelists deceive. Even if the Puritans in a stolen moment might read a novel or like Jonathan Edwards condescend to acknowledge that the reading of a well-contrived piece of fiction could benefit a preacher's pulpit style, they maintained the guilty suspicion that the novel was immoral; later many came to regard it as undemocratic as well. This attitude has never been completely overcome even by the twentieth-century descendants of the Puritans.

Government leaders sometimes warned that the passion for novels was a national moral threat. Even Hannah Foster, a highly successful early novelist, was not thoroughly convinced her own books were suitable for young readers. Yet the majority of the first American novelists, despite formidable opposition, valiantly defended their vocation by insisting that their stories were based on fact, which they then pretended to take pains to authenticate. Novelists in Anglo-Saxon countries were obliged for a period to present their novels as if they were thinly disguised fact, employing ingenious techniques in an effort to simulate reality—the epistolary form of narrative, the author's introductory disclaimer of any fictional distortions apart from minor changes to protect the "innocent," and the witness on the part of the author that his, or more likely her, purpose was a highly moralistic one. It was necessary to warn young ladies of potential danger to reputation and honor, to present a plea for true religion, opposing the forces of infidelity, and to provide instruction in patriotism and family loyalty.

Heroines in early novels were usually orthodox in religion and conduct, and any deviation from the rigid ethical code was fearfully and swiftly punished. Respect for parental authority, almost always in conflict with the star-crossed love of the heroines, was preserved. Only villains were given to moral cynicism and religious skepticism; only they struggled against the established order and questioned traditional religion.

Yet despite the pious disclaimers and the care with which these spinners of yarns abundantly employing incest, Gothic terror, and gore attempted to maintain a veneer of propriety, the novel was still suspect and only succeeded in gaining admittance into the more upright homes when it started assuming the masks of history, biography, and New Testament Christianity./2/

The Christological Novel is Established by Two Clergymen: Jesus as Royal Foundling

The first memorable attempt to Christianize the novel by the introduction of Jesus himself as a fictional personality was made by the Reverend William Ware, a Unitarian minister, who wrote *Julian: Or, Scenes in Judea*, a sentimental, rambling, yet highly learned narrative. In *Julian*, Ware demonstrated how the techniques of popular entertainment fiction could be applied to a retelling of the Christ story. He was to have many imitators and disciples in the genre in the years to come. Many of the conventions he established are still followed and can be clearly identified in books by Taylor Caldwell, Frank G. Slaughter, and others. Julian, the prototype hero of the American Christological novel, a figure that has now become very familiar to readers, is a Romanized Jew visiting his ancestral homeland of Judea. He is a philosophical skeptic who hears of an extraordinary teacher moving about among the local Jews. With a curiosity that he expresses in long-winded letters and asides to minor characters, he follows reports of the movements of this strange teacher, pondering what his significance must be. To satisfy the reader's desire for information, edification, and instruction, Julian takes time to review the words of the Hebrew prophets regarding the promised messiah. At the same time he has the opportunity to observe and relate in detail the first-century conflicts in Jewish society between, for example, the quisling Sadducees and the rigidly legalistic Pharisees, described in Julian's epistles much in the manner of Nathaniel Hawthorne's New England Puritans./3/

Julian, like the hero or heroine of many a nineteenth-century novel, reveals himself to be a truly compulsive letter writer, articulate, even verbose. He writes his mother his impressions of Judea, telling her about John the Baptist, whom he sees, describing the baptism of Jesus, which he witnesses, and acquainting her with the mother and family of Jesus after he meets them in Nazareth. While to Ware Mary was neither a virgin goddess nor the Mother of God, she was nevertheless a nineteenth-century gentleman's ideal of womanly dignity and loveliness. Julian describes her accordingly.

Ware cleverly employed the epistolary style of the British novelist Samuel Richardson in a narrative using Bible characters. He blended in amazing fashion nineteenth-century sentimentality and New England Unitarian rationalism, but he was unable to give his story a conclusive ending. Jesus, whom Julian describes as an illusive, mysterious figure, never really comes to life. Within days after Jesus is crucified, Julian hears rumors that he has risen from the dead. With the riddle of Jesus' nature still unsolved, he finishes his epistles on the following note of expectancy: "Doubtless they [the wonders he has related] sufficiently proved him to be a messenger and a prophet of God, at the same time that they failed to prove him the Messiah who had been foretold, for whom Israel had waited so long, and still waits" (270).

Perhaps the ambiguity of Ware's portrait of Jesus is not totally the result of an opaque style. There is the impression that the author himself had reached no final conclusion about the nature of Jesus. When later asked to define Ware's Christology, his brother-in-law, the Reverend Joseph Allen, responded:

> As to the exact type of Mr. Ware's Unitarianism I cannot speak with confidence, and I am inclined to think that he had no very sharply defined views in regard to the nature and rank of Jesus Christ. I know, however, that he regarded Him with the deepest veneration, as a being of super-human origin, whose mission was miraculously attested, and whose authority was truly Divine; as the Son of God in a high and peculiar sense, as the one Mediator between God and man. My impression is that he would not have been willing to be classed with any sect of ancient or modern times, in such a sense as to be responsible for the views attributed to such sect. (Sprague: ix)

Ware's contribution to the founding of a flourishing genre in American popular literature is significant. Yet intense as he was and as laborious as his fictional efforts appear to have been, he was neither a true master of rollicking popular fiction nor an orthodox Christian. His work was necessarily low-key, especially in comparison with the firebrand who was to follow. The Reverend Joseph Holt Ingraham, a Mississippi Episcopalian and firm defender of creedal Christianity, had established himself in youth as an amazingly successful potboiling novelist, author of *Captain Kyd: Or the*

Wizard of the Sea and *Lafitte, the Pirate of the Gulf*, to name only two of
the best sellers he had effortlessly churned out. It was easy for him to provide correctives for any Ware limitations he might have perceived, when
in 1855 he released, with the greatest solemnity, his masterpiece, *The
Prince of the House of David: Or, Three Years in the Holy City*.
Ingraham simply applied to the story of Jesus the adventure formula he
had perfected in the secular fiction written largely before his Christian
conversion, borrowing from Samuel Richardson, and perhaps from Ware
as well, the epistolary style.

Ingraham was no fireside dreamer but had led a life as hectic as had
many of his fictional heroes. He had at various times been a seaman, a
South American revolutionary, and a "professor" in a school for girls.
While temporarily residing in Nashville, Tennessee, where his brother
was associate rector of Christ's Church Episcopal parish, Ingraham had
provided heroic assistance during the mid-century cholera epidemic that
had devastated the area. Already feeling his first pastoral promptings, he
had also served as an unordained chaplain to prisoners in the state peni-
tentiary. With his usual penchant for dramatizing all his experiences, he
had turned out another racy romance, *The Secret of the Cells*, inspired
by his prison ministry.

Ordained a priest at the age of forty-two, Ingraham served congregations in Alabama, Tennessee, and Mississippi. Looking for new and
ever more effective ways of putting his generous talents to work in
spreading the Gospel, he accepted the suggestion of his clergyman
brother that he employ the proven skill of his pen to unfold the riches of
the Sacred Word for many who never opened a Bible but nevertheless
liked popular fiction. *The Prince of the House of David*, one of the
great best sellers of its time, was the result. Written, according to the
author, in three months by midnight oil in hours stolen from pastoral
duties, the book reached vast masses of people who had been untouched
by the efforts of Ware. Though written primarily for the unchurched, it
was in God-fearing homes that the book assumed an honored place
beside the Bible on reading tables. Following the precedent of devout
medieval authors, Ingraham repudiated the fiction of his youth, using his
royalty checks to purchase copyrights of his earlier nonreligious books.

The only literary man of prominence who commented on *The
Prince* at the time of publication was Timothy Shay Arthur, the austere
author of the temperance classic *Ten Nights in a Bar-Room*. Arthur, a
minority voice for once, dismissed Ingraham's book as one "we shrink
from reading," the reason being that "a page or two was sufficient to
create the same feeling that we have when an imaginary head of the
Saviour is presented, and from which we soon withdraw our eyes, as

from the desecration of a sacred thing" (142). The general public, however, did not share Arthur's squeamishness. By 1931 the book had sold close to five million copies and was still in demand./4/

Ingraham acknowledged two aims in writing *The Prince of the House of David*. He wished, following his brother's suggestion, to present the Christ-story in its full drama and excitement to those who rarely opened a Bible or frequented a church, to create for them the illusion of immediacy, of actual firsthand participation in "the advent of the Son of Mary, Christ the Lord" by allowing the reader to follow, step by step, the eyewitness account of Adina, Ingraham's heroine. (Ingraham refers to himself as "editor" rather than "author.") He also boldly stated in his preface his intention to tempt "the daughters of Israel" to read his narrative, in the expectation of at last converting a part of "stubborn Jewry," through his amassing of proofs that Jesus was their expected messiah: "For the Israelite as well as the Gentile believer this volume appears and if it may be the means of convincing one son or daughter of Abraham to accept Jesus as the Messiah, or convince the infidel Gentile that He is the very Son of God and Creator of the world, he [Ingraham is referring to himself as author-editor] will have received his reward for the labors, which he has devoted to this story" (ix). The "proofs," apart from the alleged fulfillment of Old Testament prophecies, were the numerous miracles related in the book. America's Jewish population, from all accounts, however, remained unmoved!

Adina, Ingraham's heroine, is a Jewish maiden of good birth, who visits Jerusalem and sends thirty-nine copious letters back to her father in Alexandria. She manages to be on hand to witness practically all major events in the ministry of Jesus, including some that the Gospels do not record but the fertile imagination of Ingraham provides. Like many a heroine of nineteenth-century fiction, she is a half-orphan; also, as any reader of the fiction of the era might anticipate, she becomes involved at the first opportunity in a forbidden romance with a Roman legionnaire. In verbose detail she recounts her experiences, first as a curious spectator to the ministry of Jesus and later as a follower, witnessing the crucifixion and rejoicing in Jesus' resurrection.

After becoming accustomed to Adina's generally breathless narrative style, the reader may find her description of Jesus anticlimactic. She describes him as a gray-haired individual, much older in appearance than his thirty years, with a finely shaped oval face, carved with lines of care. His countenance, she says, is always melancholy (226).

Ingraham, a man with a strong sense of family and proper birth, stressed the fact that Jesus, although he appeared to be the son of a humble village carpenter, was actually a divine aristocrat, the begotten son of the King of the Universe.

Jesus as Master Magician

For all his success on the popular market, Ingraham was in three decades to be eclipsed by that man of unique and peculiar genius, General Lew Wallace, who wrote *Ben-Hur, A Tale of the Christ*. No book of its kind has ever generated more excitement. Wallace was both a gifted swashbuckling narrator and a skilled manipulator of the casts of thousands later to be popularized by the biblical films. His writing even achieved a minor epic tone; with justification he has been called the Homer of Sears-Roebuck fiction and the Virgil of the early paperbacks. Despite a dramatic and reverent appearance of Jesus at the climax of the novel, the reader was always more likely to remember the book's brilliant description of a naval battle, with the heroic Ben-Hur chained in the galleys. And, of course, no one ever forgot the chariot race.

Although Wallace had loved literature from youth, he had not been a professional writer before the publication of *Ben-Hur*, and he was never to become dependent on writing for his livelihood. He was, rather, a nationally prominent public servant. He had first achieved recognition as a veteran of the Mexican War; then later he was acclaimed as a Civil War general, a territorial governor, and a uniquely gifted diplomat. Serving as a representative of his government in Turkey, he earned the respect and personal affection of the sultan, who permitted him certain liberties and privileges never before granted to a non-Muslim.

Wallace left a colorful account of the origin of his celebrated novel. The book was conceived as the result of a train encounter with Robert Ingersoll, the nation's most vocal atheist. Ingersoll, being of "unsettled mind" and inclined to lead discussions even with casual acquaintances around to the religious concerns that obsessed him, had initiated a discussion of the divinity of Jesus. His eloquence was admittedly impressive, but Wallace, although not a professing Christian, was of open mind, not prepared to "follow him as far as the non-divinity of Christ." Wallace felt the issue of Jesus' divinity deserved more serious investigation before being either accepted or rejected. After pondering his meeting with Ingersoll, Wallace determined that the best way to conduct this investigation would be by writing a history of Jesus and his times in which the arguments for and against his divinity could be weighed. For a biblical-style seven years Wallace labored, under his favorite beech tree, in the waiting rooms of "lonesome stations," in "a cavernous chamber" of the Oklahoma governor's palace—to which Billy the Kid boasted he was coming to shoot Wallace—until his opus was completed and, in his own words, "Long before I was through with my book, I became a believer in God and Christ" (1906:936).

Wallace seems never to have admitted a fact obvious to any reader: *Ben-Hur* was a tale of revenge even more than it was a tale of the Christ. Yet despite the *lex talionis* ethics of its hero, it was accepted as a stirring, inspirational work with Christian evangelistic potential./5/ Though it was written by a Protestant for Protestant audiences, its appeal was not limited. Professor Henry Salvadori, honorary chaplain to Pope Leo XIII, put out his own version of the novel with slight modifications "in the interests of piety" and was personally commended by the pope for this noble work (1906:941). Catholic priests even wrote Wallace that they recommended his tale to their penitents (1906:955). Sears-Roebuck, by its printing of a million inexpensive copies, brought *Ben-Hur* to its largest audience. In the rural regions of North America where people had access to few books, the same exhilaration could be experienced that prompted President Garfield, from the White House, to write Wallace a letter thanking him for the pleasure he had received from reading the book (1906:940).

For those few deprived Americans who have never read the book or seen a movie or a stage version, the outline of *Ben-Hur* is relatively simple. The hero is a young Jewish prince who falls victim to treachery and for a time becomes a Roman galley slave. Trained in the Roman arts of combat, he rises in favor with his masters, is able to vanquish his old enemies, and is also successful in love. He learns of the ministry of Jesus and eventually becomes an eyewitness to the crucifixion. He is, in fact, identified as the very soldier, nameless in scripture, who lifted the sponge to the thirsting Jesus on the cross. After witnessing spectacular healing miracles, Ben-Hur becomes a follower and dedicates his restored fortune to the Christian cause, through the establishment of the Catacomb of San Calixto, which will serve as a refuge for Christians during the coming persecutions.

Though the mission of Jesus was the central backdrop to the adventure story of Ben-Hur, Wallace was wise enough to use the person of Jesus very sparingly in his novel. Even so, his Jesus is not very interesting. He is described, admittedly by the villainess of the piece, as "a man with a woman's face and hair, riding an ass's colt and in tears" (514). Despite its inadequate portrait of Jesus, no other religious novel has surpassed the excitement and spectacle of Ben-Hur, with its worldwide adventure setting, later to be copied by so many American and even European historical novels and films. Even with its defects, the book was a work of real though bizarre stature. The same cannot be said for the lesser fictions following in its wake, which quickly seized upon the Jesus "with a woman's face and hair," who performed magic feats and medical wonders, as a promising figure for commercial exploitation.

The most disastrous such offering was *Come Forth*, written by
Elizabeth Stuart Phelps Ward in collaboration with her youthful clergyman husband, Herbert D. Ward, at the nadir of a career otherwise not
devoid of achievement. In this Bible adventure story the conventions
of the *fin de siècle* Gothic romance are anachronistically transposed
into the first century, and Jesus is sent to rescue Lazarus from amorous
entanglements.

The woman who was to become Elizabeth Stuart Phelps Ward was
born in 1844 into a family prominent for its writers and clergymen. Both
her maternal grandfather and her father had been professors at Andover
Theological Seminary. She was given the name of her mother, Elizabeth
Stuart Phelps, who had earned some acclaim herself as a writer. In her
early twenties the junior Elizabeth, a spirited woman who had already
dismissed the Calvinism of Andover as "predestination, foreordination,
botheration," suffered her first genuine tragedy. After losing her fiancé on
a Civil War battlefield, she became for a time a recluse, obsessed by grief
and visions of death. Yet out of this mourning emerged her first best seller,
The Gates Ajar. Published in 1868, the book established her, in the words
of James D. Hart, as "America's foremost authority on the home life of
heaven," merited three sequels from her pen—*Beyond the Gates, The
Gates Between*, and *Within the Gates*—and provoked imitations, such as
George Wood's *The Gates Wide Open*. There was even a parody from
Mark Twain (no small distinction) entitled *Captain Stormfield's Visit to
Heaven*. Like her old friend Harriet Beecher Stowe, whom she had first
known at Andover where Mrs. Stowe was a faculty wife, Elizabeth Phelps
believed her most acclaimed book was not the work of her brain alone.
"The angel said unto me 'Write' and I wrote!" she later revealed (Hart:
121). Mrs. Stowe is said to have gone to her grave believing *Uncle Tom's
Cabin* to have been the result of inspiration.

Though *The Gates Ajar*, with its description of heavenly kitchens
filled with gingersnaps, was regarded as her masterpiece, Phelps wrote a
number of financially successful novels and was active in social movements. By 1888, when she was forty-four, she had recovered sufficiently
from her earlier disappointment in love to marry Herbert Dickinson Ward,
a clergyman seventeen years her junior and by all accounts an arrogant,
self-absorbed young man. She collaborated with him on a number of biblical romances, which, though they never reached the large audiences of her
earlier books, satisfied her special circles of readers and were generously
reviewed. The first fruit of the Ward collaboration, *Master of the Magicians*, a story of Daniel and Nebuchadnezzar, was commended by *Critic*,
Atlantic, and *Nation* for its characterization of Daniel, the Bible's noble
prophet, as "a love-lorn and unconsoled hero."/6/

Come Forth, the Christological novel still mentioned in histories of American popular writing, was published in 1891. Jesus, who magically materializes and dematerializes, does little more than appear at crucial moments in the action to rescue the heroes and heroines who have gotten themselves into amorous entanglements. The book is primarily the love story of Lazarus, a young master builder of the "affluent middle classes," who surreptitiously meets his girlfriend in the crypt in the Temple of Jerusalem, catches his death of cold, and has to be resurrected by Jesus.

Come Forth contains 318 pages of saccharine dialogue and the crudest anachronisms. The plot ingredients, from *fin de siècle* romance, include misplaced love letters, confused directions, conspiring servants, oppressive fathers, invalid beauties, and secret lovers' meetings at midnight.

Jesus the Martyred Idealist

The thirty years before the next major Christological novel appeared were a welcome respite. In contrast to the embarrassing narrative of the Wards, two serious, though unconventional, portraits of Jesus were published in 1922 and 1939. They came, respectively, from the pens of Upton Sinclair, who attempted to use Jesus as a tool for castigating the excesses of capitalist society, and Polish-born Sholem Asch, who had the noble aim of reconciling Gentile and Jew around the figure of Jesus of Nazareth, prophet for Jew and messiah for Gentile.

In the early years of the present century Upton Sinclair was America's best-known writer, with 772 translations of his books available in forty-seven languages. Sinclair was greatly respected by the international intelligentsia; his friends included Thomas Mann, Albert Einstein, Bertrand Russell, Rabindranath Tagore, Mahatma Ghandi, Carl Jung, and countless others. Before America ever reluctantly recognized Sinclair's contribution to the national cultural life by awarding him a Pulitzer Prize, a number of his influential admirers had already petitioned, though unsuccessfully, that he be honored with a Nobel Prize./7/

Sinclair is best remembered today for *The Jungle*, which exposed the conditions of the nation's meat-packing plants and led to the passage by Congress of the first pure food legislation. Other books examined coal strikes, the commercialization of art, control of public opinion by big business, and the erosion of standards of colleges and universities. With *The Mental Radio*, Sinclair embraced psychic research and contributed substantially to the modest measure of respectability that it gained.

Considering the breadth of his interests, it is not surprising that Sinclair should eventually turn his full attention to religion. *The Profits of*

Religion, written in 1918, was the first volume of a carefully projected series designed to explore what the author regarded as the "tainted bond" between capitalist economics and ecclesiastical religion. *A Personal Jesus* (1952) was an interpretive biography in which the "Man of Nazareth" was sympathetically but nontheologically viewed. Even earlier, in *Candid Reminiscences*, Sinclair had made clear his religious views, recalling his proper Episcopalian upbringing and how his poor, yet respectable and even aristocratic, family had placed him under the spiritual direction of a young priest, whom he continued to remember with fondness and respect. His considerable quarrel with the Church, he admitted, was in essence a lover's quarrel. His desire, he further claimed, was not to destroy but to recover; he felt called to restore to the public the social teachings of Jesus as he believed them to have been before the Church became the instrument of kings, before its fresh, profound, and original teachings became shrouded in mystery and dogma.

Two novels, *They Call Me Carpenter* (1922) and *Our Lady* (1938), can be termed Christological. They demonstrate a blending of socialist preoccupations with biblical lore and set the Gospel according to Sinclair in judgment against modern society. Though written in a popular rather than a self-consciously literary style, the novels were not best sellers. Neither did they arouse the ire of the orthodox, as Sinclair had predicted, because by that time the author was more usually looked upon with an amused, even affectionate, indulgence.

They Call Me Carpenter differed in a number of significant ways from the books that had preceded it in the Christological genre. Its main purpose was to present the social rather than the spiritual interpretation of Jesus' teaching, so it did not attempt, like the earlier fiction, to recreate the Palestinian setting in which the historical figure of Jesus moved. Neither did it attempt any episode-by-episode account of the ministry. Instead it brought the man Jesus into the present, where he became "Mr. Carpenter." As the book opens, Jesus is preaching on the streets of Western City, a place resembling Hollywood, and turning down a lucrative film contract offered by a famed movie maker who makes extravagent promises of fame and fortune. Jesus meets Mary Magna, a movie queen, who is laboring under an oppressive seven-year contract, from which he manages to disentangle her. While proclaiming his social message, Mr. Carpenter/Jesus begins attracting opposition. After a number of increasingly dangerous adventures, he narrowly escapes martyrdom by bounding into a convenient church sanctuary and retreating to safety within one of the church's stained glass windows.

The book impressed only those who already admired Sinclair or who had their own gripes against the Christian establishment. H. L. Mencken suggested that the book should be required reading for churchmen and that "every Episcopal bishop in the Republic should be jailed until he can prove that he has read it" (Sinclair, 1960:201–82). Others were less enthusiastic. *Springfield Republican* described the book as decidedly "sophomoric" and concluded that "a generous estimate of the work would be that Mr. Sinclair has written little more than a trivial, light and unimportant message!" (7a).

A more interesting non-Christian, though highly sympathetic, fictional portrait of Jesus was issued in 1939 from the pen of the distinguished Polish-born writer Sholem Asch. Asch designed his book to be a tool for bringing together Jew and Gentile.

Writing in Yiddish, Asch had already, through translation, helped open a fascinating subculture to the American reader. Years before the general public discovered Isaac Bashevis Singer, Asch, according to Sol Liptzin, had placed "a romantic halo around the despised townlets of his native land" (178). Realistic and honest in his depiction of eastern European Jewish life, Asch was generally viewed as a defender of Yiddish art and manners. With his Americanization, beginning with the outbreak of World War I and the later publication of his Christological novels, he became a special favorite of Gentile audiences, causing some consternation among his fellow Jews. Many felt he was rejecting the Yiddish materials which had made his reputation in order to write about Christian subjects. Furthermore, the timing of the publication of *The Nazarene* (1939) did not lend confidence. The book was issued at the peak of the Nazi conquests, which threatened altogether to wipe out Jewish life in Europe. Asch's desire to establish Jesus in the hearts of his own people was unfulfilled.

Alfred Kazin observed, with more humor and pertinence than most of Asch's critics, that "though Asch went forth in search of Yeshua [the name the author always uses for his hero], he fell among the tired lambs of the Epworth League." Yet *The Nazarene*, according to Kazin, was nevertheless of some merit since "these days Bible stories are for children, or by Lloyd Douglas" (626).

Non-Jewish reviewers were much kinder, appreciating Asch's scholarship and knowledge of Jewish history and customs. They acknowledged him a writer of genuine ethical-moral sensitivity, working in a fictional field where Jesus, supreme teacher, had been too often reduced to the role of flamboyant miracle worker. Adequately promoted, *The Nazarene* became one of the great American best sellers and is still being read.

The plot of the book is complicated, even convoluted; there is a reincarnation frametale and a double focus on "Judah Ish-Kiriot" and the

Wandering Jew of European legend. Judas is revealed as a Zealot who
betrays Jesus in order to test him, believing that he will call his heavenly
legions to demolish the political enemies of the Jews. The Wandering
Jew, who is the book's narrator, is a figure of mysterious memories and
arcane knowledge. Despite the awkwardness of the curious occult frametale, Asch's skill as a storyteller is far superior to that of the average
novelist who has chosen the Gospel story for fictional treatment. Judas
stands out as a strongly realized character. If his Jesus never becomes
very interesting, Asch at least avoids vulgarity. Though one respects its
noble aims, *The Nazarene* is not an artistic success, chiefly for this reason. The portrayal of Jesus is inadequate. Though Jesus is imaginative
and poetically eloquent, he is described as a slight figure, "face fringed
with the young beard . . . frail body . . . slender neck, the expression of
infinite pity!" He remains "the pale Galilean."

A final book by Asch deserves mention. Long intrigued by the
mother of Jesus, Asch devoted an entire novel to her. *Mary*, the final
volume in a trilogy that included also *The Apostle* (relating the struggles
in the early Church between Peter and Paul), was written with deep
affection and a need to probe the problems of mothers of extraordinary
sons. Even today it has considerable psychological interest.

Jesus, the Psychotherapist

Seven years after Upton Sinclair, the lapsed Episcopalian, ventured
into biblical fiction and over sixty years after the Reverend Joseph Holt
Ingraham's *The Prince of the House of David*, a romanticized life of
Christ appeared from the pen of another Episcopalian clergyman. The
Reverend Dr. Robert Norwood was a prominent personality, rector of
the fashionable St. Bartholomew's Church at Park Avenue and Fifty-first
streets in New York City and author of a number of colorfully entitled
historical works of fiction./8/ *The Man Who Dared to Be God*, his fic-
tionalization of Jesus' life, appeared in 1929.

The Reverend Dr. Robert Norwood was an adventurous, rather
flamboyant personality himself, known for forceful sermons setting forth
a multitude of often controversial opinions and prejudices. He disliked
prohibitionists, materialists, and most modern literature, which he pas-
sionately denounced from his pulpit as "soulless." While accepting some
of the more ludicrous occult fads of his time, he was nevertheless a ratio-
nalist when it came to Holy Scripture and Christian dogma. In his sermons he liked to present "common sense" interpretations of the miracles
of Jesus, relying heavily on the findings of psychotherapy. It was to his
embarrassment in February of 1931 that a "miracle" took place in his

own parish, after he had just delivered a series of Lenten talks on "the Resurrected Christ," in which he had mingled the highest ethics and the most enlightened rationalism. A strange configuration was discovered in the veining of the brown marble wall above his sanctuary door. Viewed with some imagination, this pattern seemed to resemble the Christ of the old masters rising from his tomb. Dr. Norwood, rarely at a loss when asked to unravel the riddles of God or humanity, suggested an explanation: "I have a weird theory that the force of thought, a dominant thought, may be strong enough and powerful enough to be, somehow, transferred to stone in its receptive state."/9/ This strange occurrence, however accounted for, attracted wide publicity and for days following its discovery pilgrims thronged to the church. The publicity also did no harm to Norwood's writing career.

Though favorably reviewed at publication, *The Man Who Dared to Be God* is likely to appear to its rare reader today not only undistinguished but downright embarrasssing, with its half-digested higher criticism and self-proclaimed "enlightened" theology. Dr. Norwood was not only totally devoid of a historical sense, but he was not even very well informed on the facts of history, which could have been easily acquired from a careful reading of a few works by the Jewish and Christian scholars who have painstakingly reconstructed much of the life of the first century. Without apology, after boldly assuming in his preface his right to do so, Norwood took liberties rearranging Gospel events, adding and omitting to suit his purposes, offering his own sometimes eccentric interpretations of selected deeds and utterances of Jesus, while few meaningful insights were provided.

Norwood, who claimed to be patterning his work after the Gospel of Luke, addressed himself to "the modern Theophilus," who in his view is not unlike that learned Greek of old, presumed to be antagonized by established religion, distressed by ritualism and formality, annoyed when he is forced to say prayers in archaic language, pleading to be saved from the "wrath and indignation" of the Almighty, and tired of contemplating an emaciated figure made of bits of colored glass on a cross above a chapel altar (xiii).

Since a convention of the genre already encouraged authors of fictionalized lives of Jesus to begin with professions of personal faith, Norwood started by declaring: "I believe in God because I believe in man; and God is real to me when I touch Jesus of Nazareth. He did not work miracles, if by that word you mean magic. So I have left out the miraculous element in the story. Psycho-therapy is not magic, it is science, however dimly apprehended. It is my belief that Jesus developed wonderful powers, and used them because he found God" (xiii).

Jesus and a Cast of Thousands:
The Great Physician and His Patients

Whereas Norwood's narrative of a simple, pastoral Jesus lacked any of the sweep and excitement of the earlier Christological fiction, the mantle of Lew Wallace was soon to fall in earnest upon Lloyd C. Douglas. *The Robe*, published in 1942, restored to biblical fiction some of the epic adventure of *Ben-Hur*. Though a later Douglas novel, *The Big Fisherman*, would present Jesus as a central figure rather than as the mere point of departure for a narrative of international intrigue and adventure, as was his function in *The Robe*, the latter novel was never to achieve the overwhelming popularity of the first big biblical spectacular. It is *The Robe* that established for Douglas a lasting place in the history of popular American fiction and religious thought.

Although Sinclair, Norwood, and Asch had written in a style accessible to a broad, anxious, general audience, their novels were highly instructional in design, their aim being "to teach with delight." Lloyd C. Douglas, Frank G. Slaughter, and Taylor Caldwell, who have largely dominated Christological fiction since the forties, are, although by no means devoid of opinions, primarily mass entertainers. Sustaining a shrewd awareness of the demands of the American market, they have fully exploited the public's enthusiasm for historical romance, particularly biblical lore. It is possible to gain some genuine understanding of the postwar "religious revival" in North America by examining their books.

Lloyd C. Douglas, who died in 1951 at the age of seventy-three, is one of the most interesting figures ever to appear on the popular American fiction scene; although he was over fifty when he wrote his first novel, it proved impossible for him to write a book that did not become a best seller. In youth Douglas had followed his father's calling and entered the Lutheran ministry, yet he had never felt completely comfortable in that brotherhood. Almost from the beginning he had expressed serious doubts concerning several theological doctrines; he seemed temperamentally incapable of believing in the possibility of human damnation or the existence of a devil. After having served several Lutheran parishes somewhat uncomfortably, he became minister of the more liberal First Congregational Church in Ann Arbor, Michigan. In 1933 Douglas retired from the conventional ministry altogether to devote himself to what Carl Bode has called "the largest parish in the world," his reading public. His books, both his early religious and inspirational discourses and his later novels, which embodied in narrative form his Christian message, reached people largely of the middle class, who, though they felt the need for guidance and were in Douglas's own words "spiritually wistful," often hesitated to stir from their homes, having developed a distaste for parish life with its bond drives and ecclesiastical politics.

With his novels attracting readers around the world, Douglas started receiving thousands of letters from admirers who wished his advice on the major problems of their lives. He conscientiously answered all letters, despite his full writing schedule, and gave what help and spiritual guidance he could. His daughters did not exaggerate when they said, "*The Robe* preached to a mighty cathedral, and its author had the satisfaction of knowing that his words had sent thousands of their readers to their Bibles and thousands who had never before turned its pages sought the scriptures with awakened interest" (Dawson and Wilson: 84).

Douglas never pretended that his novels were refined works of literary art but offered them only as "old-fashioned narratives" in which decent characters usually worked through their problems to happy reconciliations. He accepted criticism graciously, placing no great importance upon what book reviewers said about the deficiencies of his craft. The following casual allusion to his customary mauling at the hands of the professional critics is revealing:

> A few years ago Mr. Bernard DeVoto wrote, in reviewing one of my novels, "Whenever Douglas is in doubt which of two adjectives to use, he uses both of them." I made no attempt to defend myself for the accusation was true. . . . However a writer—if he has any sense at all—doesn't talk back to his critics, even when they are unfair. Not long ago, a reviewer said my composition was "almost ungrammatical." My curiosity was stirred. What kind of sentence could be "almost ungrammatical." My notion was that a sentence might be grammatical, or ungrammatical, but I hadn't previously known about this No Man's Land, this twilight where one spoke almost incorrectly. . . . (1951:37)

It is not surprising that readers of *The Robe* compared Douglas's tale of miracle and adventure to *Ben-Hur*. Generously acknowledging Lew Wallace as his literary mentor, Douglas wrote, "Eventually the time came when I felt moved to write a novel which began and ended in that enchanted city on the Tiber. Doubtless my lifetime interest in Rome aided me. I am sure I have General Lew Wallace's *Ben-Hur* to thank for much of this early preoccupation with the Roman Empire. Perhaps I should also give credit to Barnum and Bailey" (1951:168).

In *The Robe* Douglas builds upon a reader's natural curiosity to know more than the New Testament or history reveals about events associated with the life of Jesus. What happened to the possessions of Jesus? Did the Roman soldiers at the crucifixion ever suspect they were eyewitnesses to one of the pivotal events in human history? The immediate stimulus for the writing of the book, however, was a letter Douglas received from a reader of his earlier books, Hazel McCann, who was a saleswoman in a department store in Canton, Ohio. She asked a simple question that suggested to Douglas the story for which his entire career had been preparing him, "Did you ever know what became of the robe which the soldiers gambled for after the crucifixion?" When the book was completed, it was affectionately dedicated to Hazel McCann.

Marcellus, the hero of *The Robe*, is the Roman soldier whose duty it is to supervise the crucifixion of Jesus. Having scruples about his unpleasant task, he fortifies himself with wine and in his drunken state acquires Jesus' robe through the casting of lots. Marcellus returns to Rome, leads an active life, yet is haunted by the memory of the crucifixion. Later, in one of the book's climaxes, he meets face to face the celebrated Big Fisherman, Peter himself. Marcellus becomes convinced that Jesus is indeed "an eternal person, a divine person with powers that no king or emperor has ever possessed," who will, Marcellus feels sure, some day return to rule the world. After a conversion to the new Christian faith and many additional intrigues and adventures, Marcellus dies a happy martyr's death.

Earlier in his career, especially around the time he resigned his pastorate, Douglas had been troubled by his serious reservations about basic Christian dogmas. He facetiously yet a little sadly had admitted that he always felt more comfortable reciting the Apostles' Creed in Latin, precisely because he understood that language none too well. Douglas's views, however, did not remain static. After the publication of *The Big Fisherman*, a sort of sequel called forth by the popularity of *The Robe*, Carl Bode, an academic critic who had keenly observed the Douglas career with a slightly perverse fascination, suggested that a personal religious pilgrimage could be perceived in the novels, which when read closely revealed their author's growing faith in the objective reality of the miraculous and the unique divinity of Jesus. In later books less "positive thinking" and "personality improvement" were evident, according to Bode, and a greater concern with the enormous questions of divinity and immortality could be clearly discerned (1950a:817–18). Daughters Virginia Douglas Dawson and Betty Douglas Wilson, who knew first-hand the personal crises in the life of their father preceding the publication of *The Big Fisherman*, were ready to substantiate Bode's contention that at long last the author of the famous novels of faith had converted himself and had been able to say without reservations that he also believed (369). Like his literary master, Lew Wallace, Douglas had written himself into classical Christianity.

The numerous biblical novels of Dr. Frank G. Slaughter, a physician who relinquished his practice to become a full-time writer, only dimly echo the minor epic thrills of *Ben-Hur* and *The Robe*. While grand and ancient civilizations do not clash in the Slaughter books, the novels do demonstrate an unfailing awareness of the demands of the American reading public, and, since Slaughter's books are often even more popular abroad than at home, they seem to suggest the author's brilliant understanding of the demands of the reading masses elsewhere as well. Dr. Slaughter's books reach over twenty million readers in over eight different languages. It is probable that only two American novelists, Erskine Caldwell and Erle Stanley Gardner, are more widely read abroad. Though Slaughter can describe an act of violence or a seduction scene as well as either of his competitors, his readers tend to skim these pages hurriedly, moving on to the high point of any Slaughter novel, the gory description of the doctor-hero's spectacular surgical operation. After he started writing biblical fiction, Slaughter discovered he could even dispense with much of the sex, provided he made the surgical scenes graphic and detailed enough. "People keep coming up to me," he has observed, "to tell me how much they enjoyed the medical parts. No, I don't think it's just because they like blood; it's the drama that appeals to them—the thing that makes people crowd around a bad accident" (*Newsweek*, 1961:82).

So great became the demand for Dr. Slaughter's books that he was obliged to organize a fiction factory, patterned after the procedures of the "brain-teams" he had observed during his medical training at Johns Hopkins Hospital. Doctors, nurses, and technical specialists worked in surgery with rigorous coordination. Slaughter decided to employ researchers, historians, and other specialists to assist in compiling his books, and he found the results highly satisfactory. Yet despite this "brain-team" effort, each book issued in his name has continued to bear his indelible stamp; it is an original product certain to please the Slaughter addict.

It was only a matter of time until Slaughter would combine his interests in religion and medicine and write a novel about St. Luke, the evangelist and beloved physician. A religious man and an elder of Riverside Presbyterian Church near Jacksonville, Florida, Dr. Slaughter was especially drawn to the material that would give him not only the opportunity to explore first-century medicine but also to express his Low-Church sentiments and rescue, he hoped, "the Master" (as he always referred to Jesus) from cold liturgical worship.

In *The Road to Bithynia*, which turned out to be only the first of a series of biblical novels, Slaughter proved that his long-established formula could be applied to scriptural materials with few modifications.

Jesus himself, not to mention Paul, was subordinated to the description of St. Luke's Caesarean delivery of the living baby of a woman who had just died. Twenty million readers, savoring descriptions of medical skills that would do credit to a modern Christiaan Barnard, were not greatly distressed that St. Luke appeared more interested in surgery and amorous adventures than in writing a Gospel.

Slaughter's image of Jesus and method of handling him in fiction is best observed in three novels in which Jesus features as a character—*The Galileans* (1953), *The Crown and the Cross* (1959), and *Upon This Rock* (1964). *The Crown and the Cross*, a biographical novel of Jesus, should have been Slaughter's magnum opus, but it actually turned out to be the least interesting of his biblical romances. Slaughter's Jesus is not a very interesting character, as one can see from the description of him. He is "meek and mild" and considered "too quiet and unassuming to be a success in any trade." Later on in his career when, nearing its close, Jesus casts the money-changers out of the Temple, the disciples are aghast: they have never before seen Jesus behave in this manner, so totally out of character!

Almost all biblical novelists—if we can judge from statements made by Ware, Ingraham, Sinclair, Wallace, Caldwell, and others—seem to have had clear intentions in writing their books, whether to convert the Jews, arouse the proletarian masses, prove to the Ingersoll radicals the plausibility of Jesus' divine claims, or fulfill a childhood ambition. Slaughter has stated his design simply:

> I do not claim any particular purpose in writing Biblical novels. However, they and the period do interest me very much and, while I carefully avoid theology and particularly eschatology and any charismatic sequences, I suppose the fact that they interest me so much does indicate something, though I'm not sure exactly what. At the moment I am a bit hipped on the failure of liturgical religion to reach people today and certainly Christ was preaching something of this, so I cannot say that working on these books doesn't actually influence strongly my own thinking and approach to life. I do feel that I know all these people at least as well as I know my own family and I feel a strong kinship with them. But my point of view is more that of a technician reconstructing a period, than one who is consciously trying to mold the thinking of a reader./10/

Whatever his methods and motivations, Dr. Slaughter has for many years invariably pleased his readers. He was only being honest, not boastful, when he said, "No publisher ever lost a dime on Frank G. Slaughter" (*Newsweek*, 1961:82).

Capitalizing on the American fascination with doctors, if not always with carpenters and incarnate gods, Taylor Caldwell's *Dear and Glorious Physician* retains the same international setting that has been employed by the best of the Christological novelists. Her characters shift back and forth from the court of Tiberius to the hovels of Galilee. Her Romans are the usual circus-loving, conquering men-at-arms readers have come to expect. And, like Slaughter, Caldwell focuses attention on St. Luke, the individual who, considering the tastes of the American fiction-reading, soap-opera-watching public, risks upstaging Jesus himself.

Caldwell, always fascinated by the personality of St. Luke, started writing *Dear and Glorious Physician*, if her own words are to be credited, while she was still a girl in England but was unable at that time to finish it. Years later, as a famous author established in the United States, she resumed the work. Harriet Beecher Stowe and Elizabeth Stuart Phelps Ward would surely have understood her meaning when she observed that, after this long period of gestation, when she was finally able to return to her writing it came very easy: "It seemed almost as if it were being dictated" (*Newsweek*, 1959:104).

Her conscious preparation for the book, quite apart from what had been going on in her subconscious mind, was intensive. With her husband, Marcus Reback, she read over one thousand histories of the period. In order to familiarize themselves further with ancient medicine, the Rebacks consulted a famous medical specialist, Dr. George E. Slotkin. They wanted to make certain every medical reference in the book would be entirely accurate. The year before the book was published, the Rebacks spent two weeks in the Holy Land. Because of Mr. Reback's Russian-Jewish origin, he was able to assist his wife immeasurably in getting into the atmosphere and "feel" of orthodox Judaism (*Newsweek*, 1959:104–5).

Nineteen fifty-nine, the year of publication of *Dear and Glorious Physician*, was an even better year than usual for books on doctors and medicine, and religious writings too were flourishing—there were publications by Fulton Oursler, Norman Vincent Peale, Bishop Fulton J. Sheen, and Dale Evans Rogers. Compared with the style of the average religious novel, Caldwell's slick yet responsible prose made her book seem commendable in a field sometimes subliterary. Her intelligence, historical sensitivity, and—perhaps most of all—her clearly defined Roman Catholic Christology (little effort was made to compromise with her pluralistic reading public, which seemingly did not mind anyhow) led her to write one of the more graceful, though still flawed, Christological novels in the history of popular American fiction. Edward Wagenknecht, a scholar who has always been noted for his fair criticism of popular fiction, reviewing the book in the *Chicago Sunday Tribune*, noted: "Though Miss Caldwell's story telling skill never fails in it, though her picture of the ancient world is amazingly vivid, her book is by no means all of a piece. Occasionally it reminds one of the religious tales of Henry van Dyke: sometimes it even recalls Bulwer-Lytton and Disraeli. On the other hand, its descriptions of operations are almost unreadable and its evocations of the sinfulness of pagan Rome suggest Hollywood" (2).

Despite its garish moments, *Dear and Glorious Physician* is one of the very few American Bible novels to present a structured and reasonably interesting portrait of Jesus. Caldwell's consistent theological stance, whether one agrees with it or not, lends the work an integrity that is lacking in less secure interpretations. Caldwell had obviously given some thought to the second article of the Christian Credo and had attempted on her pages to suggest a figure who was both true man and true God. When the Nazarene carpenter looks at a well-wrought plowshare, he takes as much pleasure in it, the reader is told, as he took in creating the Pleiades, as the Second Person of the Trinity. The novel, of course, centers on Luke, physician and evangelist. Caldwell presents Jesus opaquely, which is perhaps the only way to introduce him in fiction with any measure of success. She reveals him through the eyes of his mother, his family, and other associates from different stages in his ministry.

Eighteen years after the generally dignified and reserved *Dear and Glorious Physician*, Caldwell published another Christological novel, *I, Judas*, which must take its place among the most eccentric books of its genre yet written in the United States. In composing her book, Caldwell, a writer rarely in need of assistance, for once sought the help of another author, Jess Stearn, a man obviously less skilled in writing than Caldwell but with some reputation as an authority on reincarnation, Edgar Cayce, and ESP topics in general. Though Stearn is given credit as coauthor and was no doubt employed as a consultant on psychic issues, the fiction clearly bears the characteristic stamp of Caldwell.

The genesis of *I, Judas* is painfully curious, according to the author's own account. Following the death of her husband, Marcus Reback, grief, ill health, and hearing difficulties had thrown Caldwell into a serious depression. Upon the advice of friends, she had consented to be hypnotized by a Hollywood practitioner recommended by astrologer Sydney Omarr. Stearn was then commissioned to record the results of her hypnotic sessions. A book resulted, in which Stearn reported how Caldwell under hypnosis was regressed to a number of previous lives. According to his account, she had been, in various incarnations, a maid to George Eliot, the English writer; an Italian nun and follower of Savonarola; and, most pertinent of all, Hannah-bat-Jacob, the mother of the biblical Miriam of Magdala (Mary Magdalene). If this hypnotic data were indeed authentic, then Caldwell was no mere novelist who had chosen on several occasions to fictionalize New Testament personalities; she was an eyewitness who had seen Jesus face-to-face. Even though Caldwell permitted her hypnotic sessions to be publicized, she was careful to make no claims and continued publicly to profess her skepticism. Yet she became, to the best of our knowledge, the only Bible novelist that others have seriously proclaimed an eyewitness observer to events related (Caldwell and Stearn, 1973).

How did this reputed eyewitness view biblical events? *I, Judas* presents a new Gospel, in harmony with the revelations of Caldwell's hypnotic sessions. Judas Iscariot is a serious and gifted revolutionary, dedicated to the cause of Jewish liberation. He betrays Jesus to force the messianic hand and is then betrayed both by the Romans and by the Jewish Sanhedrin, which had promised that Jesus, if indeed brought to trial, would be acquitted of all charges of treason and blasphemy. Judas believes in Jesus' divinity, yet sees him also as the savior of the Jewish people in the political messianic sense. This interpretation of Judas as a Zealot is, of course, by no means new and has even made a previous appearance in fiction, as we have seen. Caldwell describes Jesus as tall and blue-eyed. When he is not paraphrasing the Gospels in *I, Judas*, he mouths nonbiblical yet very pious clichés. The righteous indignation reported on a number of occasions in the Gospels is considerably softened by Caldwell, who finds the experience of genuine anger contrary to his character. Jesus also appears to be something of a sentimentalist. He is seen caressing flowers and speaking to them as if they were sentient creatures. While women adore him and flutter around, he is totally asexual. It is observed that he does not look at women as do other men!

While affirming the divinity of Jesus, Caldwell departs from her earlier Roman Catholic orthodoxy. No doubt a result of her occult explorations and collaboration with Stearn, one of the most significant passages of her narrative presents her new understanding of what it means to be "born again." It should be remembered that in 1977 "born again" was a very familiar phrase in the national media. Caldwell wrote:

> To Nicodemus, one of the Pharisees intrigued by his teaching, Jesus made clear his belief in reincarnation. Nicodemus, a guiding light of the Great Sanhedrin, stole into our camp one night as I [Judas] was making an accounting to the Master. He had fretted over Jesus' references to man reborn. He looked at me askance, but the Master quickly reassured him that he could speak plainly. . . . Jesus told him, "Let me say again . . . that no man, unless he has already ascended from the earth, descends from heaven. Even the Son of Man must be lifted up so that whoever believes in him shall not perish but shall have eternal life." (152)

Jesus continues to teach, "Only the spirit, Nicodemus, is born again, for the body is but the temple of the spirit" (152). It is not surprising that the book includes that Gospel episode of the man born blind and brought to Jesus with the questi1 "Did this man or his parents sin that he was born blind?" Yet Caldwell's Jesus resists any temptation to give a further lecture on reincarnation but simply repeats the reply already known to readers of the Bible.

During her hypnotic trances, according to Stearn's earlier report, Caldwell had recounted in detail the scene in which Jesus forgave the woman taken in adultery. Since it is suspected that she may have been an eyewitness to it, Caldwell makes no apology for taking liberties with this episode in her novel. The woman is clearly identified as Mary Magdalene. When she is brought to him in disgrace, Jesus says, "Let him who has not lain with this woman or any other, let him cast the first stone" (180). Thus, Caldwell and Stearn take one of the basic ethical principles of Jesus and make it particular and limited in their rephrasing of the Gospel episode.

Judas, according to Caldwell, loved Jesus more than all the other disciples. Disheartened and disillusioned after the crucifixion, he wrote his last testament and hastily prepared his death. An epilogue added to the manuscript attributed to Judas describes the resurrection, which Judas tragically misses by only a few days.

The Stenographer's Christ:
Our Lord the Positive Thinker

At the same time as the twentieth-century adventure romances were being written, another type of Christ narrative was making its appearance, that which Robert Detweiler has called the "straight narrative" and identified as a fictionalized version of the *Leben Jesu* of the German scholars./11/ In this category belong Fulton Oursler's *The Greatest Story Ever Told* and Jim Bishop's "days" in the life of Jesus—*The Day Christ Died* and *The Day Christ Was Born*.

With sweeping armies, collapsing empires, and splendid lords and ladies, Douglas, Slaughter, and Caldwell sought to entertain, titillate, and instruct the American masses. On a less grandiose scale, two veterans of *The Reader's Digest*, Fulton Oursler and Jim Bishop, attempted to teach these same readers—identified as the stenographers, file clerks, and sales people of America—the powers of positive thought through a retelling of the Christ story.

Fulton Oursler's *The Greatest Story Ever Told* enjoyed a quick and thorough financial success. Within a week after publication in 1949 it topped the nation's best seller list and remained in that position for several months. Two hundred newspapers all over the United States syndicated the narrative, and translations soon appeared in all countries of Europe outside the Iron Curtain. It was not long in overtaking those perennial best sellers of religious fiction, *Ben-Hur* and *The Robe*. Paperback editions brought the book to thousands of additional readers. Sales passed the three million mark in the 1960s, and Oursler, formerly known chiefly as a Macfadden editor-in-chief and *Reader's Digest* senior editor, became unquestionably America's most familiar Christological novelist./12/

Oursler's book was an acknowledged attempt to write the American life of Jesus, which would be inoffensive to Catholic, Protestant, or Jew. Between 1949 and 1964, while it went through numerous printings, the book received extravagant praise from Norman Vincent Peale, J. Edgar Hoover, and the brother of Justice Felix Frankfurter of the Supreme Court. Dr. Peale designated it "one of the most distinguished books of our time." John A. O'Brien, head of the Department of Philosophy of the University of Notre Dame, avowed it would "do a world of good," and J. Edgar Hoover suggested it was a book worth taking into eternity./13/

Oursler labored eleven years on his book and by the time it was published he had become, after many struggles and partly as a result of writing the book, a devout Roman Catholic./14/ Yet many of his readers were never aware of his affiliation. Though his son, Fulton Oursler, Jr., is a bit presumptuous when he states "by his voice and pen he became a herald—a precursor of the spirit of John XXIII, and the ecumenical hopes of our time" (466), Oursler is certainly the prime religious conciliator of "pop" fiction. As other writings reveal, he became the sort of Roman Catholic who did not speculate on the pronouncements of the Church but accepted them absolutely. Yet in his popular fiction he was never assertive of his own denominational views. *The Greatest Story Ever Told* was in fact usually made available in two editions, one for Protestants and the other for Catholics, the only difference being the official imprimatur on the latter.

April Oursler Armstrong recognized that "the trademark of my father's books on Scripture was their enthusiastic acceptance by leaders of all faiths" (203). She noted her father's "native genius of being ecumenical, and of staying within the area of agreement." What Fulton Oursler knew instinctively she claimed she was forced to learn painstakingly when, at her father's death, it fell to her to finish his last book, *The Greatest Faith Ever Known*. She achieved her father's effortless effect only after careful tutoring by the man Oursler had referred to as "my Protestant pastor," Dr. Norman Vincent Peale, old friend and associate of the family.

The dramatic scenes of *The Greatest Story Ever Told* were first presented, even before the publication of the book, in a series of radio plays, which were, needless to mention, successful even beyond expectations. Before going on the air, all received the unqualified approval of a board of clergy affiliated with the major faiths of the radio audience, including Judaism.

Though Oursler took his narrative outline from the Gospels, his indiscriminate mingling of archaic diction with contemporary conversation and his free additions of prosaic dialogue between biblical figures is immediately jolting to the reader today. *The Reader's Digest* mentality that pervades the book is evident even in the chapter headings: "Joseph Dreams a Dream," "Shepherds at the Back Door," "Two Pigeons, Please," "The Caterer is Amazed" [about the miracle at Cana], "The Tax Agent Resigns," "A Young Girl Dances," "Pilate's Fireplace." The narrative episodes follow Jesus from his nativity to the crucifixion, with a few low-keyed pages at the end devoted to his resurrection. Unfortunately, the portrait of Jesus, even from childhood, is not a very attractive one. He is too prim, priggish, and joyless. He grows up as a gentle, athletic boy with superhuman abilities. He senses everything more acutely than the average boy; in fact, his senses are "the most perfect faculties since Adam." He rapidly grows to manhood, and before anyone realizes what has taken place he has acquired a circle of rustic followers and is planning an evangelistic tour, much in the manner of a first-century Billy Graham. Early in his ministry Jesus does permit himself one indulgence, a wedding feast, even though Oursler declares, "He did not often attend parties of this kind; He was too thoughtful, too studious, too solitary for such festivities" (103). Yet even his joyous miracle performed there, which gave the wedding guests such pleasure, was unable to make the gloomy Jesus cheerful, the reader is told, and he walked back toward Nazareth "in deep, reflective silence."

After the publication of *The Greatest Story Ever Told*, Oursler, like a number of other American religious novelists, suddenly found himself regarded as a father confessor and religious authority. His opinions were freely sought on moral, ethical, and spiritual matters, and his responses were widely quoted, along with those of Dr. Graham, Dr. Peale, Bishop Fulton J. Sheen, and Rabbi Joshua Liebman, the other popular religious spokesmen. And like Lloyd C. Douglas, Oursler took this vocation so newly thrust upon him seriously, if the words of his daughter are accurate. She relates that her father would often spend the evening on long-distance telephone in order to cheer up some despondent reader who had poured out problems to him in a letter that had arrived in the morning mail (Armstrong: 123).

Oursler embarked on two sequels, *The Greatest Book Ever Written*, in which he applied his colloquial diction to the Old Testament, and *The*

Greatest Faith Ever Known, his rendering of the Acts and Epistles of the New Testament and the missionary endeavors of the apostles. The last volume of the trilogy was interrupted by his death but eventually was completed, largely by his daughter, April Oursler Armstrong.

Unlike Oursler, Jim Bishop was a cradle Catholic who never, it would appear from his writings, seriously deviated from his inherited faith. His preparations to be the journalistic reviewer of the two most important days in Christian history began very early. As a boy in New Jersey he had often watched his father, Lt. John M. Bishop of the Jersey City Police Department, write official reports on the dining room table of their home. Young Bishop became intrigued by his father's sparse prose, which he would later imitate when he became a journalist and the author of a series of dramatized studies of history. Bishop is best known for his "day" form of historical reconstruction, which involves accumulating the minutiae—authentic and hypothetical—of a period in history in order to recreate vividly one twenty-four-hour sequence in the life of a famous personality. His "day" books began with *The Day Lincoln Was Shot* (1955), which was generally acclaimed as an interesting experiment and a lively recreation of a dramatic crisis in American history. His series continued, to include in the next decade *The Day Kennedy Was Shot*. Two years after the successful book on Lincoln was published, Bishop applied his now-tested formula to sacred history in *The Day Christ Died*./15/ Three years later the less ambitious volume, *The Day Christ Was Born*, appeared, replete with full-color reproductions of nativity scenes from the old masters.

Bishop's preparations for writing *The Day Christ Died* were thorough; he spent fourteen months in research alone, going through an estimated two million words of scholarship pertinent to the subject./16/ He spent seven weeks in the Holy Land attempting to retrace step by step Jesus' path to the cross. Both His Holiness Pius XII and President Eisenhower endorsed his efforts. The aristocratic pope, somewhat touchingly, is said to have expressed his pleasure that this was not to be a scholarly book but rather a simple one written for the multitude of ordinary believers. President Eisenhower shared his own impressions of Jerusalem with Bishop, and the two discovered that they were startlingly in agreement about a certain "telescoped" diminutive quality found in the Holy Places.

The Day Christ Died was decidedly ecumenical in appeal, though Catholic reviewers received it somewhat more favorably than Protestant ones. James Lloyd of *Catholic World* wondered how anyone, provided he had "some reverence and belief" (109), could fail to like the book, which was so fully in accord with Church tradition. Professor Reinhold

Niebuhr reviewed the book for the *New York Times*, demonstrating soundly that profound thinkers are not the best critics of popular books. Niebuhr was unimpressed and, somewhat irrelevantly, took Bishop to task for his failure to write a proper neo-orthodox life of Jesus, something Bishop certainly never had the remotest intention of doing. Not only did Bishop accept the Johannine narrative as fully historical, complained Niebuhr, but he failed as well to deal rationalistically with the "miracles" of Jesus. Even more objectionable, from Niebuhr's point of view, was the author's unquestioned acceptance of the virgin birth of Jesus, which to many Christians, contended the theologian, is "not a validation but a hazard to faith" (10).

A more pertinent review was Donald Malcolm's "Another Day! Another Dollar!" which appeared in *New Republic*. After expressing humble amazement in the presence of a man who could publish in the same month an account of the last twenty-four hours of Jesus' life and a series of equally detailed articles in *American Weekly* on Jayne Mansfield, Malcolm registered distress with Bishop's paraphrasing of episodes from the Gospel of John and concluded his critique by saying, "I am not qualified to judge whether Mr. Bishop's offenses against theology are as great as his offenses against literature, but I have my suspicions. In fact, with the calm expectation that events will bear me out, I have already begun work on a book of my own to be titled: *The Day Jim Bishop Was Struck by Lightning*" (18).

In his preface-apologia Bishop set forth mind-boggling ambitions for his book. He wanted to show Jesus among his own people with "a journalistic historian's approach rather than that of a theologian." If possible, he also wanted to probe the self-imposed limitations of Jesus when he came here as man, and, finally, "I wanted to understand his relationship with God the Father and God the Holy Ghost" (1957:xi–xii). Although Bishop is presumably concerned with only one day in the life of Jesus, he reviews the entire ministry through the use of numerous flashbacks. His narrative follows Jesus step by step through his path to the cross and the tormenting hours there, providing factual historical commentary to assist the reader in understanding exactly what is taking place. A sense of immediacy is the goal, almost as if the event in truth were being reported by *Time* or the local newspaper. The resurrection was, of course, another day, and Bishop's book closed with a summary explanation of the crucifixion, along with a statement of assurance of a rebirth for all mankind through a new dispensation to be ruled by a Jesus who, even in the sepulcher, still lived and promised life to all.

It is not surprising that Bishop, after once immersing himself in the first century in preparation for *The Day Christ Died*, returned to the material three years later and produced a second book, this time a slight one, on the first day in the earthly life of Jesus. In *The Day Christ Was Born* the "day" style of journalistic-history, however, became a more artificial device than before, and the author could not pretend to hold himself to a focus on the single day. To compensate, Bishop loaded his second book, more than his first, with what he called "my imaginings," adding many awkward scenes and much clumsy dialogue.

Bishop would probably have objected to the unqualified classification of his books as fiction, and they are not generally so treated in libraries or literary discussions. They are, however, pseudo-reportage at best and not scholarly treatises nor, obviously, eyewitness accounts of what they purport to disclose. Bishop does not hesitate in either book to add conversations for which there is neither scriptural warrant, source in Christian tradition, nor even very much point. He is able to describe the parents and associates of Jesus, although the Bible gives no indication of their physical features and pious tradition on these points is contradictory. While such descriptions could be easily allowed as necessary prerogatives of the novelist, other habits are less easily excused. Bishop is rarely without a ready interpretation of any event related in the Gospel narrative, even though it may have perplexed theologians and scholars for many centuries.

The Christological Novel and the "Death of God"

In the last two decades some more daringly venturesome fictional interpretations of Jesus' career have appeared on the popular market. Frank Yerby's *Judas, My Brother* is a departure and, for a less assured writer, might have been considered a highly risky venture. As it was, *Ebony* labeled the book "Yerby's supreme challenge." Long a best-selling novelist who has always scornfully dismissed the critics when they have accused him of pandering to popular tastes, Yerby, without apology, produced a book that expressed his profound distaste for theology, religion in general, and Christianity in particular, a Christological novel that would seem certain to offend millions. Though born and educated in the southern Bible Belt and exposed early in life to the special vitality of black American Christianity, Yerby makes his dislike for popular religion evident from the first page of his book. It is a credit to his staying power as a novelist that his book, nevertheless, has enjoyed a good sale, even in a publishing market that does not normally welcome iconoclasm.

Except for evidence of the vast body of historical information Yerby quickly absorbed in preparation for the book and the knowledge of the Holy Land he gained through extensive travel there, *Judas, My Brother* reads much like any other Frank Yerby pot-boiler, with its allotment of steamy formula sex scenes and episodes of sadistic violence. Yerby can handle Hebraic names with ease and sometimes uses them pretentiously; almost immediately his reader meets "Nathan bar Yehudah," the narrator, and "Yeshua," the Nazarene carpenter. Yerby's Jesus has a collection of brothers and sisters, solid village types. He alone is different, a vascillating and contradictory figure, attractive though he is in certain ways. He frequently says confusing things and is constantly racked with self-doubt. His healing powers on occasion are considerable, but they are unreliable and sometimes depart from him at critical moments. When he prophesies, his words as often as not go unfulfilled; for example, at one point (even as the Gospel relates) he sends his disciples out in pairs telling them to expect extraordinary events, events that do not come to pass. Yet Jesus is also courageous and shrewd, a man who inspires love, even in the one who betrays him. In Yerby's account, Jesus briefly survives the cross, is rescued by his friends, seen by others long enough to account for the origin of "resurrection myths," and is later quietly buried in an Essene cemetery.

Like a few of his literary predecessors, Yerby chose as his hero Judas, the Gospel figure he possibly most admires and certainly finds most intriguing. Yerby's Judas is more a man of the Enlightenment than a Jew of the first century. From his rationalistic vantage point, Jesus frequently appears to be a madman. Rather than the greed suggested by the Gospels, the vice that taunts Judas is lechery, a more interesting frailty surely in any Yerby novel. Judas betrays Jesus through human jealousy— the woman he loves dotes on "Yeshua"—yet there is a further difference in temperament and philosophy that rankles Judas. Judas does not die, as the scriptures relate, but survives to marry a prosperous widow and live out his days in wealth and comfort, though probably with something of a guilty conscience, Yerby hints in conclusion.

To his fast-paced narrative, Yerby appended a collection of pretentious though interesting notes in which he further stated his views on his subject, acknowledging his obvious debt to Hugh J. Schonfield's *The Passover Plot* and conceding a certain obligation as well to the plots of "Loukas, Markos, Mattithiah, and Yohannon—good novelists all," though much of what they wrote, he could not resist adding, "was obvious nonsense" (527). Yerby summarized for his reader several conclusions of his personal investigation of the Gospels. The death of Jesus, he said, was "very close to suicide." He concluded further that "Yeshu'a" was an Oriental mystic of two thousand years ago, whose most profound concepts "have little or no relevance for modern man" (529). Yerby reiterated in conclusion his belief that rational people are seldom very religious.

Disregarding the antireligious propaganda that blatantly fills this book, one can say that Frank Yerby wrote another of his predictable, rollicking, rambunctious narratives, supplying a veneer of history to a formula story of the sort that has brought him financial success in numerous novels since the beginning of his career. Yerby's distaste for religion is obviously real and deeply felt. In earlier books he had sometimes depicted religious atrocities; here he seethes with rage. It should also be added that the rationalistic and anti-Christian views expressed in the book are by no means original; in fact they have long had a certain "pop" currency of their own.

Not only major trends in popular piety and impiety but even theological fads occasionally have inspired, or at least shared common ground with, fictional portrayals of Jesus. In the sixties there briefly occurred the "death of God" tempest in a theological teapot, popularized by the newsmagazines and divinity schools looking for sensational speakers on controversial topics. Denominational journals enjoyed debating the pros and cons of this "atheistic" movement from within Christianity itself, and Christian youth journals published satires of it. Ostentatiously presented as the theological or antitheological trend of the future by thinkers who quoted Dostoevsky, Nietzsche, Camus, and the literature of the European absurdists, this theological novelty, though not the genuine anguish that formed the basis of some of its speculations, vanished rather quickly and was soon overwhelmed by back-to-the-Bible Evangelicalism on the right and liberation theology on the left.

"Death of God," which relied heavily on the reading of contemporary secular literature by a small band of theological academicians, did encourage or find congenial a modest literature of its own. In 1968, A. J. Langguth copyrighted his first novel, *Jesus Christs*, which used "pop" conventions yet had serious intentions and was received accordingly, adequately reviewed as an important first novel and even closely studied in some theological cliques. Faintly echoing Dostoevsky, Langguth appears to owe much to the literary milieu that produced Ionesco, Beckett, Camus, and Tom Stoppard. His work was enthusiastically read by William Hamilton, one of the "death-of-God theologians," who wrote an entertaining and appreciative review for *New Republic*, entitled "The Jesus Who Keeps Coming Back."

It is not surprising that Hamilton praised the book as highly "relevant," using the favorite jargon word of the sixties, a book that would fittingly "infuriate, delight, and help" most readers. Hamilton pronounced the work to be "a mixture of Joseph Heller and Nikos Kazantzakis, in the form of Pascal's *Pensees*" (34). Langguth's novel was further praised not only because it accorded with Hamilton's notions of religionless Christianity but also primarily "because it wrestles seriously and comically both with the

meaning of Jesus and with the problem of becoming Jesus in the time of
the death of God" (34). The book, Hamilton correctly observed, contains
"black religious jokes, short stories, science fiction, and a comic revision of
the Fourth Gospel," all "tied together for the reader when he sees that the
death of God is the real subject of this novel." Hamilton believed the
proper audience for Langguth to be Contemporary Man, who has indeed
"come of age" and must proceed on his own without God.

   Jesus Christs, called by E. B. Fiske in his *New York Times Book
Review* discussion "a tightly written series of fables for a scientific age,
vignettes of man's religious quest" (31), is unabashedly a comic, though
actually not a very witty, fiction about a Jesus who turns up at various
times in history, including the present. He appears at a Congressional
hearing but gets "bleeped" every time he refers to the Divinity; for a
time he leads the communal life of a West Coast hippy and becomes a
guerrilla lookout (this was the time when the Vietnam War was much on
the public mind). Jesus also goes to college, becomes a prisoner of war,
and is a television guest star. He keeps returning, dying and getting
resurrected or reincarnated all over again, trying to correct his mistakes.
As antihero and picaresque traveler through the range of American
society, he turns up again and again.

   The episodic novel builds to a climax in a scene where Jesus is incar-
cerated and supervised by a Nazi-like guard. In an exchange rather too
obviously inspired by Dostoevsky's "Grand Inquisitor" legend, the guard
confronts Jesus with several attacks on Christianity, derived chiefly from
Eric Fromm and D. H. Lawrence. Christianity, the guard charges, has
demanded an impossible perfection, inflicted guilt, and rejected the life
of the senses. The guard suggests that Jesus might save himself by being
certified insane, and Jesus responds with a nervous twitch! Finally the
guard tells Jesus that though he rejects him he cannot shake off his hold,
the weird fascination he exerts. The crucial episode is a none-too-subtle
parable, certainly to Hamilton and others of like mind, of the modern
world "come of age," on its own, yet haunted by the image of the
Christ.

   Langguth's book is significant in its rejection of the Christ of popular
piety and in its seeking to come to grips in a literary way with some issues
being seriously debated during the decade in which it was written. Langguth is less successful, if indeed this was his intention, in demonstrating the
continuing fascination of the figure of Jesus, the mythological figure of
Christ, if one wishes, for the modern world. Langguth's Jesus is not a very
enlightened nor especially appealing savior. The chief flaw of the book is,
however, that it lacks genuine sparkle; it just plain is not very interesting.
Today it is not often mentioned, turning up occasionally for comment in

science-fiction circles. A used paperback copy can generally be purchased in huckster rooms at science-fiction conventions.

The Cosmic Jesus: Rockets and Spacesuits

Science fiction, which has become in recent years the single best-selling literary category, offers many unusual and frequently startling opportunities for presenting Jesus as a fictional personality. Some of the most effective social criticism and satire can also be found in science-fiction books. Since science-fiction readers pride themselves on their modernity and heterodoxy, they allow liberties to their writers that other popular authors lack. While a woeful lack of imagination is evident in many authors of the straight American Christological novel, science-fiction writers, whatever their other flaws may be, are among the most visionary and imaginative to be found anywhere. They make predictions that have a habit of coming true within a few decades, and they pride themselves on helping their readers deal with "future shock," the cultural disorientation experienced from attempting to cope with the future rushing all too rapidly into the present.

Several writers who have introduced Christian subjects and themes into space fiction have been British, but their influence has been widely felt in the United States. C. S. Lewis's space trilogy, in which he transported his orthodox Christian theology into outer space, is perhaps the best-known writing of this type and is still the most stylistically satisfying./17/ In the first volume of the series, *Out of the Silent Planet*, Lewis's hero, the dedicated and conservative Professor Ransom (who bears a remarkable resemblance to Lewis's friend, Professor J. R. R. Tolkien), is kidnapped to another planet, which turns out to be Mars. There he gains a nonterrestrial perspective on Jesus' advent on earth. While Jesus is frequently referred to under his Martian name, he makes no direct appearance in the narrative.

Other science-fiction writers—in England, France, and the United States—have investigated Christian and occasionally Jewish, Islamic, and Buddhist theological ideas as they might apply in outer space. Some bold attempts have even been made to present Jesus himself in the intergallactic context. Philip José Farmer, a highly prolific and constantly inventive American writer, placed a man called "Jesus" among a strange collection of Martian Jews in his 1979 book *Jesus on Mars*. In "The Man" (1949) Ray Bradbury, an American writer known as much for his poetic style as for his scientific ideas, wrote of a ship's captain who lands on another planet the day after the advent of Christ there. When he is unable to discover the whereabouts of the messiah, the captain's exploration becomes a classic quest.

Robert Silverberg, most widely known for his short story "Good News from the Vatican" (in which a computer is elected pope), published *Up the Line* in 1969. The crucifixion is presented as a popular tourist attraction for time-travelers, jaded adventurer-tourists from the future. Other science-fiction writers have expanded Silverberg's initial idea. Garry Kilworth's story "Let's Go to Golgotha" (1975) even went a step further, suggesting that the rather bewildered mob jeering Jesus during his crucifixion consisted largely of time-travelers who had landed in Jerusalem for the occasion.

The science-fiction possibilities are endless, when Einsteinian principles, understood or even misunderstood, are extrapolated into events of religious history. Arthur Porges in "The Rescuer" (1962) tells of a man using a time machine to go back to the first century and attempt a rescue of Jesus from the cross. But the best known—or most notorious—use of Jesus in a science-fiction work remains Michael Moorcock's *Behold the Man*, first published as a short story in 1966 and later expanded by the author into a full-length novel. A modern time-traveler actually ends up becoming the crucified Jesus in this tale. Though the work of a British author, *Behold the Man* is regarded as a germinal story in American science fiction and is often, despite embarrassing crudities, included on various lists of the outstanding science-fiction stories of the century.

From the orthodox Christian and often quite touching biblical space extrapolations of C. S. Lewis, the Anglican layman now especially revered by American Evangelicals, and Anthony Boucher, a gifted American Roman Catholic editor, critic, and science-fiction writer, to the more wildly and grossly adventurous fictionalizing of Moorcock and others, science fiction has asked significant questions of theology and Bible studies. The dialogue between theology and absurdist fiction and drama by now seems exhausted, but science-fiction fandom, with its youthful vitality and tremendous intellectual resources, seems ready for dialogue with religion. Science-fiction writers have sometimes brilliantly examined the cosmic implications of existing world religions and myths. They have invented new religions for the needs of the civilizations they have imagined in the immensity of space. The religious concept of immortality and the implications of increasing longevity have been widely explored, along with questions of ethics and morality. But the cosmic Christ, who turns up on other planets and galaxies, has been by far the most interesting idea./18/

Jesus in Imaginative Literature: A Final Assessment

The writers of the fictional accounts of Jesus' adventures may not be remembered as masters of their country's literature, but they are revealing to students of society and popular religion. Their writings, even when they are graceless or embarrassing in their pretentions to knowledge, have answered a need of vast numbers of people whose religious or irreligious sensibilities can at least be suggested by examining these books, which have been so avidly read and often treasured. The mass-market religious narratives today in part serve the function that in previous ages was reserved for saints' lives and miracle legends. These novels are not for poets or theologians but are popularized versions of the faith—often garbled, to be sure, and blended with the non-Christian myths, preoccupations, and superstitions of their time.

Many of the novels are little more than fictionalizations of self-improvement concepts promoted by the writers of popular theology and edification, such as Norman Vincent Peale, Rabbi Joshua Liebman, Bishop Fulton J. Sheen, Catherine Marshall, Dale Evans Rogers, Pat Boone, and others./19/ Yet more serious considerations of Jewish-Christian brotherhood, so essential in a pluralistic society and so pressing after the Nazi experience, have found expression here too. More recently, skeptical theological fads and even popular antireligious doctrines have also appeared in fictional embodiment. Most of the writers have wished to convey lessons they felt important and at the same time entertain their readers.

The novelists, like the edifying nonfiction writers, have been largely middle class in moral, ethical, social, and religious attitudes, with the exceptions of Upton Sinclair, Frank Yerby, A. J. Langguth, and the science-fiction writers. Rarely have they recommended policies and conduct that were unconventional, revolutionary, or even very different. Complexity of characterization has rarely been found in their fiction; there have been few whisky priests, suicidal saints, or God-haunted murderers such as can be found in the serious Russian, French, and British novels of Christian persuasion. Even with the odd examples—Asch, Yerby, Sinclair, Langguth—the actions of characters have been generally predictable, especially to the reader already familiar with the respective author's work. Though most of the novels have been highly favorable to Christianity, they have generally not been dogmatic. Their Christianity has often been as creedless as Hinduism, though the language used has echoed on occasion the great affirmations of classical Christianity. American pragmatic preoccupations have been quickly recognized; these books usually advocate exercises in "self-mastery" and provide guaranteed techniques for achieving "peace of mind." God, in the view of the majority of these novelists, is much like a folksy grandfather, a bit old-fashioned and eccentric perhaps, but not much to be feared. He rewards abundantly and only punishes the most incorrigible villains. His rewards, chiefly health, success in love, prosperity, and business or professional recognition, also seem largely bestowed in this life. Though the reader is assured that all will be well in life and in death, the writers rarely commit themselves to definite views of an afterlife (at least not since Mrs. Ward) or humanity's ultimate cosmic destiny, though we have seen how one writer has promoted a belief in reincarnation and two others have used reincarnation as a useful fictional device.

These novels have a number of superficial and obvious appeals. They give their readers a vicarious, shallow stimulation, or, in the rare instances, antireligious excitement. They probably still provide an excuse for some serious, religious folk to delve into the violence and salacious adventure for which popular American fiction has become known, though the soap operas on television, with their presumed "relevance" to the problems of life, may have taken over this function.

In a majority of these novels we find a direct reflection of the Christology of popular American Protestantism for the decades in which they appeared, and judging from the fact that a number of these books have been the work of Roman Catholics, it would seem that the same theologically homogenizing influences were operating on them as well. The novels of the first half of the twentieth century, even those written by Roman Catholics, despite their professions of orthodoxy, would seem to display only the vaguest understanding of the classical Christian definition of the nature of Jesus. There is, in fact, an antitheological bias implied in most of these books. The reader is presented a Jesus of American culture, stripped of "theological accretions"—trimmings that have, the authors often believe, made him distasteful and incomprehensible, that have obscured the vitality of his personality and the force of his message. In this manner traditional Christianity has been sacrificed to a bland and colorless American religious pluralism. In the last few years American popular religion has taken new directions, and it remains to be seen how the novelists will mirror the charismatic movement, the Evangelical revival, the changes within Roman Catholicism, and the new emphases in Judaism.

Orthodox religions, it is often observed, tend to produce the most moving and lasting art. Indecisive versions of the Gospel have seldom inspired impressive art works. The British author Dorothy L. Sayers, known for detective stories and Christian apologetics, wrote the scripts for *The Man Born to Be King*, the most successful series of radio plays ever broadcast on the BBC. These plays about the ministry of Jesus received both critical and popular acclaim. Sayers was uncompromising in her belief, based on both observation and personal experience as a writer, that a sound theology is essential to any artist who would treat the Christ story. In words not directed at American popular writing but nevertheless pertinent, she noted:

> A loose and sentimental theology begets loose and sentimental art-
> forms; an illogical theology lands one in illogical situations; an ill-
> balanced theology issues in false emphasis and absurdity. Conversely;
> there is no more searching test of a theology than to submit it to dra-
> matic handling; nothing so glaringly exposes inconsistencies in a
> character, a story, or a philosophy as to put it upon the stage and
> allow it to speak for itself.(3)

Incarnate gods are no doubt difficult subjects for modern novelists, unlike epic poets, who used to handle them with ease; yet no truly remarkable secular portrayals of Jesus are evident in American literature either. In popular writing there appears no willingness to view him in courageous existentialist fashion as a magnificent, misguided idealist, another Sisyphus, if one wishes, tragic example of a brave man in defi-ance of the indifferent universe that surrounds him, symbol of human-ity's hopeless longing for immortality and for a universe in which his sufferings become meaningful. Yerby's personal anger at the Christian religion, as well as his adherence to a tested formula plot, mitigated any force his secular portrait might otherwise have had. At present it is hard to take the Jesus portrayals of Langguth and the science-fiction writers as serious philosophical statements, although tantalizing possibilities are being suggested.

The problems of presenting Jesus in literature are admittedly enor-mous. Most Americans will have strong preconceptions; regardless of their religious commitment, very few will view the founder of Christian-ity impassively. The physical appearance of Jesus alone has occasioned endless discussion, without biblical authority to follow and with contra-dictory traditions in the history of Christian art. How is one to present the words of Jesus in a novel? The words quoted by the evangelists are wise and eloquent; even the most skilled authors, when they find it nec-essary to add conversations in fictional episodes, find their powers pressed to the limit. Competing with Matthew, Mark, Luke, and John is admittedly a tall order, despite what an author may think of their histor-ical veracity. Even Frank Yerby had to admit they were splendid story tellers.

While Christian readers have a right to expect that a purportedly Christian work of art will in its view of reality conform to a doctrinal interpretation they can recognize, unless they belong to a radically unorthodox sect, these Christians will not deny that Jesus was indeed a historical personality as genuinely human as any other man who ever lived, who thus belongs to the cultural heritage of all people, whatever their religious profession. He is then as valid a subject for non-Christian literary treatment as are Julius Caesar, Alexander the Great, Napoleon, and Abraham Lincoln./20/ When the admittedly non-Christian novelist, as in the case of Asch or Yerby, is attracted to the personality of Jesus and introduces him in a work of fiction, it is right only to demand that the author abide by the same principles that would be followed if Thomas à Becket or Columbus were the subject. The historical facts should not be so distorted that a false image is projected or the integrity of the real personality, to the degree the subject can be known historically, is violated.

The total or partial artistic failure of the majority of the treatments of Jesus in American literature should not immediately lead to the conclusion that the undertaking is impossible, therefore worthless, and to be renounced. To the secular humanist, Jesus will generally appear as one of those rare individuals inspiring to all humanity, a martyr-hero whose greatness transcends his own historical period in a message for all ages. Convinced Christians have the deeper responsibility of expressing their experience or perception, limited though it may be, of the eternal mystery of the Incarnation. A skilled work of popular art, like fine art itself, can expand human experience and increase understanding.

NOTES

/1/   According to James D. Hart, "Literary taste is not an isolated phenomenon. The taste of the largest number of readers is shaped by contemporary pressures more than is the taste of the highly cultivated reader, who has a deeper background of aesthetic experience and knowledge to guide him. Books flourish when they answer a need and die when they do not. The needs of the greatest reading public are various: they include clarification of ideas already in circulation; emotional statement of feelings that people are prepared to accept; popularization of desirable information heretofore obscured; satisfying appeal to forms of entertainment currently considered amusing or exciting. . . . Yet in some way or another, the popular author is always the one who expresses the people's minds and paraphrases what they consider their private feelings" (285).

/2/   The popularity of the historical novel in America has been discussed by Ernest E. Leisy and by James D. Hart, who observed, "Critics who liked novels but who still felt a taint attached to 'mere fiction' contended that if a historical romance were written and set in America it would be pure. Therefore, they cried, let us have our own Waverly" (79–80).

/3/   Obviously the fine scholarly work on the Pharisees by Joseph Klausner, Paul Goodman, and Martin Buber was not available to Ware. His Pharisees are fictional villains, by no means a historically valid portrayal.

/4/   Full information on the sales of the book appeared in *Publisher's Weekly* 119 (February 21, 1931): 940.

/5/   The anonymous writer of "The Winner of the Chariot Race" (*Nation* 80 [February 23, 1905]: 148–49) aptly observed that "Jesse James is a divinity student in a white choker when compared with Messala [the book's villain], who, in spite of his 'air of passionless hauteur characteristic of the fine patrician face,' was 'cruel, cunning, desperate, not so excited as determined'—a soul in a tension of watchfulness and fierce resolve."

/6/   *Critic* 17 (July 5, 1890): 2; *Atlantic* 71 (July 18, 1890): 133; *Nation* 51 (September 25, 1890): 252.

/7/   For some understanding of the extent of his following among European intellectuals, see Sinclair's book *My Lifetime in Letters*, where he discusses his friendships thoroughly.

/8/   The Reverend Dr. Robert Norwood's books included *His Lady of the Sonnets* (1915); *The Witch of Endor* (1916); *The Modernists* (1918); *The Man of Kerioth* (1919); *The Heresy of Antioch* (1928); and many more.

/9/   Quoted in an unidentified newspaper clipping this writer discovered in a library copy of *The Man Who Dared to Be God*.

/10/   Quoted from a personal letter from Dr. Slaughter, January 14, 1968.

/11/   Detweiler's brilliant essay is the finest discussion of the topic that exists. The present discussion in no way improves upon Detweiler's work and claims value merely because it enlarges the scope of the concern. An interested reader is also referred to the splendid essay by Warren G. French, "A Hundred Years of a Religious Bestseller," *Western Humanities Review* 10 (Winter 1956). Although French concentrates on one book, he provides a provocative view of the genre as a whole.

/12/   Books written by three of Oursler's children—Will Oursler, Fulton Oursler, Jr., and April Oursler Armstrong—provide full information on the sales history of their father's most popular book.

/13/   These endorsements of Oursler's friends were widely quoted in promotion of the books and can be found on the dust jackets of earlier hardcover editions.

/14/   He had been reared a Baptist but had nearly drowned at the time of his immersion and had never fully recovered from the trauma. The early part of his life was spent in skepticism of all organized religions and in devotion to liberal movements and fads.

/15/   Less notable was the book he sandwiched in between his two major works, *The Golden Ham* (1956), a biography of Jackie Gleason. It deeply offended the performer, who, unlike Lincoln or Christ, was immediately on the scene to register his protest. Replied Bishop to Gleason's objections, "I went from Lincoln to Gleason to Christ, and neither of the other subjects has complained yet." His remarks were quoted in *Time* 19 (May 13, 1957): 82.

/16/   Bishop listed as his primary sources: Matthew, Mark, Luke, John, Cyril of Jerusalem, Flavius Josephus, Edersheim, Gamalid, Danby, William, Ricciotti, Lagrange, Kugelman, Hoenig, Benoit, Goodier, and Prat. These references are included in *The Day Christ Died* (vii). Needless to add, the book topples over with the weight of sucn documentation.

/17/   Lewis's books, which have appeared in numerous editions, include *Out of the Silent Planet* (1938), *Perelandra* (1943), and *That Hideous Strength* (1945).

Though Lewis was an Anglican layman, his clear affirmation of basic Christian dogmas in his apologetic writings has made him a special favorite of American Christian Evangelicals.

/18/   Since science fiction is sometimes witty and satirical, the scenario has been suggested, waiting to be fleshed out by a capable writer in the genre, of a civilization from outer space that knows Earth culture only from its television transmissions inadvertently beaming in their direction. The entire planet is converted by an earthly television evangelist it views regularly and is frantically trying to figure out how to transfer its wealth into the "dimes and dollars" requested by the religious leader.

/19/   The earlier nonfiction has been competently evaluated by Schneider and Dornbusch. The conclusions of their study tend to substantiate the present observations of the fiction.

/20/   The legitimacy of the historical romance and historical novel seems well recognized; major writers work within the genre and professional historians to provide useful critical commentary.

WORKS CONSULTED

Armstrong, April Oursler
    1968   *House With a Hundred Gates*. Garden City: Doubleday.

Arthur, Timothy Shay
    1856   "The Prince of the House of David." *Arthur's Home Magazine* 12 (February): 142.

Asch, Sholem
    1939   *The Nazarene*. Translated by Maurice Samuel. New York: G. P. Putnam's Sons.
    1941   *What I Believe*. Translated by Maurice Samuel. New York: G. P. Putnam's Sons.

Bishop, Jim
    1957   *The Day Christ Died*. New York: Harper and Brothers.
    1960   *The Day Christ Was Born*. New York: Pocket Books.

Bode, Carl
    1950a   "Lloyd Douglas: Minority Report." *Christian Century* 67: 817–18.
    1950b   "Lloyd Douglas and America's Largest Parish." *Religion and Life 19: 440–47*.

Caldwell, Janet Taylor
    1959   *Dear and Glorious Physician*. Garden City: Doubleday.

Caldwell, Janet Taylor, and Jess Stearn
    1973   *The Search for a Soul: Taylor Caldwell's Psychic Lives*. Garden City: Doubleday.
    1977   *I, Judas*. New York: Atheneum.

Dawson, Virginia Douglas, and Betty Douglas Wilson
    1952   *The Shape of Sunday*. Boston: Houghton Mifflin.

Detweiler, Robert
    1964   "Christ in American Religious Fiction." *Journal of Bible and Religion* 32 (January): 8–12.

Douglas, Lloyd C.
    1948   *The Big Fisherman*. Boston: Houghton Mifflin.
    1951   *Time to Remember*. Boston: Houghton Mifflin.
    1966   *The Robe*. New York: Pocket Books.

Fiske, E. B.
    1968   Review of *Jesus Christs*. *New York Times Book Review* (March 10): 31.

Hackett, Alice P.
    1956   *60 Years of Best Sellers, 1895–1955*. New York: R. R. Bowker.

Hamilton, William
    1968   "The Jesus Who Keeps Coming Back." *New Republic* (April 6): 34.

Harper, J. Henry
    1912   *The House of Harper: A Century of Publishing in Franklin Square*. New York: Harper and Brothers.

Hart, James D.
    1950   *The Popular Book: A History of America's Literary Taste*. New York: Oxford University Press.

Ingraham, Joseph Holt
    1874   *The Prince of the House of David; Or, Three Years in the Holy City*. Boston: Roberts Brothers.

Kazin, Alfred
    1943   "Neither Jew nor Greek." *New Republic* 59 (November 1): 626.

Langguth, A. J.
    1969   *Jesus Christs*. New York: Ballantine Books.

Leisy, Ernest E.
    1950   *The American Historical Novel*. Norman, OK: University of Oklahoma Press.

Lerner, Max
    1957   *America as a Civilization: Life and Thought in the United States*. New York: Simon and Schuster.

Liptzin, Sol
    1963   *The Flowering of Yiddish Literature*. New York: Thomas Yoseloff.

Lloyd, James
    1957   "The Day Christ Died." *Catholic World* 185 (August): 109.

Malcolm, Donald
    1957   "Another Day! Another Dollar!" *New Republic* 134 (June 10): 18.

Mott, Frank Luther
    1947   *Golden Multitudes*. New York: Macmillan.

Newsweek
1959   "Dear and Glorious. . . ." 53 (March 9): 104.
1961   "Prognosis: Bad." 67 (January 16): 82.

Niebuhr, Reinhold
1957   "The Way to Calvary." *New York Times* (May 19): 10.

Norwood, Robert
1929   *The Man Who Dared to Be God.* New York: Charles Scribner's Sons.

Oursler, Fulton
1947   *The Greatest Story Ever Told.* Garden City: Doubleday.

Oursler, Fulton, Jr.
1964   *Behold this Dreamer: An Autobiography.* Boston: Little, Brown.

Sayers, Dorothy L.
1943   *The Man Born to Be King.* New York: Harper and Brothers.

Schneider, Louis, and Sanford M. Dornbusch
1958   *Popular Religion: Inspirational Books in America.* Chicago: University of Chicago Press.

Seitz, O. C.
1931   "A Prince of Best Sellers." *Publisher's Weekly* 68 (February 21): 940.

Sinclair, Upton
1923   *They Call Me Carpenter.* Chicago: The Paint Book Company.
1943   *Our Lady: A Parable for Moderns.* Hollywood: Murray and Gee.
1954   *A Personal Jesus.* London: George Allen and Unwin.
1960   *My Lifetime in Letters.* Columbia, MO: University of Missouri Press.
1962   *The Autobiography of Upton Sinclair.* New York: Harcourt, Brace and World.

Slaughter, Frank G.
1951   *The Road to Bithynia.* Garden City: Doubleday.
1959   *The Crown and the Cross.* Cleveland: World.
1963   *Upon This Rock.* New York: Coward-McCann.

Sprague, William B.
1874   *Annals of the American Unitarian Pulpit: Or, Commemorative Notices of Distinguished Clergymen of the Unitarian Denomination in the United States.* New York: Robert Carter and Brothers.

Springfield Republican
1922   "They Call Me Carpenter." (October 8): 7a.

Wagenknecht, Edward
1959   "Dear and Glorious Physician." *Chicago Sunday Tribune* (March 1): 2.

Wallace, Lew
1906   *An Autobiography.* New York: Harper and Brothers.
1922   *Ben-Hur.* New York: Harper and Brothers.

Ward, Herbert D., and Elizabeth Stuart Phelps Ward
    1891   *Come Forth*. Boston: Houghton, Mifflin, and Co.

Ware, William
    1856   *Julian: Or, Scenes in Judea*. New York: C. S. Francis.

Yerby, Frank
    1970   *Judas, My Brother*. New York: Dell.

IV

Bible Country:
The Good Book in Country Music

Charles Wolfe

People with a casual knowledge of country music tend to assume that most of the genre consists of either songs generated from old mountain folk ballads or the more modern honky-tonk-lost-love songs. Almost unexplored and always unheralded is the vast body of sentimental songs that has always formed a basic core of country music: songs that are not so much about lost love as they are about a nostalgia for the past, a longing for home, the loss of mother or dad. Such songs went out of fashion in mainstream pop music in the 1920s; they survived and flourished in country music and have secure homes today in bluegrass bands and on the stage of the Grand Ole Opry. Much more than the folk ballads or honky-tonk laments, the sentimental songs—what used to be called "heart songs" by older country singers—are full of stereotyped images and emotions that repeat themselves over and over in song after song. As of yet no one has compiled a glossary of these images, but such a list must certainly include the icons of the rose, the log cabin, mother, the pine tree, the supper table, twilight, and the old Bible. The present study is an attempt to trace this last icon, the Bible, as it has appeared in the sentimental country song over the last one hundred years.

For practical purposes, we will examine here only those songs which were either a product of commercial country music or songs which were a direct influence on country music. We will not include various sorts of church songs or Gospel music songs, though both of these genres contain many songs using the Bible as a key image. (Indeed, many late nineteenth- and early twentieth-century Sunday school songbooks have entire sections devoted to songs about the Bible.) While Gospel tradition and commercial country music do overlap in several areas, the two genres are quite distinct and have followed quite separate paths of development. The study of Gospel music in the twentieth century is today only in its infancy, and as a discipline it is thirty years behind the study of country music. In future years, when the full story of religious music in the South has been documented, a parallel study should be done on the Bible metaphor in Gospel and church music.

One particular set of images seems to dominate many of the early country songs about the Bible: this is an association of the Bible with mother and the past. Nostalgia for the past has always been a staple in American music of all sorts from the 1840s on; commentators have for years remarked on the unique place motherhood has in the American system of values. It should not be surprising, then, to find the third powerful icon, the Bible, associated with them. Nor should it be surprising to find that most of the early Bible songs are built around the general theme (or even title) of "Mother's Bible." In the last hundred years at least a dozen songs have appeared bearing this title or a similar title, and probably more appear as unpublished manuscripts in the files of the Copyright Office. An examination of this song complex is thus a natural starting place for an exploration of Bible songs in general.

Modern scholarship is showing that country music has as many roots in nineteenth-century popular music as it does in folk music, and certainly the complex of mother's Bible songs reaches back into pre–Civil War Tin Pan Alley. During the 1840s a number of family singing groups toured around the country, doing concerts of popular songs; one of the most successful of these groups was the Hutchinson Family of New Hampshire. Known as "the tribe of Jesse" (after the father, Jesse Hutchinson), the family eventually numbered some sixteen children, most of them talented singers or instrumentalists or composers. In one of their song collections, a bound folio of sheet music published in New York by Firth and Hall in 1843, appears the text of the first enduring mother's Bible song, a composition entitled "My Mother's Bible." Though marked by stilted nineteenth-century diction, the words contain most of the images and sentiment to be found in all the later mother's Bible songs.

MY MOTHER'S BIBLE

This book is all that's left me now!
Tears will unbidden start!
With falt'ring lip and throbbing brow,
I press it to my heart.
For many generations passed
Here is our fam'ly tree!
My mother's hands this Bible clasped,
She dying gave it me.

Ah, well do I remember those
Whose names these records bear!
Who round the hearthstone used to close,
After the evening prayer;
And speak of what this volume said,

In tones my heart would thrill:
Though they are with the silent dead,
Here they are living still.

My father read this holy book
To brothers, sisters dear!
How calm was my poor mother's look,
Who yearned God's word to hear!
Her angel face! I see it yet!
What thronging mem'ries come!
Again that little group is met
Within the halls of home!

Though the song was to remain popular throughout most of the nine-teenth century (it appears in over a half dozen collections during that time), its authorship is in doubt. The original 1843 version attributed the composition to "J. J. Hutchinson," one of the family members, but later versions attribute the same song to Henry Russell (music) and George P. Morris (words). Russell (1812–1900), an Englishman by birth, was known as more of a showman than a fine singer, and he claimed credit for over eight hundred songs, including "Woodman, Spare That Tree," which he coauthored with Morris. The Hutchinson Family is known to have popu-larized some of Russell's other songs, and some similar collaboration might have yielded "My Mother's Bible." Neither Hutchinson nor Rus-sell, though, was known as a religious composer; Russell, indeed, was satirized during his career for his excessive preoccupation with songs about *old* things; one of his critics in Boston once wrote that a Russell program included every antique but "the old boot jack." Thus, the first effective Bible song in any form of American music was born not from a a religious impulse but from a nostalgic one.

The Hutchinson–Russell song contained a set of key images that quickly proved themselves with the popular American temperament—a dying mother, the simple joys and faith of childhood, the physical Bible as a legacy and as a symbol of the past. They were to recur time and time again in the music of the next hundred years, especially in folk and country music. There is no direct connection to show that the Hutchinson–Russell song got into southern vernacular music or into early° country music, but its images were promulgated by another writer who is very much a part of the fabric of that early music, Charlie Tillman.

Born in Alabama in 1861, Charlie Tillman was a self-educated musi-cian who had begun singing and composing in his mid-twenties. Soon he had a national reputation as an evangelist, song leader, and singer, and in 1893 he substituted for Ira D. Sankey as a song leader for a mammoth World Convention of Christian Workers held in Boston. Sankey, who along with Phillips Bliss and Dwight Moody did the most to popularize the new, lively "Gospel hymns" that eventually evolved into Gospel music, encouraged Tillman to write songs and helped to publicize and promote them. Soon Tillman had produced a battery of songs that were to become staples in southern Gospel music, including "The Old Time Religion," "When I Get to the End of the Way," "Old Time Power," and a song that has entered folk tradition, "Life's Railway to Heaven." Tillman made his headquarters in Atlanta, where he began publishing his own songbooks (some of which were to sell over a quarter of a million copies) and working with famous preachers of the time, such as Sam P. Jones, the energetic evangelist who converted Tom Ryman, the Nashville riverboat captain who in turn built Ryman auditorium, for years the home of the Grand Ole Opry.

In 1893, the same year he went north to work with Sankey, Tillman wrote his version of "My Mother's Bible." The song was originally designed as a duet, and the words were credited to evangelist M. B. Williams. The text ran as follows:

MY MOTHER'S BIBLE
by
Charlie D. Tillman

There's a dear and precious book,
Though it's worn and faded now,
Which recalls those happy days of long ago.
When I stood at mother's knee,
With her hand upon my brow,
And I heard her voice in gentle tones and low.
> *Chorus*   Blessed book (blessed book), Precious book
> (precious book),
> On thy dear old tear-stained leaves I love
> to look,
> Thou art sweeter day by day,
> As I walk the narrow way,
> That leads at last to that bright home above.

As she read the stories o'er,
Of those mighty men of old,
Of Joseph and of Daniel and their trials,
Of little David bold,
Who became a king at last,
Of Satan with his many wicked wiles.
> *Chorus*   Then she read of Jesus' love,
> As He blest the children dear,
> How He suffered, bled, and died upon the tree.
> Of His heavy load of care,
> Then she dried my flowing tears,
> With her kisses as she said it was for me.

> *Chorus*   Well, those days are past and gone,
> But their memory lingers still,
> And the dear old Book each day has been my guide,

> And I seek to do His will,
> As my mother taught me then,
> And ever in my heart His words abide.

Over the next twenty-five years, Tillman saw the song increase in popularity and appear in a number of turn-of-the-century songbooks, including A. J. Showalter and E. G. Seweil's *Gospel Praise* (Nashville: Gospel Advocate Publishing Company, 1900), in James Atkins and William J. Kirkpatrick's *Young People's Hymnal No. 2* (Nashville: Methodist Episcopal Church Publishing House, 1912, officially sanctioned by the Methodist Episcopal Sunday School Board), and in paperbacked shape-note collections, such as E. T. Hildebrand's *Song and Story* (Basic, VA: Hildebrand–Burnett Company, 1920). In future years the song was to develop into a standard in church collections; it appeared in an official Army–Navy hymnal and in *The Broadman Hymnal* (Nashville: Broadman Press, 1940), for years the hymnal of the Southern Baptist Convention. Probably because of its early popularity at camp meetings and revivals, the song also went into folk tradition in several parts of the country; folklorist Roger Abrahams collected a version from noted balladeer Almeda Riddle in Arkansas in the 1960s. She said she had learned the song as a child, from her mother.

Tillman's song also has the distinction of being the first Bible song to be recorded in the country music tradition. In 1924, barely a year after recording companies had recorded an old Georgia fiddler named John Carson and thus inaugurated the boom in "hill country" music, Columbia records brought several Atlanta area musicians into their New York studios to record some of this genuine down-home music. In addition to fiddlers and banjoists, one of those making the trek was Charlie Tillman himself, who, along with his daughter, Jewell Tillman Burns, had decided to commit some of his singing to posterity. One can only wonder at what Tillman, then age sixty-three, thought of the new-fangled recording machines that surrounded him in the studio or what the jaded recording executives thought of his stately songs. They recorded six titles, including Tillman favorites like "Old Time Power," and "My Mother's Bible." The record was issued on 28 January 1925, on Columbia 15025, one of a series of southern Gospel records by such now obscure groups as the Alcoa Quartet, the Wheat Street Female Quartet, and the Paramount Quartet. It sold some three thousand copies while it was kept in the catalogue—not exactly a best seller even in those days and selling even fewer than Tillman's other recordings, which sold five thousand to eight thousand copies each. Nonetheless, it preserved Tillman's performance of his own song and made his song accessible to a wider audience; Columbia issued it on its "Old Familiar Tunes" series, thus offering it to the same southern audience that was buying fiddle tunes, old ballads, and old love songs.

The song continued to be recorded by other old-time country artists during the twenties. In April 1925, just three months after Tillman's Columbia record was released, two fellow Atlanta singers, Mr. and Mrs. J. Douglas Swagerty, recorded a "cover" version of it for the rival General Phonograph Corporation (Okeh 40457). In December 1927, the Allen Quartette, yet another Georgia singing group, recorded a version for the same company (Okeh 45168); and in early 1928 West Virginians Frank Welling and John McGhee, two of the most popular country recording artists of the time, recorded a lively version in Chicago (Paramount 3108, Broadway 8204). Whereas the earlier versions of the song had been rather staid renditions with organ or piano accompaniment, the Welling and McGhee version featured a lively tempo sparked by two guitars, one played Hawaiian style. The Welling and McGhee record was also issued on the Broadway label, a "stencil" issue designed for the Montgomery Ward catalogue, thus giving the song even wider distribution.

As Tillman's song gained wide circulation both in Gospel and country music circles (and the two musics became increasingly distinct forms from the 1920s on), a number of other different "Mother's Bible" songs cropped up, all similar in tone and theme to Tillman's. One of the first, "Mother's Book," appeared as early as 1904 in L. L. Pickett and O. B. Culpepper's *Gems No. 2*. This song is credited to Mrs. W. T. Morris (words) and L. L. Pickett (music) and contains a refrain very similar to that of Tillman's song:

> Dear old book (Dear old book), my mother's book
>   (my mother's book),
> Day by day it ever guides me on the way,
> As its well-worn leaves I read, there I find my
>   daily need,
> As I journey on to mother and to God.

Also in this song are the characteristic images of a book with worn and torn pages and a child standing at mother's knee while she reads. The more modern Gospel music publishers—the ones specializing in publishing annual books for singing conventions and sponsoring quartets to popularize their wares—got into the act in the early 1930s, when the two major publishing companies, Stamps–Baxter and James D. Vaughan, each came up with their own "Mother's Bible" songs. The Vaughan version appeared first in the 1932 songbook *New Gospel Voices* with words credited to James D. Vaughan and LaVerne Tame, and music to Charles S. Bradford. The exact title was the same as Tillman's and the Hutchinson Family's, "My Mother's Bible."

> There's a dear old book, a holy book,
> Which my mother read each day,
> I can see her there in the fireside chair,
> Her hair has turned to silv're gray,
> "My child," she would say, in her sweet tender way,
> "The Bible is better than gold,
> Heed its every command, on its promises stand,
> Till you enter the Heavenly fold."

This song uses the idea of a Bible as a guide but omits the image of the old, torn pages. The Stamps–Baxter version dates from two years later, 1934, and features words by the Reverend W. P. Long with music by Frank Stamps, one of the founders of the company and a major influence on southern quartet styles; the song, called simply "Mother's Bible," appeared in *Leading Light*, Stamps–Baxter's 1934 book, published in Dallas. Though mother stained this Bible with tears, the burden of the song focuses on the desire of the speaker to return to the simple, heartfelt religion of his youth; this religion is closely associated with mother but not so much with the Bible. The overall song model continued to be a potent force in Gospel singing as reflected by the fact that as recently as 1974 a song called "Mama's Bible," written by Ruby Moody, a well-known country Gospel composer who has worked a lot with Grand Ole Opry star Hank Snow, appeared in a collection published by radio evangelist J. Bazzell Mull in Knoxville. (This was Mull's *Our Recorded Songs Number 3*.)

Companies like Stamps–Baxter and Vaughan made their impact on the development of country music, and many of their songs found their way into the repertoires of singers of the 1930s and 1940s. But the country singers themselves began their own crop of mother's Bible songs as well, recording them, performing them on radio, and circulating them in songbooks they sold over the air. As early as 1929 Frank and James McCravy, two popular singers from North Carolina, recorded a song entitled "My Mother's Old Bible is True" for the Victor company in New York (Victor V-40265). The record sold only some twenty-three hundred copies at the start of the depression, but the McCravys later publicized the song over their NBC network radio show, "Fireside Songs," which reached a huge audience. In 1935 Luther Baucom, a member of a popular North Carolina band named The Tobacco Tags, wrote "Mother's Torn and Faded Bible," which began:

> There's an old and faded Bible,
> With my blessed mother's name,
> It's the only token that she left to me,
> Its cover is all broken,
> And its pages all are torn,
> But the story of the savior is the same.

Chorus
    Oh, that Bible my mother left to me,
    It's a treasure I will cherish evermore,
    Tho' its cover is all broken,
    And its pages are all torn,
    It will guide me to that happy golden shore.

Though delivered at a breakneck tempo, with accompaniment of guitar and two mandolins, and performed in a setting quite different from Tillman's—the 1930s country radio show—Baucom's song contains all of the sentiment and imagery of Tillman's original, even to the image of the old battered book as a guide to "that happy golden shore." The song was a standard from 1935 until 1941 with the Tobacco Tags; they published it in two of their songbooks and recorded it for Victor records in 1935 (released on Bluebird 6668-A).

Yet the mother's Bible song that survives in country music today is really none of the above, but a song popularized by bluegrass stars Don Reno and Red Smiley in the 1950s, entitled simply "Mother's Bible." The song was composed by banjoist-singer Don Reno and originally recorded by the duo on King records in 1952 (Cincinnati: King 1263). Though Reno and Smiley were noted throughout the country for their flashy, influential instrumental technique, they also delighted audiences with old-fashioned close-harmony singing. "Mother's Bible" was designed for such duets (as was Tillman's original), and Reno and Smiley made it a standard with bluegrass musicians. It is still heard today at festivals and concerts across the country, the only mother's Bible song that really is. The song, which includes the standard images of faded Bible, mother's knee, and the nostalgic past, has this chorus:

    Mother's Bible (oh how dear), with the covers worn
        and old,
    Mother's Bible (much more sweeter), but much more to me
        than gold,
    And she told me (yes, she told me), just before she went
        to sleep,
    If I read it (and believed it), Jesus then my soul
        would keep.

It is impossible to assert that all the offshoots of the nineteenth-century mother's Bible songs were directly influenced by the prototypes. No one can say with certainty that the composers of the later songs had the earlier ones in mind or that they had even heard them. Some may indeed be deliberate imitations, but it is far more likely that the number of these songs linking the images of Bible, mother, and nostalgia reflects how potent these images are for the popular American mind. Many of the later Bible songs that were to emerge in country music in one sense or another developed the basic themes set forth in the original "Mother's Bible" complex.

In the 1920s, many Bible songs sung by professional entertainers were also widespread in folk tradition. On 20 June 1928, Missouri folk song collector Vance Randolph visited a Pentecostal meeting in a tent near Joplin, Missouri. One of the songs that caught his ear was called "I Believe This Dear Old Bible," a song of "many stanzas," each one of which ended with "I believe this dear old Bible from beginning to the end." Randolph printed what he could remember of the song in his 1950 volume of Ozark Folksongs (86) and sent it out into the world for other folklorists to deal with. Meanwhile, in Eastern Kentucky, three young singers were learning the song in and around the school they attended in hilly Rockcastle County. Doc Hopkins, the oldest of the group, became a solo singer; Karl Davis and Hartford Taylor formed a duo and became known as Karl and Harty. For over twenty years the three, broadcasting their music over powerful radio stations in Chicago and Cincinnati, were heard by millions in the South and Midwest. One of the songs that they used repeatedly in their programs was a version of the song Randolph heard.

I BELIEVE THAT GOOD OLD BIBLE

I believe that Father Adam was the first created man,
That Eve was made his wife according to the maker's plan,
They lost their home in Eden, the Lord they did offend,
I believe that good old Bible from beginning to the end.

I believe that master Abel was killed by master Cain,
That Noah went into the ark to keep out of the rain,
I believe that little David killed Goliath with a sling
I believe that good old Bible from beginning to the end.

I believe that Job had patience, and also lots of boils,
The Lord had pity on poor Job and saved him from the soil,
To shade him from the burning sun and ease his bitter pain,
I believe that good old Bible, from beginning to the end.

I believe that King Belshazzar saw the writing on the wall,
When Daniel translated it, he knew it meant his fall,
I believe the Lord this warning to the drunken king did send,
I believe that good old Bible, from beginning to the end.

I believe that Pharaoh's army was drowned in the sea,
That Moses and the Israelites from bondage did go free,
I believe good old Elijah to Heaven did ascend,
I believe that good old Bible from beginning to the end.

I believe that Christ was crucified and died upon the tree,
He ascended up to Heaven to prepare a place for me,
I believe that in like manner, He's coming back again,
I believe that good old Bible, from beginning to the end./1/

"I Believe That Good Old Bible" was only one of a number of songs championing the literal belief in the Bible and, by implication, the "good old ways." In fact, these songs form the core of country music's first really big group of "fad" songs. In July 1925, just at the time the record industry was truly realizing that a market existed for a genre called "hill country music," the famous Scopes "Monkey Trial" (about the teaching of evolution) took place in Dayton, Tennessee. Newspapers around the South had a field day with the event, and record companies rushed singers into the studios to record songs about the trial. The result was over a dozen different recordings of a good half dozen songs, all of them naturally taking the antievolution stand. The singers perceived correctly that for most southerners the trial was an assault on the literal truth of the Bible, and some of the songs made reference to the Bible in this respect. The most popular of the songs, Carson Robison's "The John T. Scopes Trial," recorded by Vernon Dalhart (Columbia, CO15037–0) and selling over one hundred thousand copies, began with the stanza:

> All the folks in Tennessee are as faithful as can be,
> And they know the Bible teaches what is right,
> They believe in God above and His great undying love,
> And they know they are protected by His might.

But a more direct commentary about the Bible was to emerge from the pen of Uncle Dave Macon, a Middle Tennessee singer and composer who was to become one of the first stars of country music and in later years a fixture on the Grand Ole Opry. Uncle Dave came by his religion honestly; he included a number of sacred songs in his canon and knew the Bible well enough even to preach a sermon occasionally. In his first recording session after the Scopes trial—he had been a recording star for some months—he recorded an original composition called "The Bible's True."

THE BIBLE'S TRUE

Spoken: Now I don't believe in evolution or revolution, but when it
            comes to the good old Bible from Genesis to Revelations,
            I'm right there.

            Evolution teaches man came from a monkey,
            I don't believe no such a thing in the days of a
                week of Sundays.

Chorus: For the Bible's true, yes I believe it,
            I've seen enough and I can prove it,
            What you say, what you say, it's bound to be that way.
            God made the world and everything that's in it,
            He made man perfect and the monkey wasn't in it.

Chorus: I'm no evolutionist that wants the world to see,
            There can't no man from anywhere, boys, make a monkey
                out of me.

Chorus: God made the world and then he made man,
Woman for his helpmate, beat that if you can./2/

Because Uncle Dave's song was not specifically tied to the Scope's trial, it did not become dated and he continued to sing it in later years. Though he never published it, the song migrated around Tennessee by word of mouth and has been collected as a folk song.

Many members of the country music audience in the 1930s and 1940s were fundamentalist Protestants and had a vested interest in the literal veracity of the King James Testament. The Scopes trial was only one challenge to this interest; a later one occurred some twenty years later when a furor arose over the publication of a "new Bible." In 1949 Cambridge University Press completed a translation of the whole Bible into basic English, rendering passages like the twenty-third Psalm into such antiseptic prose as "The Lord takes care of me as his sheep; I will not be without any good thing." Summing up the feelings of many Protestants, evangelist and singer Johnny Masters, leader of the Masters Family and then one of the most popular country-Gospel groups in the country, wrote a song called "They've Made a New Bible." Recorded for Columbia records in 1949 (Columbia Harmony HL-7298), the song begins by relating the King James Bible to the Pilgrim fathers who settled this land. Yet, the refrain goes, "In these awful times, it's no good so they say, / They've made a new Bible, throwed the old book away." Jesus said there would be false prophets, a later verse reminds the listener and then exhorts, "Keep the old Bible, don't be fooled by man."

Masters's association of the Bible with patriotism might well have grown out of a couple of Bible songs that emerged during World War II. One was "The Bible on the Table and the Flag Upon the Wall," a hit for Gene Autry, probably the most popular country singer in the early 1940s and a standard on the Grand Ole Opry broadcasts featuring Wally Fowler's Oak Ridge Quartet, before going to Hollywood to become a cowboy.

Even more potent was a recitation from the late 1940s called "The Deck of Cards." This piece was first recorded by an Arkansas singer named David Myrick, under his professional name of T. Texas Tyler, on an independent Hollywood label called 4-Star (4 S 1228). Tyler's version stayed on *Billboard*'s hit charts for eighteen weeks in the spring of 1948, rising as high as number two in the ratings. The narrative tells of a soldier during the Italian campaign who was caught in a church service holding a deck of cards; brought up for discipline before his commanding officer, the soldier explains the religious significance of the deck of cards and how it acts as a Bible for those who do not have one. The ace reminds him that there is but one God, the deuce that the Bible is

divided into two parts, the Old and New Testaments; the trey suggests
the Father, Son, and Holy Ghost, and the four reminds him of the four
evangelists, Matthew, Mark, Luke, and John. The recitation goes through
the entire deck in like manner, each card suggesting to the soldier some
aspect of the Bible.

Tyler's version of the recitation became a country standard in the
late 1940s. Cowboy singer Tex Ritter did a "cover" version of it that
made the charts, as did some ten other singers, including non-country
performers Phil Harris and Wink Martindale. During the Korean War,
Red River Dave and others recorded an updated version called "The
Red Deck of Cards," about a prisoner of war who was not allowed by his
Communist captors to have a Bible. In later years Red Sovine did "The
Viet Nam Deck of Cards." Other versions included Cowboy Copas's
"Cowboy's Deck of Cards" and Ferlin Husky's "Hillbilly Deck of Cards."
Such adaptability should not be surprising, though. The idea of the reci-
tation itself dates from at least the Revolutionary War, where it was
known as "The Soldier's Bible" or "The Gentleman Soldier's Prayer
Book." It was found in sermons by the nineteenth century and was trans-
ferred to the American West at the dawn of the twentieth century.
Quite possibly the concept could be traced as far back as the Middle
Ages. It is not surprising that it emerged as a hit record again in 1959,
when Wink Martindale rerecorded it.

A fourth type of Bible song, much more direct and overtly moralistic, is in some ways much more typically American: the type of song that
simply admonishes its listeners to read the Bible and use it as a guide.
One of the first of these in the mainstream country genre (as opposed to
Gospel and church music) was Karl and Harty's "Read the Bible,"
recorded for Columbia records in February 1940 and featured by the
team over their daily Chicago radio show for years. The tone is set by
the first stanza: "Oh, my friend, are you downhearted? / Do you feel
that you are lost? / Read the Bible, my friend, read the Bible." The song
is simple, direct, with no fancy metaphors or twists; you will find no
consolation in fellowship, the listener is warned, nor in "an empty heart
at prayer"; the Bible is essential. In a later song, "A Bible Lesson," not
recorded but circulated widely via radio transcriptions, Karl and Harty
give some specific examples of their dogma; each verse describes a particular malaise or problem and offers a specific Bible passage for comfort. Yet another popular song by the same team was a "spelling song"
called "B-I-B-L-E." Karl and Harty did a lot of this type of song; an
early 1934 hit was a version of an old revival song, "I'm S-A-V-E-D,"
and another was "I'm F-R-E-E from S-I-N." Such spelling songs had
been around since the early days of country music (when a favorite was

"C-H-I-C-K-E-N Spells Chicken") and are represented today by Tammy Wynette's "D-I-V-O-R-C-E." The "B-I-B-L-E" song probably came from an old Sunday school song little children used to sing that went:

> The B-I-B-L-E,
> Yes, that's the book for me,
> I stand alone on the word of God,
> The B-I-B-L-E.

Boys and girls would usually raise their Bibles high in the air during the singing of this song.

Karl and Harty, more than any other country singers, consciously used Bible songs—most of them original—in their repertoire, and they were much appreciated for doing so. They were one of the first close-harmony "brother" style acts, and their singing influenced countless others, including the Blue Sky Boys and the bluegrass giant Bill Monroe. Throughout most of their career they used religious or sentimental songs as staples in their performances, singing at a sprightly tempo, with high, clean harmony. By the 1940s, when the juke box was replacing the radio and songbook as a prime market for country music, they were forced into doing songs like "Fifty One Beers," "Tears in my Beer," and "Seven Beers with the Wrong Woman." They did not like these songs, felt the music was changing too fast, and got out, but not before penning, almost ruefully, one more Bible song, "When I Laid My Bible Down."

The admonition genre did not belong completely to Karl and Harty, though. In fact, the most successful of all such songs came from the pen of bluegrass musician Don Reno, introduced earlier as the composer of the latest "Mother's Bible" song. In 1951, returning from a trip, Reno was involved in an automobile accident in West Virginia; during his recuperation, he wrote a song called "I'm Using My Bible for a Roadmap." It was recorded at Reno and Smiley's first recording session in 1952, a session devoted entirely to the then thriving genre of bluegrass Gospel music. Ironically, by the time the company got around to issuing the song (on King 1945), Reno and Smiley had given up music and Reno was in the grocery business in Asheville, North Carolina. The song was a hit, though—it was to become probably the best-known bluegrass Gospel song—and soon Reno and Smiley were back together singing it before all sorts of audiences. "There'll be no detours in Heaven," the song begins, and continues to use the road metaphor to describe the pilgrimage to Heaven. "I'm using my Bible as a roadmap, / My last stop is Heaven some sweet day." The song and the metaphor were both so effective that in later years Reno wrote a follow-up song entitled, "Since I've Used My Bible For a Roadmap," also recorded for King.

Other admonition songs referred the listener to a specific passage in the Bible. The Bailes Brothers, famed of the Grand Ole Opry and one of the leading acts in the late 1940s, admonished the listener to "Read Romans Ten and Nine" (Columbia, 1946, CO20529), while Molly O'Day, the most popular female singer of the 1940s, had a hit with Lonnie Glosson's song "Matthew 24" (Columbia, 1947, CO20534). Both were somewhat apocalyptic in nature; "Matthew 24" begins by saying "I believe the time is coming for the Lord to come again, / I believe the end is nearing every door," and suggests "compare today with Matthew 24." Less specific in its reference was Carl Story's recording of "Four Books in the Bible" (Mercury, 1951, 6359), a song by Odell MacLeod that begins, "Do you want to know what's the matter with this old sinful world," and suggests that the answer is in the "four books of the Bible, Matthew, Mark, Luke, and John." "There's a Page in the Bible" (King, 1946, 1659) by the Brown's Ferry Four (which then included Grandpa Jones and the Delmore Brothers) is like Karl Davis's "Bible Lesson," suggesting that there is a page in the Bible that will answer troubles: "There's a page in the Bible that the right way will show."

As popular as these admonition songs were, though, none could compare with the commercial success of the first big country hit about the Bible, a lonesome lament called "Dust on the Bible" (Columbia CO2008). It was a song that in some ways harkened back to the earliest motifs of the old, worn Bible, but the sentimental images of mother and heaven are missing. Here the Bible becomes a symbol of the earlier rural values from which an industrialized blue-collar audience has fallen away. Walter Bailes first encountered the idea of going into a home and finding a dusty, unused Bible from a young minister in West Virginia, who used the story in a sermon. The story stuck with Walter (who is today himself an evangelist), and in 1946, when he and his brothers were moving Grand Ole Opry audiences with their sentimental, highly moral songs, he cast the story into song form. "Dust on the Bible, dust on the holy word," reads the first line. Audiences across the South responded; the song was a hit for the Bailes Brothers, and in later years also became a hit for The Blue Sky Boys and Wade Mainer. Preachers even based sermons on it, returning it to the pulpit from whence it had sprung.

In the same vein—the Bible representing values the modern world has grown away from—was Canadian singer Wilf Carter's 1940 hit, "Let's Go Back to the Bible" (Victor Bluebird B-8875) and Hank Snow's 1952 hit "Married by the Bible, Divorced by the Law" (RCA Victor 4733). The latter song, written by Johnny Rector, Pee Wee Truehitt, and Neva Starns, laments the "strange world we live in," with all its divorces and compares it with "the days of Ma and Pa." Another song, Bradley

Kincaid's "Brush the Dust from that Old Bible" (Capitol 1276), even links this theme to the threat of atomic holocaust, a timely idea in 1950, when the record was released.

The most recent Bible song to hit the country charts was Claude Gray's 1960 recording of "Family Bible" ("D" 1118). The song was actually written by Willie Nelson, one of today's superstars, when he was just getting started, and was sold to Gray for a reported fifty dollars. The song reflects Nelson's conservative Texas upbringing and his total absorption in the country tradition: the old, torn family Bible is a "key to memories" of a rural farm family sitting around the dinner table after supper, with father reading from the Bible and mother softly singing "Rock of ages, cleft for me." In fact, the song is in many ways a modernization of the original "mother's Bible" complex, with the Bible representing the past, childhood, and the joys of a stronger faith in simpler times. The song has remained a favorite with singers even today, especially bluegrass and country Gospel groups.

Though "Family Bible" was the last individual song to attain wide popularity, a 1975 album by a modern country group certainly deserves mention in any survey of this sort. This is a set of LPs by the Statler Brothers entitled *Holy Bible—Old Testament* (Mercury SRM-1-1051) and *Holy Bible—New Testament* (Mercury SRM-1-1052). This ambitious project, reportedly some eight years in the planning, was realized by the Statler Brothers, a Virginia quartet that started out singing Gospel music and switched to a highly successful brand of Nashville country music some fifteen years ago. (Only two of the members are really brothers, and none is really named Statler; the quartet is formed around two brothers, Don and Harold Reid, with Lew DeWitt and Phil Balsley, and they took the name Statler from a box of tissues they found in a hotel room.) In a response to their fans' request for more of the Gospel songs that made them famous, the quartet began working, about 1968, on a series of original songs about biblical characters. In their notes to the album, the brothers explained, "We all grew up in Christian homes thinking we knew the Bible, but as we began getting to it a little deeper we found out there was more to the Book than we had learned in Sunday school. We began to see the characters in the stories as human beings. We began to realize they had the same problems, temptations, fears, doubts that you and I have." One of the stated goals of the record is to take these Bible characters "off the pedestal and put them on the street."

The result is not a song, or songs, about the Bible as a whole, as most of the other songs discussed here have been, but a series of songs about individual characters in the Bible. Of the twenty-two songs, fifteen are original. There are songs about Abraham ("Have a Little Faith"), about

Adam and Eve ("Eve"), about Samson, Solomon, Noah, and, in *The New Testament* set, songs about the twelve apostles, about Paul, and several about Jesus. The songs are performed in lush Nashville studio arrangements, and each one is prefaced with a spoken introduction by one of the group. The Statlers hesitated to call their work "Gospel music"— "They're country albums with a gospel theme," said Harold Reid—but they were very successful, even by modern Nashville standards. As of 1980, sales had topped the five hundred thousand mark, and the Statlers report with pride that the "albums are often used by Sunday school teachers for their classes."

Bible songs hit a high-water mark in popularity in country music in the period from 1945 to 1955, with remarkable successes like "Dust on the Bible," "I'm Using My Bible For a Roadmap," and Don Reno's version of "Mother's Bible." After that, their popularity receded. No song directly about the Bible has shown up on country hit charts for twenty years. Perhaps the music is becoming more urban, appealing to a more eclectic audience that does not share the homogeneous rural southern values once held by most listeners to country music. Or perhaps we are all becoming more hedonistic or at least more circumspect about our religion. For whatever reason, Bible songs are more a part of the music's past than they are its present. Though such songs never played a major role in the music, they focused attention on connotations the Bible had acquired for many rural Americans—the past, the hearth, the family. As such, they form a small but unique commentary on the Bible's place in a vital and influential culture.

NOTES

/1/   These lyrics were taken from a Capitol Radio transcription.

/2/   This song was composed by Uncle Dave Macon in 1926. It was transcribed from Vocalion 15322 and 5098.

WORKS CONSULTED

Atkins, James, and William J. Kirkpatrick
        1912   *Young People's Hymnal No. 2*. Nashville: Methodist Episcopal
                                Publishing House.

Broadman Press
        1940   *The Broadman Hymnal*. Nashville: Broadman Press.

70351

Carr, Patrick, ed.
  1979   *The Illustrated History of Country Music*. New York: Dou-
                  bleday.

Hildebrand, E. T.
  1920   *Song and Story*. Basic, VA: Hildebrand-Burnett Company.

Mull, J. B.
  n.d.   *Mull's Our Recorded Songs Number 3*. Cleveland, TN: Ten-
                  nessee Music and Printing Company.

Pickett, L. L., and O. B. Culpepper
  1904   *Gems No. 2*. Louisville, KY, and Greensville, TX: Pickett
                  Publishing Company.

Randolph, Vance
  1950   *Ozark Folksongs*, IV. Columbia, MO: University of Missouri
                  Press.

Showalter, A. J., and E. G. Seweil
  1900   *Gospel Praise*. Nashville: Gospel Advocate Publishing Com-
                  pany.

Stamps, Frank, and Baxter
  1934   *Leading Light*. Dallas: Stamps and Baxter.

The Tobacco Tags
  ca. 1935   *The Tobacco Tags*. Durham, NC: Privately printed.

Vaughan, James D.
  1932   *New Gospel Voices*. Lawrenceburg, TN: James D. Vaughan
                  Publisher.

Wolfe, Charles K.
  1975   *Grand Ole Opry: Early Years, 1925–35*. London: Old Time
                  Music Press.
  1976   *Tennessee Strings: Country Music in Tennessee*. Knoxville:
                  University of Tennessee Press.

V

The Electronic Church

Perry C. Cotham

Jesus preached to no more than twenty to thirty thousand persons during his ministry, it is generally estimated. Regardless of the accuracy of this calculation, the figure is trifling in contrast to the audiences reached today by his disciples who employ the various forms of mass communication in their effort to fulfill the commission to preach the Gospel to all nations. The flow of church history and religious experience since the first century has, in large part, been given direction by the contours of the technologies that spawned great movements. The Protestant Reformation would have been unlikely without the invention of printing in the fifteenth century, which put the scriptures into the hands of the common people. Gutenberg's Bibles had been in print for fifty years before Luther nailed his ninety-five theses to the door in Wittenberg. The Reformation was indeed the child of the print medium.

The second great invention to shape religious attitudes and behavior arrived in the twentieth century. The electronic media enable modern preachers with a national audience to reach a vastly larger audience each time they speak than did Jesus or any of his apostles during their entire lives. Considered in historical perspective, this development is truly phenomenal. Furthermore, the technology is available so that, theoretically at least, a billion persons, one-fourth of the earth's population, can be reached simultaneously with an evangelist's message.

Good news indeed for many preachers! The sawdust trail of a century or so ago has been modernized into an air-conditioned television studio, equipped with all the bright lights, color cameras, trained technicians, and elaborate sets of secular counterparts. Over 95 percent of American residences have one or more television sets, and average Americans spend approximately half of all their leisure time in front of these sets; in fact, most people spend more time watching TV and listening to the radio (combined) than they spend at any other activity except sleeping. And while many Christians thrill at the potential for beaming the Gospel across the nation and around the globe, others do not share this enthusiasm. Some question whether the broadcast medium is the best or even an appropriate method to disseminate the good news. Mainline Protestant denominations have experienced a significant decline in membership during the seventies, a decline concomitant with the rise of the electronic church and Evangelicalism in general. And this development has, in large part, given rise to serious criticism of the electronic church—its validity, its ethics, its value to authentic Christian experience.

The electronic church may be viewed from various vantage points— historical, sociological, psychological, economic, legal, and hermeneutic-theological. The term "electronic church" came to currency with the unprecedented business success of televised religion in the 1970s. Consequently, any truly meaningful evaluation must await the garnering of more factual data. The scope of this essay includes providing a brief historical sketch of radio-TV preaching and surveying the contemporary scene by identifying the most powerful TV evangelists, citing those issues that are raised most often by critics, and finally noting the major themes developed by electronic evangelists and considering some of the strengths and limitations of the medium.

What is meant by the term "electronic church"? A broad meaning is possible if we include all electronic programming with religious intent and value. There are many spin-offs of the electronic revolution that have aided today's church leaders in becoming better equipped in both public and private counsel—motion pictures produced by Christians for either the screen or television viewing, video tape and film programming for religious instruction, cassette recordings of sermons and lectures, and rapid-speed computers and processing machines that permit media evangelists to identify and send "personalized" communications to select audiences. Current interest and controversy focus on one aspect of the communications revolution, and it is unquestionably the most important aspect—radio and television broadcasting.

This essay will deal chiefly with radio and television evangelism of Christian persuasion (since this by far makes up the bulk of such evangelism), concentrating on the ways in which this programming proclaims. the biblical message. The fact that numerous shows may be viewed on hundreds of stations, raising enormous sums of revenue, provides evidence enough that they are taken seriously by millions of people. And while we deal with television evangelism, we must keep in mind its role in the total context of the electronic communication explosion.

Early Beginnings

When radio transmission was made available for the public interest, use, and convenience, American preachers were ready to seize the new opportunities for enlarging their audiences through access to airwaves. Purportedly, the first religious program was the broadcast of the Sunday evening service at Calvary Episcopal Church in Pittsburgh on 2 January 1921, by the nation's first commercially licensed radio station, KDKA. Religious programming and the licensing of new stations emerged together. In 1922, Paul Rader established his own once-a-week religious radio station in Chicago with call letters WJBT ("Where Jesus Blesses Thousands"). The Moody Bible Institute set up its own radio station in 1926 (WMBI). Charles E. Coughlin, the politically oriented priest long since widely repudiated by officials of his church, began airing his broadcasts in the 1920s from Royal Oak, Michigan, and during the depression years could claim an audience of tens of millions. Coughlin's program demonstrated the potential of the medium to place power in the hands of religious demagogues. There would be no way to determine how many sermons or devotional messages, much less scriptures, have been read, quoted, and misquoted over the airwaves of American radio stations. Nearly every town of any size has a radio station, and each station has allotted time to local preachers to present their message. The Fundamentalist preacher has always been stereotyped as the "radio evangelist," and many Fundamentalists have felt that the epitome of Gospel ministry is a fifteen-minute daily outreach to the city. Serious biblical discourse was rarely in evidence; instead, the local radio show gave the town preachers frequent opportunity to rehash old sermon outlines, defend sectarian doctrines, harangue the local heathen, or grind personal axes. The format of religious programs in Small Town, America, rarely required intellectual discipline of either the pastor or the listening flock. Presentations were mostly extemporaneous at best and, quite often, there seemed to be little evidence of preparation by the speaker. Some seemed satisfied simply to turn on the microphone and start shouting. If the preacher took a vacation or held a revival in another town, the program could be taped for future broadcast.

Among those who emerged on the national scene as hucksters for God over the radio airwaves were figures like Brother Al ("That's A-L, Brother Al"); the Reverend Frederick B. Eikerenkoetter II, who became known to millions as "Reverend Ike," C. W. Burpo ("Spelled 'B,' as in Bible"), Kathryn Kuhlman, A. A. Allen, and Garner Ted Armstrong. These religious personalities developed an avid following among the ranks of Fundamentalists who regarded Billy Graham as too establishment-oriented, Billy James Hargis as too political, and Oral Roberts as too suspect after he founded a university and joined the Methodist Church.

Each of these was a colorful and dramatic radio evangelist in his or her own right, etching a unique style and message. Asa A. Allen was a

licensed Assemblies of God preacher who established headquarters
in Dallas and in 1953 launched the "Allen Revival Hour." "Miracle"
became the key word in "Triple A's" revivals and broadcasts, and no one
outstripped his supernatural claims. He frequently reported resurrections
from the dead and claimed that "miracle oil" began to flow from the
heads and hands of those attending his revivals (finding justification for
the latter phenomenon in Heb 1:9). Kathryn Kuhlman emerged in the
seventies as an energetic, theatrical advocate of miracles. Her ministry
featured a large radio and television network and a growing number of
regional personal appearances in key cities in order to conduct her miracle services. For many years, Garner Ted Armstrong has been heard over
the airwaves dispensing the plain apocalyptic truth on "The World
Tomorrow." His key to understanding current problems and events, such
as drug abuse, crime, space exploration, and ecology, is an awareness of
biblical prophecy. The main theme of "Reverend Ike," according to his
many critics, was the power of positive greed. ("Don't be a hypocrite
about money; Say, 'I like money.' Money is not sinful in its right place. I
bless the idea of money in my mind.") Ike's broadcasts were filled with
stories of financial success obtained through his efforts ("this poor sister
received a new Buick in forty-five minutes"). Ike's unabashed love for
money and material wealth and his doctrine that these are the proper
rewards of religious devotion struck some of his critics as caricatures of
the Calvinist belief that God favors the elect even in this world.

One of the most respected and enduring programs has been "The
Lutheran Hour," which premiered in October 1930 and featured a noted
Old Testament scholar and prolific writer, Walter A. Maier, as speaker.
Maier's sermon of about twenty minutes was preceded only by a choral
group singing classical church music. Thousands of pastors around the
country would rush home from their own services to receive spiritual
nourishment from this renowned teacher. Maier's own eloquence and his
emphasis on the biblical message were sources of the program's power.
"The Lutheran Hour" became the most popular religious broadcast in

the history of radio, and during his career Maier delivered 509 radio addresses. The program continues today with Oswald Hoffman, who has been the speaker since 1956. A contemporary of Maier was Charles E. Fuller, whose "Old Fashioned Revival Hour" became a national program in 1937. Fuller's avowed purpose was to broadcast the old songs and the "old Gospel message." Fuller would tell his audience, "Our one message is Christ and Him crucified, and we endeavor by God's grace to beseech men and women to be reconciled to God in Christ Jesus." His program became one of the most popular of all radio shows, steadily drawing people from all religious persuasions, an estimated audience of twenty million listeners a week, until shortly before his retirement in 1967.

The Electronic Church Today

Radio evangelism continues to this day with a similar variety in style and content to that of a generation ago. But today nearly everyone, evangelists included, considers radio speakers as second cousins to television personalities. The "electronic church" is a term applied primarily to big-time television evangelism. The expression connotes in most minds an effervescent, charismatic personality around which the show centers, a Bible-centered message, Gospel music, pleasant sounds, happy faces, images of success, warnings of doom, appeals for conversion, and, ultimately, sophisticated appeals for financial support of the broadcast ministry.

Prior to the early seventies comparatively few people paid much attention to television evangelism. Apart from Oral Roberts's specials and telecasts of Billy Graham crusades, most television evangelism belonged to graveyard and ghetto hours. But interest in television evangelism was soon to quicken, given the spirit of the times, the emergence of charismatic celebrities, the arrival of cable television, and the realization by stations that they could sell time for religion and retain the same approval from the Federal Communications Commission (FCC) as for sustaining time. And many sincere, highly motivated and ambitious evangelists discovered that through television they could reach millions of people and promote salvation just as effectively as secular entrepreneurs presented their products.

Religious broadcasting boomed into a big business in the seventies, a fact that did not go unnoticed by the national news media. The industry generated thousands of jobs and an annual cash flow of hundreds of millions of dollars. Religious observers were seeing the movement as a "new force" on the American religious scene. The National Religious Broadcasters (NRB) was founded in 1944 as a trade association for religion-oriented stations and program producers; in 1970, the association could claim about one hundred members, but ten years later that figure had multiplied nine times. Today the NRB's annual convention attracts many observers and guests to Washington, and Presidents Ford and Carter have addressed the convention, thus attesting to the political clout of religious broadcasters. The electronic church, largely dominated by the Evangelical-Fundamentalist-Pentecostal wing of Protestantism, by 1980 owned fourteen hundred radio stations and thirty-five television stations; four religious "networks" feed programs via satellite to stations and to thousands of cable-TV hookups. Mainline Protestant, Catholic, and Jewish broadcasters, who have relied mainly on free time in television's low-audience "Sunday morning ghetto" for their largely nonsectarian programs produced with commercial networks or on syndicated shows, have found themselves eclipsed.

Although there are hundreds of local, regional, and national broadcast preachers, the electronic church in the 1980s is dominated by several superstars who raise more than a quarter of a billion dollars a year for their diverse religious enterprises:

—Pat Robertson hosts the "700 Club," a daily talk show originating from Virginia Beach, Virginia, and heads the Christian Broadcast Network. Robertson claims his show is serving 700 million people.

—Jim Bakker hosts the "PTL" ("Praise the Lord" and "People That Love"), which originates from Charlotte, North Carolina.

—Jerry Falwell broadcasts "Old-Time Gospel Hour," a taped version of Sunday morning services at Thomas Road Baptist Church in Lynchburg, Virginia.

—Oral Roberts of Tulsa, Oklahoma, hosts a weekly religious show but is better known for prime-time television specials featuring varied entertainment.

—Billy Graham is the best known of the mass evangelists. Graham launched his "Hour of Decision" on radio in 1950, and the show grew in popularity. Graham's television outreach now is mainly through specials consisting of edited versions of taped campaign appearances.

—Rex Humbard of Akron, Ohio, broadcasts worship services from the Cathedral of Tomorrow, which are taped for a one-hour telecast.

—Jimmy Swaggart of Baton Rouge, Louisiana, is a colorful Assemblies of God revivalist who achieved popularity first in Gospel music. He began with a radio broadcast, "The Camp Meeting Hour," in 1969 and three years later moved into television evangelism.

—Robert Schuller of Garden Grove, California, offers morning worship services that are taped and telecast as the "Hour of Power."

These high-powered evangelists are men of charm, talent, drive, and ambition. Each projects a skillful blend of worldly and everlasting well-being, and each possesses an uncanny ability to tug at both heart strings and purse strings. Still, how does one account for the meteoric rise to power of the entire electronic church? And why these evangelists rather than others?

In explaining the rise of the electronic church, one major factor has already been noted—the expanding technologies that revolutionized mass communications also expanded opportunities for evangelism. The application of computer and communications technologies can be found in politics, government, business, and other institutional enterprises as well. The early electronic preachers knew relatively little about the audiences they were dependent upon for financial support. The mail bag was the key to support for early radio preachers, and so the typical sermon would end with the appeal to "keep those cards 'n letters coming in." Behind the scenes now of every large evangelistic association is the computer churning out vital data, maintaining highly differentiated mailing lists and storing for rapid retrieval significant information about the people behind the names and addresses. Each phone call can be registered with information about the caller stored. With the passage of time, parasites can be deleted from the list and repeat contributors can be further cultivated with seemingly personalized attention. On-line printers mass produce letters with the recipient's name scattered throughout the text and then signed mechanically by the evangelist as though it were written and typed individually for that person. The ethics of such communication methods are questionable, to be sure, but they are part and parcel of the American bureaucratic lifestyle, as everyone knows who receives periodic fund-raising letters from local and national officials and organizations. Without these letters electronic evangelists would not be able to reap the large financial resources that are necessary to underwrite their organizations—or, the funds could certainly not be as easily raised.

Still, advancement in communications technology is inadequate to explain why the electronic church is controlled and operated by evangelists of the Fundamentalist-Evangelical-Pentecostal persuasion. Two additional factors are important. First, there is a drift or trend of the entire American culture toward conservatism. This shift to the right is not reflected merely in religious attitudes but also in voting booths across the land. Throughout his entire presidential campaign in 1976, Jimmy Carter shared his faith as a "born-again" Christian. During the same year, George Gallup discovered that fifty million of the adults also considered themselves to be "born-again" Christians, and 1976 was declared by the news media to be "the year of the Evangelical."

Conservative religion seemed to flourish with renewed appeal and a favorable image it had not enjoyed since the days of the Scopes trial in 1925. (Viewers of *Inherit the Wind* may easily forget that millions of Americans, many journalists included, were admirers of William Jennings Bryan.) Religiously or politically, the sixties were years of ferment and unrest. The assassinations of President John F. Kennedy, Martin Luther King, Jr., and Robert Kennedy, the Vietnam War, the resignations under duress of Vice President Agnew and President Nixon, and assorted major and minor political scandals—all of this led to widespread disillusionment. We lost confidence in business. We lost confidence in government. We saw that liberal policies were not necessarily the answer to intractable social problems but often led merely to pouring more and more tax money into problem areas and the establishment of new bureaucracies and expansion of old bureaucracies.

In the churches, mainline Protestantism lost much of its appeal. Emphasis on the social Gospel and a call for direct action no longer seemed practical or satisfying to many churchgoers. Christians often felt that the pulpit had drifted away from substantive biblical messages and away from biblical authority and was offering little more than social and political comment or an exhortation that was no more authoritative than if it had come from Eric Severeid. And so conservative religion, based on clearly acknowledged biblical authority and promising to offer "ultimate answers" and "meaning" in the midst of complexity and disillusionment, experienced a resurgence. Liberal denominations declined in membership; Fundamentalist and Evangelical churches grew. And along with that Evangelical renaissance, giving its own impetus, was the electronic church.

The other major reason why the electronic church is predominantly utilized and controlled by Evangelical and Fundamentalist Christians is that the available technology is compatible with and can be supported by their theological stance toward proselytism. Since broadcast time is not free in this country, someone must pay. And who should feel more obligated to pay than those who feel their souls have just been rescued from peril by a message heard over the tube? Evangelicals take quite literally Jesus' "Great Commission" to "go into all the world and preach the Gospel to every creature." Some of the most popular shows are filled with one emotional appeal after another for a decision for Christ ("Just accept Jesus into your heart right now in order to be forgiven for all your sins, and then call us at the toll-free number on the bottom of your screen").

Obviously, mainline Protestants have a different view of the conversion process, a process involving instruction, reason, and reflection. Such a process may be conducive to developing mature disciples, but it is certainly not conducive to fund raising. Many Methodists, Episcopalians, or Presbyterians, for example, would find it inappropriate if not outright abhorrent to ask another person, "Do you know Jesus?" or "Are you saved?" High-pressured proselytism is simply anathema to their traditions. Furthermore, what appeals to traditionalists in terms of worship experiences would not be attractive to mass audiences and vice versa. Most Protestants would be uncomfortable with strong emotional appeals for anything, with altar calls, and with lowbrow Gospel music. Speaking of the traditionalists, Jerome Hadden points out that "what appeals to their tastes in worship does not appeal to the masses who think that Bach is a beer and Haydn is the quarterback of the Rams."/1/

My purpose here is not to analyze the vast criticism aimed at broadcast evangelism by church leaders and lay opinion makers, except to point out that far and away the chief criticism is that the electronic church flourishes at the expense of the local congregation. This is also the oldest criticism. There is a very deep and well-justified concern not only that the electronic church moves deeply into the ranks of churchgoing Americans and convinces them that a worship viewed in the comfort of their den is sufficient spiritual experience but also that the money going to support the broadly based ministries of electronic evangelists is money that would have gone into the coffers of the local congregation. No one has been more outspoken on this point than the noted University of Chicago church historian Martin Marty. Marty described this competition between the electronic and the local church:

> Late Saturday night Mr. and Mrs. Invisible Religion get their jollies from the ruffled shirt, pink-tuxedoed men and the high-coiffeured, low-necklined celebrity women who talk about themselves under the guise of born-again autobiographies. Sunday morning the watchers get their jollies as Holy Ghost entertainers caress microphones among spurting fountains as a highly professional charismatic (in two senses) leader entertains them. . . . Are they to turn off that very set and then make their way down the block to a congregation of real believers, sinners, offkey choirs, sweaty and homely people who need them, people they do not like but are supposed to love, ordinary pastors who preach grace along with calls to discipleship, pleas for stewardship that do not come well-oiled? Never. Well, hardly ever. . . . Since the electronic church, you remind me, at least "preaches Christ" and thus may do some good, let it be. Let its members pay for it. But let the church catch on to what is going on, and go its own way, undistracted by the offers of "cheap grace" or the language of the cross without the mutual bearing of the cross. (Fore: 6)

The realization that small-town congregations may be losing the battle of interest and funds to the television evangelists inspired Merle Allison

Johnson to write a book entitled *How To Be Happy in the Non-Electric Church.*

Electronic evangelists go to great lengths to refute vigorously the alleged "robbing Peter to pay Paul" effect of their ministries. They are sensitive about such a charge, and the avowed purpose of their broadcast evangelism is to complement and support the programs of the local congregation. As Robert Schuller told his audience upon returning from a conference in New York that dealt with this issue, "The church is not an electronic TV set. The church is a caring institution where people love and care for people." Perhaps the debate can be settled soon by the conduct of empirical research. Preliminary reports are already beginning to suggest that, contrary to fears, the electronic church is not hurting the local congregation./2/

The Role of the Bible in the Electronic Church

It is customary for electronic church preachers to declare vociferously that their message is biblical. Several questions suggest themselves. Is the "whole counsel of God" indeed proclaimed from the television pulpit? Is biblical exegesis sound? Is there a clear hermeneutic? Are sound applications drawn from biblical narratives? Are solutions to problems of everyday life biblical and practical? Are the full demands of Christian discipleship made clear? Is there an emphasis on objective truth and experience? Are the biblical God and the biblical Christ depicted? Does the electronic church make it clear that there is more to biblical proclamation than the utterance of words? What if, in some distant century, all Bibles had been destroyed and all that researchers of that future civilization discovered about twentieth-century spiritual experience were videotapes of Christian television shows? What portions of the Bible would have survived and how would our spiritual experience be described?

These are questions of gravity and they must be answered by looking at the stance of the electronic church as a whole rather than by focusing on any one broadcast show. Unfortunately, the general norm in biblical exposition seems to be more eisegesis than exegesis—the scripture means exactly what the preacher says it means and nothing more. All too often exposition is characterized by shallowness and superficiality. Viewers will look in vain for an in-depth, enlightened, critical approach to the scriptures or to systematic Christian doctrine. Television preachers engage in much "proof-texting," the taking of individual scriptures from context and citing them in support of some contention. They generally avoid the prophetic literature of the Old Testament and the New Testament epistles but are effective in reciting and dramatizing the narratives in the life of Jesus and famous characters of both Testaments.

Electronic preachers seem not to have a clearly defined hermeneutic. They give little or no consideration to cultural factors operative during biblical times that may have influenced the writings and show little or no evidence of familiarity with historical and critical methodologies in biblical interpretation. Several issues are neglected: Is the Bible the word of God or does the Bible contain God's word? Does God have a revelation for us outside the canon? How was the canon determined? Are all books of equal authority? How was the authenticity of Jesus' words established? Are there significant differences between biblical apocalyptic passages and numerous noncanonical apocalyptic materials? Did the biblical authors edit other materials that are included as their writing? What literary forms were employed by biblical writers? Is the Bible self-interpreting? Is its meaning self-evident? Who is competent to interpret it? If we seek answers to these questions from electronic preachers, the answers must come inferentially, for the preachers themselves seem to have given little consideration to these questions. The overall impression is that the Bible must be read literally, that all biblical materials are of equal value, that God does give subjective revelation to individuals apart from the canon, that church tradition and the ruling of great councils are irrelevant, that the Bible is inerrant by any standard—historical, scientific, theological—and that critical methodology is fruitless.

Factors Affecting the Role of the Bible in Electronic Evangelism

If this overview of the place of the Bible is accurate, how do we account for such a dreary video picture? To contend that the weaknesses in electronic evangelism are the same weaknesses inherent within Fundamentalist preaching in general is insufficient, although the statement is true enough. I offer three explanations that relate to (1) the nature of the television medium; (2) the nature of broadcast ministries; and (3) the nature of electronic spiritual experience.

First, when religious folk enter the television industry, they enter the world of entertainment. Television in America is viewed for only two reasons. First and foremost, it is viewed for entertainment. There is nothing particularly profound about that statement; anyone who has studied mass media in this nation is aware of this fact. A distantly second reason people watch television is to gain information, yet even here informative shows may be selected primarily for their entertainment values. Audiences are self-selecting according to what they find to be the most entertaining and most worthwhile programming. Television evangelists find themselves pitted against highly financed commercial competitors and are aware that they must compete favorably by packaging religion entertainingly.

This accounts for the wide-ranging adoption of the same entertainment formats employed so successfully in nonreligious programming. Opting for the daily talk show format or some variation of it is pure pragmatism on their part. Pat Robertson, Jim Bakker, Oral Roberts, sincere as they may be, are the Johnny Carsons, Phil Donahues, and Dinah Shores of television religion. "The 700 Club," "PTL," and "Praise the Lord" (the latter two are separate shows) provide good imitations of the "Tonight Show"—a lavish studio set with modern equipment, a live audience, a host and a co-host who engage in innocuous chatter and laughter (which some, to borrow Sören Kierkegaard's terms, have described as "pious twaddle"), interviews with guest celebrities and musical soloists, all interspersed with musical presentations, station breaks, and the religious equivalent of commercial interruptions and appeals. The main differences are that the jokes are always clean, the interviews tend to be even more predictable than their secular equivalents, and the music employs pious lyrics though it is otherwise identical to popular music generally.

Ideas and lines of analysis that are complex enough to make intellectual demands on an audience are not very entertaining, and the television medium does not easily adapt itself to sustained analysis. Any message of substance is likely to be reduced to a few catchwords and slogans. "Praise the Lord" is the best-known slogan in pop religion these days, and it may be injected with enthusiasm at any time in one's own monologue or during the testimony of another. "Thank you, Jesus" is appropriate at the end of any Gospel musical number, and the host may want to exhort the audience to "give the Lord a hand of praise." Jimmy Swaggart commends to his audience the Pentecostal spirit of an ordinary working man who, when asked the time of day would reply, "Hallelujah! Praise the Lord! Glory to God! Thank you, Jesus! It's 1:15." Oral Roberts has been a pioneer in electronic evangelism and is responsible for bequeathing a number of shouts of praise. Two decades of Roberts's slogans became the shouts of the neo-Pentecostal, charismatic revival: "Expect a miracle," "Our God is a good God," and "Something good is going to happen to you." Hundreds of thousands have exclaimed "I found it!" and committed themselves to have "seed-faith" and make a "blessing pact." It is anyone's guess what future slogans and shibboleths will emerge, but one may hope an exclamation of praise heard one evening (20 February 1980) on "Praise the Lord" will not take hold—"Let the bride of Christ become as big as she can!"/3/

A second reason for the paucity of serious biblical exposition is that the broadcast programs by top television evangelists are only a part of the larger whole of their individual ministries. That successful television programming reaps enormous harvests of revenue is evident to any media observer. Television preachers are competing directly for the same consumer dollars that viewers dole out to advertising sponsors. Gospel superstars hope to get on every outlet possible, because every station added to the schedule enlarges the audience and increases income to the producer. The revenue that flows in is often in excess of what is necessary to produce and sustain the programming. Thus, the most powerful electronic evangelists feel that the generous response from their clientele is a sign from the Almighty calling them to engage in various multimillion-dollar building programs.

One viewing of any major show informs the viewer of these magnificent pet projects. Jim Bakker describes how he received the idea for Heritage Village, a miniature version of colonial Williamsburg, from a direct revelation. Funds raised by the "PTL" maintain "Heritage, U.S.A.," a recreational mecca that resembles a modern Olympic village. A massive Polynesian-style pyramid, designed to house Heritage University, dominates the site and awaits more funds for completion. Money raised by Oral Roberts has been used to build a modern university facility named in his honor. Under present construction nearby is the "City of Faith" ("God laid this on my heart to build," Roberts announces), which will include a thirty-story hospital, a sixty-story diagnostic center, and a twenty-story cancer center—"where prayer and faith will come together." Jerry Falwell maintains Liberty Baptist College with television revenue, just as Pat Robertson underwrites Christian Broadcast Network University with viewer loyalty. Robert Schuller long urged his viewers to send money to complete construction of the $15 million Crystal Cathedral. Both Jimmy Swaggart and fast-rising evangelist James Robison ask supporters to send money for urgently needed multimillion-dollar office headquarter complexes.

Several evangelists use their programs for other types of promotion, such as announcing and plugging their personal appearance tours throughout the country, and they may save the really high-powered huckstering for these occasions. Books, cassette tapes, and records may be offered. Jimmy Swaggart frequently offers special deals on record albums he recorded that have been "an untold blessing to multiple tens of thousands." Rare indeed is the electronic evangelist who does not use a family member on his program. Faithful viewers easily recognize the visages of Richard Roberts, Robert A. Schuller, Donnie Swaggart, Tammy Bakker and numerous Humbards, to cite a few.

The national religious broadcast that shuns all solicitation for funds is a rare and respected genre indeed. Such a show, however, would be unlikely to compete favorably for outlet exposure with "PTL," "700

Club," Roberts, or Schuller. Many observers feel the evangelists are caught up in a vicious circle: money—and plenty of it—is essential for a continuing television program, from which time must then be taken in order to ask for more money. An interesting quantitative study would involve counting the total number of minutes sacrificed to fund raising in these most popular shows. Such a study might be implausible since the pitch for money is subtly interwoven with the message from the scriptures. Therefore, serious, in-depth exposition of the Bible cannot be expected from the leading shows until the preachers find other ways to finance their programs and diverse building projects. For example, one evening on a program televised 6 May 1980, Oral Roberts stopped to plug his "City of Faith." He resumed the sermon, only to stop again and interview a pre-med student at Oral Roberts University and the doctor who is dean of the ORU School of Medicine. The result was a double plug for the university and for the City of Faith. In the midst of a long prayer, Rex Humbard paused and cried out, "And God, give me people who will send us monthly contributions."

The eagerness of the audience to respond generously to appeals for money is in itself a fascinating psychological phenomenon. How are such cash flows generated? First, there may be an appeal to the scriptures. There are two main scriptures used in fund raising. One is Jesus' statement in Acts 20:35 ("It is more blessed to give than to receive"), and the other is Luke 6:38 ("For whatever measure you deal out to others will be dealt to you in return"). An element of spiritual self-interest is also involved. Viewers are promised a multiple return on money that is contributed. Contributing to these programs and personalities (probably most gifts are given to the personalities, albeit unconsciously) is an investment in something larger than oneself. Giving is a literal "joining of the club," as signified by the reception of a certificate, Faith Partner Bible, or the like. The giver is reassured that he or she is a spiritual person, a "fisher of men," a fellow soul-winner for Christ. Appeals for funds are not likely to be abated any time soon and in fact will likely increase as the value of the dollar is eroded by inflation and as building costs continue to rise—undoubtedly, both inflation and building costs, the evangelists sometimes suggest, are ploys of the devil to test the faithful's sensitive nerve leading to the pocketbook.

The talk-show host has a somewhat different format with which to make direct appeals than does the electronic preacher. For example, in 1979, instead of his "700 Club," Pat Robertson hosted a telethon special that copied from beginning to end the methods of the old cerebral palsy telethons. A panel of men and women waited anxiously by phones to receive pledges that were rushed by attractive young people to Robertson, who, as breathlessly and enthusiastically as Jerry Lewis, read out the list of the latest donors ("New York, $300 . . . Kentucky, $300 . . .Kentucky, another $100 . . . and now let's switch live to our New York affiliate").

The talk-show host also has numerous natural breaks in which to inject appeals for funds. He implores during pauses or at the conclusion of each spell of witnessing or rehearsal of a conversion event ("Are you right with your neighbor? With your family? With your God? Have you accepted Jesus as your personal Savior? If not, accept him this very moment while I pray for you and then get up and go immediately to your phone and call us"). Each talk show continuously flashes the number viewers may call, and the camera often pans a staff of volunteers oblivious to the excitement of what is happening on the set because with earnest and pained expressions they are engrossed in counseling phone respondents. Throughout the show, whether during interviews, songs, or even prayers, viewers are certain to hear the sound of ringing phones in the background—proof enough that the perishing are being rescued around the country.

Other methods of presenting emotional appeals for support exist. "Brick-and-mortar psychology" has long infested American religious experience and may be anticipated as an important force that will continue to shape the future of the electronic church. The phrase "brick-and-mortar psychology" refers to the well-established fact that people will donate money more readily to erect buildings than to support more ephemeral and intangible goals. Videotapes of edifices are beautifully produced and edited, revealing all the color of nature's grass, flowers, trees, and landscape as backdrops (naturally Charlotte, Garden Grove, and Virginia Beach fare better in regard to their backdrops than does Tulsa). Evangelists are fond of detailing their struggles to build their cathedrals, hospitals, and universities. On one show, while Tammy Bakker, the wife of Evangelist Jim, sang with great emotion the song "It is Finished" (a song about Jesus' redemptive work on the cross), taped segments showing the unfinished and vandalized Heritage University headquarters were splashed on the screen with more appeals for money, though the similarity between Christ's atoning death and the Bakker's building project seemed slight.

The major evangelists report regularly what they are doing to stretch the viewers' salvation dollars. Some of the appeals are low-keyed and obviously earnest, such as those by Jimmy Swaggart, and others are blunt and to the point, such as an appeal by Dwight Thompson (aired 20 February 1980): "God has given me a message. Now you pray and write me, enclosing the largest check you can." Prayers and checks are usually asked for in the same breath.

Free gifts, the sale of special merchandise, or other requests for audience response constitute another major method of retaining audience interest, soliciting funds, and enlarging a mailing list. Such methods hearken back to the days of earlier radio evangelists. C. W. Burpo's audience "heard" him entering the "throne room" from whence, he assured listeners, he would send their messages up to heaven. A. A. Allen's listeners were offered a free "prayer cloth" guaranteed to cure the recipient's physical and financial ills. Among the sacred merchandise hawked by radio evangelists were large-print Bibles, calendars, greeting cards, Bible-verse yo-yos, ballpoint pens with an inspirational message, inspirational "truth-pacs," bumper stickers, record albums with heart-touching stories and songs, books, and magazines.

The catalogue of come-ons for the religious superstars today is just as varied if not as astonishing, and the offers and giveaways often appear to be the evangelical equivalent of indulgences, their hawkers modern Tetzels. Books are still popular giveaway items. Billy Graham alone has given away millions, some of which, such as *Halley's Bible Handbook*, have been highly worthwhile offers. Robert Schuller offers a compilation of his ten most popular sermons and Oral Roberts offers *Don't Give Up!* ("You can stand in a world weakened by compromise and corruption.") Schuller's "gift of the week" is changed every few weeks; he has offered a glittering "gold" cross pendant, a ceramic tile with famous one-liners from sermons; window trinkets with colorful rainbow and appropriate quip (a "think-it"). Pins (Falwell offers "Jesus First" and American flag models for proud lapel wearing), super deluxe special edition Bibles, miracle manuals, pictures, inscribed bricks, multiple trinkets and gadgets are among the other offers that abound with an implied promise of special blessing, personal closeness to the star, and an identity with the movement, which sometimes resembles a fan club.

Keeping viewers tuned in involves varying the context if not the basic message. Rex Humbard takes his troup to Jerusalem and an upper room for the annual communion service near Easter. He has also taped shows at Cape Canaveral and in the nation's capital. Oral Roberts prays over letters (or most likely computer print-outs of names of people who have written him) that are carried to the Prayer Tower. In 1980 Roberts laid hands on son Richard and commissioned him to go to the Holy Land with several bags of mail, over which he prayed at the Garden Tomb, Sinai, Bethlehem, the Sea of Galilee, Cana, and Mount Calvary. On the same trip, Richard sealed the names of the Covenant Family in a moisture-proof container and buried it on top of the Mount of Olives ("where Jesus' feet last touched earth and where in the Second Coming his feet will first touch down again"). On location, "I felt the spirit in me," Richard declared to his father; after this trek, Oral's granddaughter was baptized. (The show reporting Richard Roberts's pilgrimage to the Holy Land was aired in March of 1980.) On Easter weekend, Trinity Broadcasting Network staged a giant rally in Los Angeles, featuring Gospel music, a dramatic reenactment of the crucifixion, a fervent sermon dealing with the Second Coming and imminent judgment, and a strong emotional appeal by Dwight Thompson for decisions for Christ. On 27 March 1980, "Praise the Lord" featured one lay preacher, Arthur Blessitt, who had just returned with pictures of his traipsing through the Bible lands dragging a twelve-foot cross ("I just wanted to cram that cross down the devil's throat," he told the audience).

Finally, there is a third explanation for the diminished quality of biblical proclamation and spiritual experience in the electronic church. This consideration is vitally important in contemplating the value of electronic religion, though hardly as significant as other factors relative to the role of the Bible. Put succinctly, the electronic church is *not* a church.

The term "electronic church" is a misnomer. And the danger comes when people on the fringes of Christian faith confuse the excitement of show-biz Christian programming with the message, ministry, and worship of the church in terms of some local, visible community. Compared with the glitter of electronic worship, the services of the local church are lackluster. The church on the tube is transmitted from a carefully controlled studio and is experienced in the safe, comfortable environment of a den or living room. That is not the same as sitting with an audience that includes less fluent preachers, sniffling toddlers, restless teenagers, sleepy parishioners, an off-key song director, an out-of-tune organ, and hearing-impaired grandparents.

The "electronic church" is another example of the depersonalization of our lives that has been lamented by sociologists for three decades now. There cannot be a church without the intimate, interpersonal relations between all kinds of people of shared faith or spiritual history. On television, a Bible message is proclaimed, obviously; the lordship of Jesus is confessed; there is a call to repentance and renewal. Yet there is no sacramental dimension to television worship, nor is there any meaningful sense of being in community with a group of believers. One may watch in living color the rite of baptism administered by Robert Schuller, witness Rex Humbard taking holy communion with his followers, or listen rapturously to even outstanding church music—but none of this spectator activity is equivalent to or a substitute for participation in the life of a particular religious community.

Biblical Themes and the Electronic Church

The electronic pulpit treats a wide range of biblical subjects and human problems, and most of these can be subsumed under five categories: (1) deity, (2) conversion, (3) Christian life, (4) Christian world view, and (5) eschatology. How these themes are developed may be determined by attending to the content of messages by electronic preachers on these subjects, by observing spiritual phenomena either experienced or reported on these programs, and by noting the scriptures used most frequently on the shows.

The Doctrine of the Deity

The chief statement about the deity can be heard in the opening and closing lines of most shows and interspersed throughout the programs: "God loves you and so do we" or "Jesus loves you and so do I." There is seldom a hint that God might mediate his love and concern through less obvious human instruments. The depressed, the frustrated, the suffering, and the lonely are offered cheer by that one reassurance—at least God loves you.

The God of the electronic church is that familiar God of American Fundamentalism—the celestial, beneficent grandfather above the bright blue who is ready "to turn minuses into pluses and scars into stars" if only we exercise "possibility thinking." This God is trinitarian, manifesting himself in the overlapping roles of Father, Son, and Holy Spirit. The familiar faith in an omniscient, omnipotent ("There ain't nuttin' my God cain't do," declared one Gospel music performer), yet personal, loving, comforting God, who forgives sins, answers prayers, and helps his followers solve personal problems by his direct spiritual presence and guidance, is the kind of religion promulgated by the electronic church.

The seventies have been termed the "Me Decade," symbolizing the emergence of books on self-improvement, self-help, and pop psychology in general. The emphasis was a retreat from the social and political activism of the sixties. Perhaps much of the unrest and upheaval of the sixties led to the disillusionment, frustration, uncertainty, and search for meaning of the seventies. The God of the tube, a God for the times, is One who cares more about individual problems than social justice. God is not the Universal Spirit of the deists, an impersonal, uncaring, bureaucratic authority who controls our lives through science, medicine, and government. The God that loves and cares directly for each individual is the only one who can instill comfort and reassurance in a stressful world, proclaim the evangelists. God has a plan for each individual life. "God is the architect that gives us the plan," notes Rex Humbard, "but we are the builders."

The beneficence of God cannot be overemphasized by his superstars on the tube. There is absolutely nothing that his children might desire that they could not request in prayer—a raise in pay, physical attractiveness (professional vocalist Diana Pilcher appeared once with Robert Schuller and told him God helped her lose 113 pounds—"It's God's work within me making the choice of fruit over cake"), or good grades in school ("Isn't Jesus so smart!" said one youngster on "Praise the Lord"). God can work financial miracles and can deliver the material goods. All you have to do is ask for it (Heb 4:15 is a popular scripture on this score). Ernest Angley delivers a sermon entitled "God I Want It All," the title being a transition phrase while he catches his breath and moves to the next item we can demand from God—money, material possessions ("I want to be loaded down daily with great blessings"), good health ("Sickness doesn't make you humble. Not so. Jesus was the most humble man who ever lived and he was never sick."), freedom from anxiety, and unabated joy ("I have more joy than you can get out of a million barrels of anything").

The belief in God as a benevolent resource is seldom put as crassly by other preachers as by "Reverend Angley" or by "Reverend Ike," but that view permeates the message offered by most electronic preachers who hold to a "health and wealth theology"—turn to Christ and God will bless Christians materially wherever they are. Turn to Christ and your life will work. (One wonders if the video evangelists would explain the widespread poverty in India and Africa as a consequence of the non-Christian religions practiced there.) Jim Bakker relates one prayer incident where a man who requested a brown Winnebago camper received just that. Such incidents are recited countless times on Christian talk shows. Electronic Christianity is not a counterculture; it is a superculture, an actualization of the best of everything that the world and life have to offer.

One aspect of the Fundamentalist God, however, does receive rather scant mention: God's individual judgment, vengeance, and retribution. Unlike Bible-thumping Fundamentalist preachers of old, electronic preachers ground their approach in love, not in fear or threats of hell. They are capable of fire-and-brimstone preaching but generally adapt themselves to the "cool" medium of television, forever smiling and reaffirming, "God loves you, and so do we." Largely missing is the lofty sense, traditionally proclaimed by the Jewish and Christian religions, of God's far-reaching judgment of all people and all nations and God's power over history and eternity.

Jesus is acknowledged widely and enthusiastically as God's Son and the Savior who can forgive and heal individuals. But his servanthood is not proclaimed as fervently as his divinity. And his redemptive work is centered more in his death and resurrection than in his entire life and ministry. To Robert Schuller, Jesus was the greatest possibility thinker and the greatest success in history: "Christ is the super success of all times because his declared manageable objective was to influence the world and seen 2,000 years later, you have to admit that he did succeed. I am not following a loser, I am following a winner."

Electronic preachers have always labored to depict God as our constant companion and continual confidant. Such efforts are not peculiar to television evangelists but may also be seen throughout popular culture, Gospel music, and folk art. Figures of speech can be colorful and imaginative, though crude. To Jimmy Swaggart, the Holy Spirit is the "Great High Sheriff of Heaven." In his powerful campaign sermon (aired 16 March 1980), "Missing God's Last Train to Heaven," Swaggart quips that "the lantern of salvation is being waved by the heavenly conductor at the depot," and then, mixing metaphors, he asks, "Will the landing lights be on for you when you touch down in eternity?"

Not only has God sometimes been too crudely anthropomorphized, but the priceless words and phrases of Christian theology—"love," "grace," "miracle," "born again"—have often been devalued and trivialized through continual, careless usage. C. S. Lewis's Screwtape, from his perch in hell, would easily approve the metaphors that have surely diminished the reverence for the deity. Any sense of the numinous is likely to vanish when one is told, "Call on Jesus. Remember, he is willing to help you twenty-four hours around the clock" or, "Just call the heavenly operator. The exchange is J-E-S-U-S and you've got a direct line." Ernest Angley asserted on 30 March 1980, "Jesus is the one to sweeten you; that cup of coffee will never do it." In describing Jesus' encounter with Satan, Paul Crouch declared, "Jesus made Satan eat crow in the bowels of the earth." This language may provide great entertainment on "Hee-Haw" but cannot help jolting the listeners who learned to say their prayers from the King James Version of the Bible or the Book of Common Prayer.

The Doctrine of Conversion

Efforts at conversion of viewers, especially on the talk shows, are central. No other theme is quite as prominent in either the spoken word or in the lyrics of Gospel music. With little emphasis on crosses to bear, only converts to gain, the thrust of evangelical television has too often become a soul-hunting numbers game—the more dramatic the conversions and the more prestigious and photogenic the converts, the better the ratings for the show. Thus, in the merging of show business with pop religion, we have the advent of celebrity Christianity. For the elite converts, conversion was not from sinners to disciples, but to stars. Often no period of gestation seems to precede the new birth, nor is incubation always necessary after birth. The reborn Christian who has flare or previous notoriety is ready to ride the star witness circuit. Power and personality, not service and suffering, thus become too often the marks of Christian faith.

"Born-again Christian"—terminology is important here. As Ernest Angley put it, "I don't tell anyone I'm a Christian. Anybody can be a Christian. I say I'm a born-again child of God, heaven-bound." The expression "born-again Christian" is not new—it of course goes back to the discussion between Jesus and Nicodemus recorded in the Gospel of John. But it was given new popularity by the national media in the seventies by Jimmy Carter's affirmation of faith and by the conversion and subsequent public appearances of Charles Colson, a former Nixon dirty-trickster.

The doctrine of conversion as taught by the typical electronic evangelist is decidedly different from the doctrine of conversion taught in most Protestant churches. Evangelicals on the whole have tended to value a dramatic conversion experience, where God reveals himself unmistakably and overwhelmingly in the events of their lives. Rex Humbard's experience is typical. The Holy Spirit spoke to his heart when he was thirteen, drawing him to God. "I didn't know much about theology, but I knew someone was dealing with my heart." Then Christ is usually described as taking over a person's life. There is a climactic moment of rebirth, and some shows offer the phone respondents "a new birth certificate" for completion by the convert, who adds the date of his arrival in the "spiritual delivery room." Salvation is actually "such a simple step," declared a guest preacher on "Praise the Lord." "Look at Zaccheus. He was saved right there in his own home, somewhere between the sycamore and the salad." The same show is transmitted from a set that has a large, stage clock (a "prayer clock" with a heart in the middle of it) and a soul meter that rolls up the number of new converts reported as the ministry progresses.

By contrast, the mainline pulpit sometimes has virtually ignored the experience of conversion. The emphasis instead has been on a gradual reorientation of life, more like a seeking pilgrimage that grows out of maturation and character development. Through an individual's commitment, study of the Bible, prayer, and a genuinely pious lifestyle, God progressively reveals himself, it is believed. But, because perfection is an elusive ideal, there will always be something more for which the Christian may strive—a realization that should keep the disciple humble and persevering.

According to electronic preachers, any change that takes place is not maturity but conversion. And, as Jimmy Swaggart put it, "There's no such thing as a Christian getting a little more saved. These new converts are just as saved a second after they've accepted Jesus as they will be when they are in heaven." Little attention is given to "preventive salvation" by raising young ones in the "nurture and admonition of the Lord." Most of the emphasis is on remedial salvation or the rescue operation with all its drama and excitement. The new convert simply changed sides: the basically good alcoholic, the victimized prostitute, the high-powered politician caught in a complicated web of corruption, the reluctant drug pusher, or the high-principled safe cracker will now join the righteous. Of course, each was intrinsically good before finding Jesus. It is small wonder, then, that people can say that they found in Christ what they could not find in drugs or promiscuous sex. Same people, same lofty ideals—but now on a different side.

The chief strategy on Christian talk shows that is employed to gain new converts is borrowed directly from advertising—personal testimony. Nothing is quite as engrossing as the testimony of a "new-born babe in Christ" who has a good song to sing and a great story to tell. Take, for example, Brenda Stevens, a former Miss Massachusetts and runner-up in the Miss America pageant. For the "700 Club" (aired 13 April 1980) she sings "Five Rows Back," the moving ballad of a woman responding to the Gospel invitation while the congregation sang "Just As I Am." Then she related her own story to Robertson: "I experienced very high highs and very low lows." Though she was very talented, her marriage was breaking up and she felt rotten enough to threaten suicide. Although she had consulted a psychiatrist, it was only after her reading of Oral Roberts's *Daily Guide to Miracles* that "the blinders just came off." Now she is witnessing, singing, and praising God—and promoting her new album.

And there is Laverne Tripp, telling Paul and Jan Crouch (4 March 1980) about a dramatic "encounter with Satan's power." The devil tried to get him to take his life at age thirty by convincing him that he was never really saved anyway and that at least if he killed himself he would miss the tribulation. "Filthy liar" exclaimed Paul about the devil; "Jesus!" gasped Jan. Laverne continued, "I could have been one of the most popular country music singers in the world, but thank God he delivered me before I was so trapped and so enslaved to drugs, racketeering, and worldliness. Now I won't sing anything but praise for the Lord." The story was a moving one, and Paul makes a special appeal: "The door to the ark is open tonight. Jesus is about to come. The end is near. There's nothing you can start and nothing you can stop to make you good enough to come to Jesus. Come just as you are. Move quickly to your phone right now. Hold your prayer requests until later. I ask that every line be open for salvation calls only."

Of course, the testimonial has always been important in church history. A religion that believes in sudden salvation is tempted to measure the height of one's rise by the depth of one's fall. A great sinner provides the most impressive testimony to redeeming power. New converts, from the apostle Paul on, have always provided the role models for the recalcitrant.

What too often distinguishes the born-again television personality is a certain arrogance of having arrived—suddenly, and often without the "dark night of the soul"—at the happy ending. It is birth without sweat and labor. And then there is such an emphasis on the details of the sinful past (Christian converts from the Charles Manson cult provide good examples of this), which seems to romanticize the "before" in order to accentuate the "after." The past loses some of its sordidness (a perverse kind of *felix culpa*, "fortunate fall") when its recounting can be turned into books, records, and personal appearances on the Gospel circuit. Surely it pays more to serve Jesus today than in previous centuries.

The Christian Life

The cost of discipleship is so great, the Jesus of the Gospels counseled, that men and women should analyze the cost and benefits before making a decision. The warnings of Jesus and the experiences of his disciples as told in the narratives of Acts depict the Christian lifestyle as one of long, dull marches through the wilderness: pain, struggle, and humiliating defeats. But Christian living all too frequently comes off looking fairly easy in the messages of the electronic church. The pain and struggles of the Christian life do not make for good script copy unless they are rehearsed as a quick, summarized prelude to a victorious conclusion. No place remains for failure or defeat. "I don't have any sympathy for the theological strain that tries to glamorize or glorify failure," comments Robert Schuller. "The tragedy is that if I allow myself to accept, believe, salute, endorse, or approve failure I am really saying that I accept the fact that some human beings are suffering today and I don't care."

Most media evangelists agree that the Christian is in battle against a literal devil. He not only "goes about the streets like a roaring lion" (1 Pet 5:8 is quoted often) but, in the words of Swaggart, he is "blowing, blustering, and hollering, 'I'm going to kill you.'" If the devil did not exist, the electronic church would have to invent him to have a butt for jokes and one-liners. In many sermons the devil comes off looking less like the Miltonian prince of darkness than like the school bully who gets his kicks by picking on the good kids on the playground. "Christians have the power to pull that ole boy over and give him a ticket," declared Paul Crouch about the devil. Reflecting on the full house at an Easter rally, Dwight Thompson declared, "Oh the devil has a migraine tonight that he'll never get rid of." Possibly the most frequently quoted scripture by electronic preachers is one popularized by Oral Roberts in dismissing the Adversary: "Greater is he that is in you than he that is in the world" (1 John 4:4).

Is there an adequate view of evil? Herein is a major deficiency in the doctrine of the electronic church, certainly from the viewpoint of mainstream Christianity. First, there is little conception of societal or corporate sin. There is no strong prophetic call to social justice. Everyone knows about individual sin—lying, killing, adultery, coveting. But corporate sin is more difficult to comprehend—that a whole society can sin and individuals within that society cannot exempt themselves from the sin or some kind of action to remove it. Perhaps there is not time, even on the talk shows, to treat corporate sin adequately, but it is difficult to imagine the Old Testament prophets drawing top Nielsen ratings with their stern calls for social justice.

The view even of personal conduct and human frailty is also scarcely adequate. Many evangelists venture to take strong stands against drinking, drugs ("which will scramble your brains"), smoking (Swaggart draws smiles by pointing to the irony of church members who step outside the church building for a cigarette because they do not want to defile the house of God), and promiscuous sex (Humbard proclaims that the idea that illicit sex is acceptable "is a lie from the pits of hell and the devil created it"). Many of the personal testimonies relate escapes from alcohol and drug addiction. Correspondingly, notions of salvation relate to actualizing full human potential and realizing all possibilities. However, prescriptions given are inadequate from either a psychological or a theological viewpoint.

The explanation and defense of the Christian lifestyle and fellowship are also inadequate in most television religion. There are quick and easy solutions to all kinds of personal problems. In fact, television's stock-in-trade is an endless stream of easy answers to difficult questions; if the problems on police dramas and situation comedies can be resolved satisfactorily in sixty or even thirty minutes, why cannot spiritual problems? Solutions are possible if one "prays hard enough" or "believes enough." The local church with its supportive fellowship may be circumvented, even viewed as a kind of prop or kindergarten for weak Christians. ("Forget baptism. Forget the church. Bring your problem directly to

God," counseled one TV preacher.) Not all electronic evangelists counsel such self-help formulas. In fact, a number urge viewers to get involved in a local congregation, but enough cast aspersions on church life and activity to cause grave concern.

The aspect of individual spiritual experience that is emphasized more than any other is private prayer. There is absolutely no concern or item for which a preacher or his viewers cannot pray. All it takes to make any subject prayerworthy is an agreement between the talk show host and a viewer (Matt 18:19 is one of the most quoted scriptures in the electronic pulpit). And the true believer may expect a direct answer from God. Heard frequently in interviews are such statements as "God gave me this song," or "God told me to get on that subway," or "Jesus told me to return home." One evening on the "700 Club," Sister Beatrice of Baltimore read excerpts from sixteen notebooks of material dictated to her by the Lord (one message was signed "H.R.H.," His Royal Highness). According to her testimony, the Lord healed "Sister B of Baltimore" of angina, cancer, poor vision, and varicose veins. Jesus then told her, "you're as fit as a fiddle" and later told her "you've come a long way, baby." Ben Kinchlow, interviewing Sister B with all the seriousness (and charm) of Dan Rather, laughs at those poor, incredulous souls who reject the idea that the Almighty speaks directly to people, even in slang.

Because television prayer is folksy and conversational, talk show hosts can be known to fill available time with lengthy prayers (". . . and we thank you, Jesus, and pray through him. Amen and don't go away 'cause we'll be right back after this break"). Because the Trinity Network had persistent satellite difficulty, the host one evening cried out in prayer, "Oh, God, touch that piece of machinery and make it work beautifully."

Prayer and the life of piety in general are linked to private, subjective experience. Feeling right about yourself and your world is what really matters. And there seems to be literally nothing that God will not do to help you feel right. On an Oral Roberts special broadcast of 29 March 1980, Cheryl Prewitt (Miss America 1980) was presented to the viewers along with a film clip of her coronation by Bert Parks. Miss Prewitt told how after an automobile accident at age eleven her body was set in a cast and there was no medical hope of survival. But she did survive, manifestly, and this was just the beginning of many miracles. Later as a teenager, Miss Prewitt discovered that one leg was shorter than the other by two inches. After three months of praying ("because I could not be happy with a short leg") she attended a Kenneth Hagin revival. "I centered my mind on Jesus Christ. . . . I watched my leg grow two inches right there in front of my eyes. . . . I felt the most loving warmth . . . the most beautiful experience I've ever had," she avowed. The audience applauded and Roberts joined her in front of the camera to plug the City of Faith before delivering his sermon "Our God is Able."

Perhaps this is the most troubling feature of electronic religion. Faith is tied to a money-back guarantee of God's protection, healing, and overall well-being; religious experience is grounded in subjective feelings rather than anything resembling objective reality. It is hard to find any message addressed to those who must continue to suffer because God grants no special healing. Little wonder that patients in one hospital were forbidden to watch the "PTL Club" because of the "disturbing effect" on those patients./4/

The Christian World View

"There are millions of born-again believers who are no longer passive and non-competitive, and we are tired of ourselves and our leaders being portrayed as bumbling squares, and our religious beliefs being mocked by immoral shows, comedians, and other show-business personalities. We plan to form a media and legal task force to monitor all communications." The speaker is Anita Bryant at a press conference before the National Religious Broadcasters (Bethell: 88–90). The statement reflects a renewed desire of Evangelicals to get organized and involved in the political process. Though without a regular show, Anita Bryant definitely has been an electronic preacher through her "God and Country" television specials and personal appearances.

The electronic church possesses a powerful potential for reshaping American culture along the lines of the morality determined by its most influential evangelists. Television evangelism as a whole is not yet in the vanguard of this movement, but it is a potentially powerful mouthpiece and power base for the "sleeping giant" of American politics—fifty million born-again Christians. The contemplation of this fact creates apprehension among mainline Protestants, incumbent politicians, and the national news media. Since there is a moral dimension to all great political issues, religious program viewers are likely to hear evangelists venture into political preaching. Inspired by the successful militancy of people like Anita Bryant, Fundamentalists and Evangelicals have kindled a new militancy and fervor that have not been exhibited since 1925.

Evangelicals tend to be cynical about Congress, legal institutions in general, and government bureaucracies. After all, the perfectibility of humanity without God is not one of their doctrines. Most oppose extensive social legislation and regard evangelism as the most effective means of political and social reform. They are largely against big government, the homosexual-rights movement, abortion (the last two being "assaults on the Christian family"), and the Equal Rights Amendment; they grant their blessing to capitalism and its material fruits, the censorship of pornography, a balanced budget, prayer in public schools, and a strong national defense. Frequently, the Christian talk shows deal with these issues. Pat Robertson sends his followers a monthly newsletter offering his financial tips and interpretations of current events—all laced with biblical citations. Jerry Falwell, using his program as a power base, founded Moral Majority, an organization to mobilize believers for political purposes and "Clean Up America" rallies. Falwell has vowed on many occasions to bring "atheistic" public education to its knees and to replace it with a free enterprising Christian school system.

James Robison, a Baptist preacher from Texas, is one of the most blatantly outspoken of the political moralizers; he does not hesitate to use his national program as a power base for his own organization. His major theme is "America needs a spiritual healing. . . . we have runaway government and runaway inflation. If we don't come back to God this nation is finished." Robison begs his television audience for funds to continue his crusade: "God has broken my heart over this nation. I am weeping over this nation. People say to me, 'You are the only hope we've got.'" He then hawks his book *Save America to Save the World*. So controversial has Robison become that an FCC (Federal Communications Commission) official upheld the right of a Dallas area station to cancel his program ("a continuing problem") because of his attack on homosexuals.

Jerry Falwell's pulpit at Liberty Baptist College is by far the most influential Fundamentalist forum for exploring and exploiting political issues. Falwell misses few preaching opportunities to declare that America's greatest need is for a moral revolution and a spiritual awakening. The "Old Time Gospel Hour" does not merely blur the distinctions between politics and religion; at times it completely merges the two, and the viewers who came across the program while turning the channel selector would be as likely to think they are watching a political rally as a worship service. The traditional red, white, and blue colors abound, "I Love America" rallies are plugged, and patriotic hymns are sung. Falwell also speaks for a simplistic Zionism that has won applause from some Israelis: "God's promise to Abraham was that he would bless those that blessed the Jews. So we have his promise that, as long as we uphold Israel, he will uphold us." Among the political evangelizers there are two favorite scriptures, both from the Old Testament—2 Chr 7:14 and Prov 14:34.

What kind of clout electronic preachers can wield on the political scene is unclear mainly because overtly political preachments violate the federal fairness doctrine. But subtle insinuations that liberal policies are inconsistent with New Testament Christianity are heard and have elicited considerable criticism from politicians, national leaders, and print journalists. There is no doubt that people who underwrite the efforts of political evangelists and join conservative organizations are sincerely looking for fair and legal answers to a lot of frustrating problems. Religious broadcasters do their followers a grave injustice when they oversimplify ethical and social issues and engage in bumper-sticker warfare that cannot address itself to the realities of civil liberties in a pluralistic society.

Eschatology

"The climax of history is near. Jesus is coming soon!" Such is the chief message about the future from the electronic church, whose preachers, on the whole, seem convinced of an imminent and immediate return of Jesus to the earth. Not all electronic preachers emphasize this theme, and in fact some avoid it altogether. But those who avoid the topic constitute a small minority, and the theme is present to one degree or another in the preaching of Oral Roberts, Jim Bakker, Jerry Falwell, the Alamos, even Billy Graham, and many others of less stellar status. As one declared, "We are in the last hours of history. This will be the generation that will roll out the red carpet for the Lord Jesus Christ."

The order of events is generally agreed upon. The final trumpet will sound, and the saved ones will be gathered up into the clouds in rapture to be spared the seven-year tribulation on earth. Next, the mighty battle of Armageddon is the glorious event in which the forces of evil are finally and totally annihilated. Jesus will then return to the earth to establish his kingdom and rule for a thousand years, at the conclusion of which there will be eternal bliss or punishment for every individual who has ever lived.

This is the standard premillennialism that has been around a long time, but electronic evangelists have given the doctrines new currency. Perhaps no one has done more to propagate this doctrine in recent times than Hal Lindsey, author of *The Late, Great Planet Earth* and *The Terminal Generation* and a popular guest on talk shows. The key to current premillennialism and the timetable of events is provided by the modern Jewish nation. The Bible purportedly prophesies a restoration of the Jews to the Promised Land, Israel's rebirth, and a time of unbelief about Jesus' divinity in the early stages of its history (which is going on now). The "this generation" of Matthew 24 is taken to be approximately forty years, beginning with the rebirth of the state of Israel in 1948 and confirmed by the Six-Day War in 1967. Lindsey's timetable calls for the end of the world somewhere between 1984 and 2000. The great enemy to the north (mentioned in Ezekiel 38 as a mighty army all riding on horses) is taken to be Russia; Russia's military advances into Afghanistan and the Islamic revolution in Iran are taken as evidence that biblical prophecy is being fulfilled.

Lindsey and other apocalyptic preachers speak with great certainty. Ultraconservative political and religious styles are often highly pedantic—manifesting an elaborate concern for demonstration, scholarship, footnotes, bibliographies, and a parade of experts (one doomsdayer appearing on "PTL" was introduced as the author of four hundred books)—all dazzling the laity with the heroic striving for "evidence" to prove that the "unbelievable" is the only thing that can be believed. Lindsey and his disciples select as favorites passages from Ezekiel, Daniel (arguing that Daniel prophesied the *exact* day when Jesus made his triumphant entry into Jerusalem), Matthew's Gospel, and Revelation. In the style of the old-time revivalists who deployed charts and pointing sticks, Lindsey's sermons are delivered in front of the camera with a large map of the Middle East as a visual aid. When the sermon is over, the show's host makes another appeal to those who are in the "valley of decision," and eventually Lindsey will plug his books or tickets for his Holy Land tour.

The "new apocalypticism" that keeps viewers preoccupied with the end of the world seems not to deter evangelists from pursuing fund raising for massive structures designed to stand for several generations, barring bombs, earthquakes, and wrecking crews. This obsession with the end of time provides evangelists with ample material to keep the emotions of the sinners and wanderers stoked while they make vivid appeals for conversions and money to maintain the ministry in these crucial last hours.

"Are you ready to meet him? Did you come packed? Did you come with your traveling shoes on?" asks Dwight Thompson in an Easter rally televised by Trinity Broadcasting Network. "Before I finish preaching we may all be called into rapture. Before my clothing would hit the ground I would be catapulted into glory at the speed of sound. If the man who cleans up this place is not a Christian, he'd say, 'My, they had some party here last night.'" Graphic depictions follow of the mighty wrath to come, serving to arouse the passions and inspire militancy. That which impends may still be avoided. The beast is capable of one last resurgence of strength, enabling him to slay hosts of moral weaklings before he gasps his final breath. What is at stake is always a conflict between absolute good and absolute evil. There must be a will to fight sin and evil to the very finish of history. Nothing but complete victory will do. Obviously, religious and political apocalypticism share the same tense message and methods of doomsdayism, and both emerge during times of national doubt and malaise.

No other topic provides as much occasion for biblical reference and for eisegesis as its main method of interpretation. There appears to be little system or intellectual–theological discipline in handling apocalyptic literature; in one passage there may be statements that are taken literally and others that are interpreted figuratively. Preachers who are otherwise vague on third world geography are proclaiming with amazing certainty the boundaries of Gog and Magog and are dogmatic in identifying the forces aligned with the beast. Emphasis on the prophetic theme not only comes at the expense of other substantive biblical doctrines but also cuts the nerve to very serious occupation with social involvement with the world as it is, a problem not unique to the television age. Jesus may be portrayed merely as one of the biblical prophets who predicted the end of the world, giving the impression that this was his primary goal. That the utterances of Jesus that proclaim the world to come might also summon his followers to live and serve fully in *this* world is a possibility largely ignored by the electronic premillennialist church.

A Concluding Note

Surveys indicate that the average American, while believing in God and respecting the Bible, actually knows very little of the Bible's content or traditional ways the Jewish and Christian religions have used the scriptures./5/ Public-service religious programs by leaders of established religious groups have attempted, within the limits of the media employed, to present relevant biblical messages. But how many people watch the more substantial, less flamboyant shows, which frequently appear at less than congenial times? There is no way to know for certain. It is suspected that a majority of viewers of religious programming are already confessing Christians and that the more popular shows constitute, in the words of one observer, an opiate for the already converted.

Among the top-rated shows, viewers can learn a lot about the Bible from listening to the sermons of Billy Graham, Jerry Falwell, and Rex Humbard, among others—preachers who, apart from plugging their own programs and ministries, preach basic moral living and individual piety. There have been some worthwhile interviews on practical subjects on the religious talk shows. Graham is undoubtedly the best known and most widely heard preacher of all time, and his basic message from the Bible has stressed fundamentals most Christians can accept: all persons are sinners by nature; God's grace shown in Christ's death alone can save; the soul is immortal and God extends salvation after one's repentance and faith; in the Christian lifestyle there are moral absolutes to direct our decision making. Preachers like Graham and Falwell become less useful in biblical proclamation when they venture into sociopolitical issues. Storytelling has become a lost art in the ranks of much of contemporary American culture, but the art is alive and well in the form of biblical narratives retold and modernized by people like Jim Bakker and Oral Roberts. The thrill of such storytelling is diminished, however, when extrabiblical themes are injected into the narratives. Too often on the major programs the Bible is used as little more than a springboard to the evangelist's pet scheme or favorite project. Robert Schuller's "Hour of Power" is one of the most beautifully produced and attractive of the available programs; however, Schuller makes little use of the Bible in his sermon apart from isolated texts on which he pegs his possibility-thinking ideas.

Throughout Christian history many means have been used to communicate the Gospel: preaching, drama, music, stained-glass windows, telephone, radio, stereo. Each medium presents possibilities along with distinct limitations. The uses and abuses of television as an evangelistic vehicle are only now being explored. For better or worse, television is certain to change our religious lives, just as it has changed our buying habits, our politics, and our family relationships. Television, more than any other form of mass communication, is intimate and immediate. We must learn how to use its unique properties to best advantage. Several possibilities suggest themselves.

Brief religious spots on prime-time commercial television may develop as valuable vehicles for communicating a biblical or socially useful message. Although employing no single scripture, the brief spots sponsored by the Church of Jesus Christ of Latter-day Saints are tasteful, thoughtful, and relevant to the contemporary lives of all Americans, Christian or otherwise. Many of them have dealt with family life and the reconciling power of love. One spot urged parents to reinforce their children when they behave properly or perform well. The voice on another spot was that of a little girl who described her relationship with her grandfather and how kind and helpful he was to her while she was growing up; the spot ended with an admonition: "Give old people the chance to enrich your life." A single basic biblical message (Honor your father and mother) can be meaningfully introduced in a minute message, and it may well be established that sixty one-minute spots are more effective than a sixty-minute church service. Brevity and action seem generally essential to successful television programming.

Religious shows can continue to learn from the secular ones and need not be limited to imitations of Carson colloquies or variety reviews. Religious news programs are an interesting possibility, especially if international correspondents are used to provide the sight and sound of religious life throughout the world. Character sketches of personalties, such as Mother Teresa of Calcutta, could prove inspirational as well as educational. Television can also memorably dramatize the lives of giant personalities from the Christian past, such as Saint Augustine or Martin Luther. The ancient churches of Asia and the Christian congregations of the emerging nations of Africa can be vividly introduced into the American home. Through television American Christians can be aided in overcoming their provincialism. While escaping the elegant blandness of so many PBS (Public Broadcasting System) specials, the visual powers of television can open up the beauties of Christian art. The great religious artists of all the ages can be made familiar.

Investigative reporting of issues and problems in the Christian community, a sort of sacred "Sixty Minutes," has been suggested by one distinguished Old Testament scholar. While the present mood of Christianity, fortunately, does not suggest a return to the acrimony that often characterized the celebrated religious debates of the last part of the nineteenth century, a religious version of "Firing Line," led by a witty, urbane host, would perhaps be a rewarding as well as daring innovation. Religious programs can certainly arrange meaningful dialogue between significant thinkers and personalities representing the varied Christian traditions. Television may prove especially successful in presenting the Jewish heritage of Christianity and promoting dialogue between leaders of both faiths.

That the church should employ methods of mass media is an assertion that would be questioned by few. Christianity is the religion of the "Good News," and its central directive is to spread that news. Nor is it realistic to expect the church to rely on the print medium alone. But how the various means of electronic mass communication should be employed and for what purposes will continue to generate controversy among church leaders. If this results in the production of quality programs that would excitingly and provocatively present a substantive message, the controversy can be healthy.

Church leaders can do a better job in providing their membership with criteria by which all media offerings may be evaluated. The electronic church can give more heed to the moral dimensions of media power, submitting every method used to build an audience or to raise funds to careful ethical scrutiny. In addition, the church should do a better job in resisting being taken over by the power that television exposure gives. Unless this power is resisted, the Christian faith itself gets caught up in the ratings race, and the electronic church comes across as a mere cultural religion aping all the glitter and trappings of the values it professes to reject.

NOTES

/1/   The source was an unpublished paper prepared for the "Consultation on the Electronic Church" at New York University on 7 February 1980. The consultation was coordinated by the Communication Commission of the National Council of Churches, 475 Riverside Drive, New York, New York.

/2/   For a recent examination of this issue, see Gallup, 1982.

/3/   Documentation stating the specific date and time that shows were viewed is of questionable value. Shows are syndicated, many are edited, and all may be aired at different times in the several cities they reach. Many of the Billy Graham and Jimmy Swaggart shows are edited tapings of mass revivals and may be shown months after the initial taping took place. The dates given in this essay for selected shows indicate the times of viewing in the middle Tennessee area.

/4/   "Patients in the psychiatric unit at Wilson Hospital, Johnson City, New York are forbidden to watch the PTL Club . . . because of what hospital officials describe as a 'disturbing effect' on some patients." A brief article in *Eternity* (30 [May 1979]) explains why.

/5/   See Gallup, 1978. A *Christianity Today*–Gallup survey is clearly and concisely discussed in *Time* (December 31, 1979): 64.

WORKS CONSULTED

Armstrong, Ben
    1979   *The Electric Church*. Nashville: Thomas Nelson.

Bethell, Tom
    1978   "Common Man and the Electric Church." *Harper's* 256 (April): 86–90.

Fore, William
    1979   "The Electronic Church." *Ministry* 1 (January): 4–7.

Gallup, George, Jr.
    1978   *The Unchurched American 1978*. Princeton: The Gallup Organization.
    1982   *Adventures in Immortality*. New York: McGraw-Hill.

Harrell, David Edwin, Jr.
    1975   *All Things Are Possible*. Bloomington: Indiana University Press.

Johnson, Allison
    1979   *How to be Happy in the Non-Electric Church.* Nashville:
                        Abingdon.

Martin, William C.
    1970   "The God-Hucksters of Radio." *Atlantic* 225 (June): 51–56.

Montgomery, Jim
    1978   "Religious Broadcasting Becomes Big Business." *The Wall
                        Street Journal* 191 (May 19): 1–2.

Montgomery, John W.
    1977   "Mass Communication and Scriptural Proclamation." *Evangeli-
                        cal Quarterly* 49 (January-March): 3–28.

Sholes, Jerry
    1979   *Give Me That Prime Time Religion.* New York: Hawthorn
                        Books.

Taylor, James A.
    1977   "Progeny of Programmers: Evangelical Religion and the Tele-
                        vision Age." *Christian Century* 94 (April 20): 379–82.

Yancey, Philip
    1979   "The Ironies and Impact of PTL." *Christianity Today* 23 (Sep-
                        tember 21): 28–33.

VI

The Traveling Bible Salesman:
The Good Buck from the Good Book

Ralph W. Hyde

The Lore of the Bible Salesman

The Bible is the perennial best seller, and it is not surprising that the marketing of Bibles in the United States has taken characteristically American forms, piety mingling with commercial conventions. American business ingenuity, so highly regarded throughout the world, was very early applied to the Good Book, from which it was immediately discovered could be earned the good buck. The traveling Bible salesman holds a significant place in our national lore, though the extent to which the romantic fictional image corresponds to reality, both yesterday and today, has never been fully explored. A unique lore has developed around the Bible salesman, complete with pious sentiments, ribald jokes, and literary depictions.

The first American peddlers—young, bright, venturesome, if not always scrupulous—were often accused of purveying "wooden nutmegs and cucumber seeds, oak-leaf cigars, shoe-peg oats, polyglot Bibles (all in English) and realistically painted basswood hams" (Wright: 20–21). This Yankee peddler, a colorful feature of the native scene, made an imprint on American literature, finding his way into books by James Fenimore Cooper, Washington Irving, Thomas Chandler Haliburton, and Stephen Vincent Benét. The more specialized peddler, the traveling Bible salesman, who only in the 1970s became the traveling "salesperson" when women successfully entered the field, has also stirred the imaginations of a number of American writers. He appeared in Christopher Morley's short novel *Parnassus on Wheels*, first published in 1917. In Joe David Brown's novel *Addie Pray* (1971), a father–daughter team peddled Bibles during the depression years and practiced an assortment of con schemes. Two novels by Guy Owen, *The Ballad of the Flim-Flam Man* and *The Flim-Flam Man and the Apprentice Grifter* (1965 and 1972), showed Bible selling as a subsidiary activity of another con artist. In 1962 Alma Stone shifted perspective in her novel *The Bible Salesman*;

her hero was a young black man who was not a charlatan but a zealous Christian sincerely dedicated to placing a Bible in the hands of every plowman. But by far the most profound American fiction featuring the traveling Bible salesman was Flannery O'Connor's ironic and grotesquely humorous short story "Good Country People" (made widely available in *The Complete Stories*, 1971).

While fiction reflects the romance, humor, and picaresque roguery surrounding the public image of the traveling Bible salesman, it may not always have accurately reflected the reality of the occupation. It may never have fully comprehended what it means to sell Bibles to the American common folk. More balanced mirrors can be found in documentary films, firsthand narratives, and taped interviews of persons who have actually followed the trade at one time or another in their lives.

A Documentary Film View of Bible Selling

Salesman, a documentary film that received critical attention a few years ago, attempted an impartial look at door-to-door selling. The scenario on which the film was based follows the activities of young men employed in door-to-door selling by Mid-American Bible Company, a firm specializing in Bibles and religious materials designed for Roman Catholics. The main story line of the film focuses on the fortunes and misfortunes of one of the salesmen, Paul Brennan, who soon loses heart for his job, declines in sales, and ultimately—though this is not shown in the film itself—leaves Bible selling for the aluminum siding business.

In his introduction to *Salesman*, Harold Clurman remarks:

> Americans are a moral people: they wish to believe in what they do, have some faith beyond the mere earning of a livelihood. They know that man cannot live by bread alone. What commodity could give them greater assurance that their salesmanship is ipso facto ennobled than the purveyance of the Bible? Doesn't Dr. Melbourne I. Feltman, the designer and theological consultant as well as "the world's best seller," as he is called at a general sales conference, tell the assemblage [a group of sales trainees] that its task is a bold one, that the salesmen are doing their "Father's [God's] business?" (The Maysles Brothers and Zwerin: 7)

Selling *is* America's business; selling the Bible combines the business ethos and the religious ethos, which though it is declining is by no means extinct in America./1/ Like Willy Loman in Arthur Miller's *Death of a Salesman*, Paul Brennan is on the downward slide, and the implication is clear that the fault may not be with him, that door-to-door selling may be in the process of being supplanted by other methods (we note the contemporary television pitch) and that in a consumer society with so many commodities competing for the dollar of the more mobile consumer, the door-to-door selling of Bibles, or anything else, grows increasingly difficult. In short, the documentary suggests that Paul Brennan is an anachronism, even though he does not know it. Nor do his co-workers know it, for in 1966 (when the film was made) many of them were doing all right. Nor do the several thousand young people who each summer go on the road for The Southwestern Company know they are anachronisms. For a great many of them do all right. All right indeed!

The Southwestern Company: History and Description

Nashville, Tennessee, is known for its churches, its Gospel music, and its religious publishing houses, including the Thomas Nelson Company, the world's largest publisher of Bibles. In addition to the Nashville firms, most of them church-related, which rely on mail orders, churches, religious organizations, and bookstores for the distribution of Bibles and religious literature, there is a secular firm, The Southwestern Company, long associated with Nashville but now located between Nashville and Franklin, Tennessee, whose sales are conducted on a subscription basis. The salespersons are energetic and attractive young people, mostly college students, who work during their summers. The company is a surviving and thriving instance of that method of distribution which combines the roles of the peddler, the book agent, and the subscription bookseller. For over a century, agents for Southwestern have placed Bibles and other books through the method of door-to-door selling. Orders are taken, deposits are requested, and books are delivered at a later date, usually the end of summer. It is safe to say that a vast majority of people think of Southwestern, so widely celebrated in the lore of the South, when the door-to-door Bible salesman comes to mind.

The company had its beginnings about 1840; in the mid-1850s it became widely known as The Southwestern Publishing House, publisher of *The Tennessee Baptist* and an assortment of religious booklets. When the Civil War began, a shortage of Bibles developed in the South. Stereotype plates were smuggled into Nashville from the North, and Southwestern began printing Bibles and New Testaments. From 1867 to 1879 the firm published in Memphis; it returned to Nashville in 1879 as simply The Southwestern Company. The years following the Civil War saw the founding of more than one hundred new colleges, many of them in the South, where economic conditions were so desperate that many young men could find no work. The Reverend J. R. Graves, the head of the company, saw the opportunity to help these young men, to place Bibles in thousands of homes, and to establish a successful business at the same time. From 1868 on, student book agents carried Southwestern Bibles and a growing line of other books from door to door (Hilts: 11–16).

The company grew throughout the remainder of the nineteenth century, its salesmen following the westward movement. Southwestern weathered World War I and continued to prosper until the onset of the Great Depression in 1929. It managed to survive the depression years, though just barely, and then it braced for World War II, when it suffered shortages of salesmen, paper, and other necessary materials. After the war, a strong sales organization was rebuilt and the company was soon again on the move. In 1968 the assets of Southwestern were sold to the Times Mirror Company, the publisher of the Los Angeles *Times*. Though the basic method of selling did not change, new product divisions were established, and by 1972 the firm had a $20 million-a-year business. By 1974 there were some twenty-nine book titles sold by the company, of which only two were Bibles, though six were religious reference books, and six more were children's books, some with religious content (Hilts: 80–95).

Southwestern has been a peculiarly successful company, identified by a spirit that animated its officials, its sales supervisors, and its more successful student door-to-door salespersons. According to an official campaign biography of a former Southwestern president who ran for the Republican nomination for governor of Tennessee:

> This is the Southwestern mystique—a spirit that is vital to the company, nearly unique in the business world, and difficult to understand until you have talked with Southwestern sales managers, attended a sales school, and watched student salesmen at work.
>
> The Southwestern mystique is a combination of both new and old ideas in the company. The basics of the Southwestern business have remained essentially the same for more than seventy years. The selling is done by students who work door-to-door. Normally, a student sells one summer, then recruits a crew of other students to lead the following summer. In his first year he might expect to have $1,200 after expenses. In subsequent years, as his own sales ability increased and as he developed sales crews, he would find savings of $2,000 to $4,000 reachable—and some have gone over the $15,000 mark. While the earnings have risen over the years, the basic method hasn't changed much.
>
> In addition, the fundamental work ethic has been a part of the Southwestern philosophy from the beginning. *Work hard and you will succeed. Work will overcome all obstacles.* The 75 and 80 hour work week is strongly recommended at Southwestern. The most successful student salesmen get up at 6:15 A.M., make their first sales calls at 7:59, make at least 30 demonstrations each day, work until 9 P.M., and work six days a week. (Hilts: 54–55)

Apparently, working on the Sabbath has not been advocated by South-western, which, despite its expanding line of products, is still known basically, at least in the minds of the public, as an old-fashioned company that sells Bibles and Bible study aids.

Sales Methods and Appeals

That the "Southwestern mystique" has sometimes been regarded outside the company with a certain cynicism is not surprising. Reports have surfaced and sometimes been published recounting sales techniques at one time advocated by the company that were certainly manipulative if not ethically questionable. Needless to say, we are now speaking primarily of the past. Sales strategies today are much more sophisticated. Salesmen once counted on first making the acquaintance of local ministers in their assigned territories in order to capitalize on this connection in the selling itself as well as in obtaining free meals and securing discounts on lodging./2/ This, of course, followed the common practice of insurance and other salespeople in using the membership lists of their churches and clubs for solicitation.

The Bible salesman, however, could be more aggressive than most other salesmen. The following technique, described in a devastating *Reader's Digest* article of the late thirties, was widely used at one time: "In the training school the salesman refused a sale is taught to say, 'Well, Mrs. Jones, I reckon I'll just have to eat with you,' and Mrs. Jones usually submits. He is instructed to offer pay for accommodations, but I never heard of an offer being accepted" (Alexander: 37). At least in the thirties a night's lodging might be obtained in this way./3/ The salesmen were instructed to spot an attractive house and to call as night drew on. If the householder refused a sale, the salesman was to say, "Well, Mr. Jones, if I can't sell you a Bible, I reckon I'll just have to stay the night with you." It usually worked then. Salesmen were again instructed to offer to pay for the night's lodging before leaving in the morning. They were told the host would not likely charge anything, but if he said $1 or $2, this should be deducted from the price of the Bible or book (i.e., the sum would come from the sales commission), for of course any self-respecting Southwestern salesman would have used the occasion to sell the host at some point during the stay.

Reprehensible as these tactics may seem today, it should be remembered that 1937, when the *Reader's Digest* article was published, was a deep depression year. The experiences recounted in the article were those of the author's son who had sold during the previous summer./4/ In those days Southwestern sent salesmen chiefly into rural territories; now, urban communities are much more likely to be selected as a result of the national shift of population to towns and cities. In those days men would headquarter in a town or city, perhaps in the home of a minister, and retain a room to which they would return on weekends. On Monday morning they would catch a bus or, more likely, hitchhike into a nearby rural area, and, carrying their sample cases with special "thin Samples" (demonstration books, not full copies), they would trudge along the country roads, knocking at the doors of farmhouses. Even if the occupants could not or would not buy, often enough they were glad to see a Bible salesman who could enliven their dull hours with news of the outside world. For though the salesman's own travels had usually been limited, theirs had generally been even less extensive./5/

It has always been a principle at Southwestern not to advance money to its salespeople. Even the sample case was charged ($5 in 1936) to the salesman, but the charge was refunded when the case was returned. The young man reached his territory as best he could. Once there he survived as best he could. He worked then, as now, strictly on commission, which in 1936 was about 40 percent of sales; it is a bit higher today. Then a salesman was expected to meet living expenses out of deposits paid by customers on books he sold them; it is the same today.

The *Reader's Digest* article relates how the author's son made the nine-hundred-mile journey to his territory in North Carolina "at a cost of 90 cents for hamburgers" (Alexander: 37). Obviously, he hitchhiked or "hoboed," notwithstanding that he was a fraternity man from an affluent family. The father related how his son would build up to a sale by asking a prospect, "What kind of Bible have you?" The prospect usually responded that he already had more Bibles than he could read. But training school had prepared the salesman to parry that objection: of course the prospect would have a good Bible, being a cultured person; would he please show it to the salesman? When it was produced, the young man praised it but said that, while no doubt it was the best available Bible at the time it was purchased, it was now outdated. His product, he pointed out, was published much later (even though it still contained Bishop Ussher's Old Testament chronology). Now, since the prospect had been kind enough to show his Bible, the salesman would like to show his. And then the young man would be ready to launch into "Canvass No. 1," in which he did everything "but get a toe hold or half Nelson" (Alexander: 38)./6/

If the prospect was a woman, a different approach would be used:

> Suppose the housewife is busy. The following technique is quoted from the salesman's guide:
> "Explain to her that you observe she is quite busy but you have just one picture you want to show her in the Illustrated Bible. Then

you open your prospectus and show her the picture, Jesus in the
home of Mary and Martha. Then say the following: 'We are told that
Jesus was better pleased with Mary, who sat at his feet inquiring of
spiritual things, than he was with Martha, who was too busy with
household duties. Don't you think that women would be better off
today if they read the Bible more, and worried less about household
duties?'" (Alexander: 38)

The informant told of a salesman in Alabama who made extraordinary
sales among black farmers, who were in those pre–civil rights days especially disadvantaged. Later he learned that they believed they would
suffer misfortune if they refused to buy a Bible! Another salesman in
Mississippi sold eight Bibles in a poor family, and when he came back in
September to deliver he learned that no member of the family could
read or count. They had their money ready, sure enough, but he had to
count it out for them (Alexander: 40).

The legal value of records in family Bibles was a strong selling point,
whether or not the prospect could read, and many rural people were
illiterate in those days. The necessity for authentic records in family
Bibles was always stressed. From the files of the company came horror
stories salesmen could relate: for example, a woman in Oklahoma lost a
pension because she did not have a family Bible to prove her marriage
to a war veteran.

Yet salesmen, despite these pressure tactics, justified themselves. The
Reader's Digest informant acknowledged, "We were all pretty philosophical about our sales no matter how we made them. The man who
buys a Bible is getting something that will do him no harm and may do
him a lot of good" (Alexander: 40).

Undoubtedly, the need to make money was the prime motivation for
most college students in the depression years. Although financial need
continues as an important motivation, company officials in recent
years—and especially in more prosperous times when students have been
able to borrow money more easily, obtain jobs, or receive more parental
assistance—have emphasized more than ever the less tangible rewards,
such as the opportunity for young persons to learn to be independent, to
stand on their own feet, to compete in the free enterprise system. All
along, an important duty of sales managers has been to write letters to
salesmen in the field, sometimes rambling, informal, talkative letters,
which have given encouragement and advice, bolstered sagging morale,
and often slyly promoted competition among members of the same crew
to see who could outsell the others. Those who became wise to that tactic
of stirring up competition have generally praised it as effective and
"American." It kept up their mettle, and their sales invariably improved
(Hilts: 63–64).

By the summer of 1973, thanks in part to expansion made possible through the acquisition of Southwestern by *Times Mirror*, a record eight thousand men and women were in the field selling for Southwestern. Putting into practice the techniques taught them in Sales Training School in the spring, they wrote up $40 million in annual sales. They were instructed to charge the front porch of a prospective customer and knock loudly, starting their first call at exactly 7:59 A.M. and spending no more than twenty minutes with any prospect. For those who diligently followed instructions, commissions would average $1,700, with some hitting $12,000. A few who had sold for several years would earn as much as $24,000, thanks to residual commissions on the sales of those they had recruited, which were added to their own current sales commissions (*Time*: 86).

New salespeople each summer continued to go forth selling Bibles for Southwestern. No longer was their territory concentrated in the South; Southwestern well knew that the entire country had, in fact, become an extended Bible Belt. What sort of young person accepted this call? They were young, tractable, and inexperienced in selling, for the most part. The majority needed the money in order to attend college, and summer work was ideal for them. Most seem to have come from families in which, regardless of means, the work ethic remained strong. We usually call this "the Protestant ethic," or "the Puritan ethic," but perhaps "the American work ethic" is a more accurate term.

Many of the salespeople were and continue to be identified with churches in which this work ethic is particularly strong. The Church of Christ, a powerful influence in parts of the South and Southwest, is one example, and the Mormon Church is another. Thousands of young salespeople have been Baptists, Methodists, Presbyterians, or members of the Assemblies of God. Hundreds have preached in their spare time or devoted hours to volunteer work in the churches of their territories. Officials of Southwestern repeatedly have stated that their business is free enterprise in its most unadulterated form, capitalism at its purest. Meld free enterprise, the work ethic, the idea that to sell Bibles is to provide a high-minded public service, and fuse this amalgam with self-interest. Project these compounded notions onto a group of inexperienced, susceptible, yet enthusiastic young people who are, moreover, further energized in Sales Training School in a week-long, eighteen-hour-a-day training course conducted by sales experts. Add the inspirational addresses they hear delivered by prominent politicians and other public figures and the interaction with a group of other young people undergoing the same training, who have as their goal the making of the greatest amount of money in the shortest amount of time. It is not surprising that these several thousand young people, fired with these compounded notions, comprise a formidable sales force.

There are, of course, individual failures. It might be further suggested that, aside from those who fail through sheer laziness, the failures are largely introverted persons, perhaps imaginative and reflective, for whom selling door-to-door is an assault upon their sensibilities, a betrayal of their inner vision of themselves. They may lack the ability to equate God and Mammon. Such persons are not salespeople, and they generally do not remain long.

Interviews with Salespersons

In order really to understand what door-to-door Bible selling in the United States has been, it is necessary to talk with persons who have themselves been "on the field." For this reason, representative salespeople were interviewed, including one woman and one black person. While Southwestern salespersons have traditionally been white Protestant males, the company has been alert to national trends, has even sold from time to time a Catholic Bible (which never, of course, even when peddled by Mexican-American youth, moved anything like the King James Version), and has recently been recruiting and training more and more women and blacks. In fact, one of the company's top salespersons of the summer of 1981 was a talented, personable black woman, a business major at Alabama State University. Her problem was never getting *in* doors, either white or black ones, but getting *out* of them, since people usually insisted she stay for a chat or a meal.

All interviews were recorded on cassette tape, with the exception of one that had to be conducted by mail in questionnaire form. The object of the interviews was to provide, in supplement or correction to the company literature and fictional lore, firsthand accounts of selling experiences and to sample attitudes of several persons who have sold Bibles and other books for Southwestern. Each informant was asked about earnings, about attitudes toward the experience, and about any unusual or especially memorable events. The only criteria for selecting informants were that persons interviewed should reflect a considerable span of time, and that at least one black and one woman be interviewed. This modest goal was achieved. The oldest person interviewed sold books back in 1931. The most recent interviewee sold in 1979 and was, when interviewed, busy assembling a crew to take into the field for the summer of 1980. Other informants sold between those years./7/

Mr. L. W. was seventy years old when interviewed on 22 March 1980 near Shelbyville, Tennessee, in his attractive ancestral farmhouse. He has been a farmer all his life, except for the short time he spent selling Bibles and books and another brief period in his youth when he clerked in a grocery store. Though he attended two years of college, he did not finance his schooling by selling books. In fact, he good-naturedly referred to himself as a failure as a salesman.

In 1931 he ventured forth in a Ford touring car with a Shelbyville friend who had organized a crew of eight young men to sell in rural areas of New York State:

R. W. H.: Was that your first trip to the Northeast?

L. W.: That was my first trip.

R. W. H.: What kind of reception did you have?

L. W.: Well, you know, that '31 was one of the hardest years. They all said that 1931 was the hardest year on the book field.

R. W. H.: The fact you were southerners, did that make any difference?

L. W.: No, I don't think so. We had—we had—I just couldn't sell books. And times was hard and people just didn't want to turn loose money.

R. W. H.: You sold a lot of books besides the Bible, didn't you?

L. W.: I sold Bibles, dictionaries, Mary Lyles Wilson's cookbook. . . . We had Bible stories, children's Bible stories, and I've got one of the books out here now. I believe it's *American Business Guide* and several different sizes and kinds of Bibles.

R. W. H.: You had a big Family Bible?

L. W.: And a big Family Bible.

R. W. H.: Which was pretty expensive. And then you had—

L. W.: Teacher's Bible and the Testaments.

R. W. H.: Do you remember the prices of any of them?

L. W.: The Teacher's Bible I do. We had two sizes in that. One was a little larger print than the other. One sold for $6.75, the other sold for $7.75.

R. W. H.: Now, the big Family Bible sold for much more.

L. W.: It sold for $12.50, I think.

R. W. H.: Now, before you left, you had a training course in Nashville?

L. W.: A training course in Nashville.

R. W. H.: About what—five days or a week?

L. W.: Something—a week. We went down on Monday. We left out, I think, on a Saturday or Sunday, headed for New York.

R. W. H.: You remember some of the techniques they taught you how to sell? How to handle an order book, and push a pencil at the customer?

L. W.:   I remember one about turning the Bible up and that All-Seeing Eye of God picture. Now, do you remember that?

R. W. H.: I remember that. In other words, you look at it upside down and show it right-side up to the person you're facing.

L. W.:   And I remember a little about the first item in that Dictionary—Bible Dictionary—was Aaron, the brother of Miriam and Moses, and so on. I remember that book, turning it up, you know, like this and reading it off.

R. W. H.: Where did you stay, in a hotel or private home?

L. W.:   We stayed in a private home. We rented this room—the three of us—rented this room for three dollars a week—one dollar a week per person.

R. W. H.: And you came in on weekends.

L. W.:   Came in on weekends.

R. W. H.: It was not a minister—did you stay with ministers?

L. W.:   No, no.

R. W. H.: Now, how about when you were out during the week, you were walking, right?

L. W.:   Walking.

R. W. H.: Where did you spend the night when you were out walking?

L. W.:   Wherever, just anywhere they'd let you stay.

R. W. H.: Did you offer to pay, or did you have to pay?

L. W.:   We tried—I think I paid twice. And after that, wherever I could stay, and they'd take me in, I'd stay.

R. W. H.: Were you instructed in the training school to find yourself a nice house when night was coming on, and if the person charged you for spending the night—he'd always ask you to spend the night—and if he charged you, you would knock it off the price of the book?

L. W.:   That's right.

R. W. H.: That's what they told you to do?

L. W.:   That's right. That's right.

R. W. H.: Well, we got the same instructions! [Laughter]

L. W.:   If you could sell him a book to help pay for your night's lodging, that's what you did. I remember the first place I had to pull out a cold dollar to stay that first night. I run up on a tight 'un.

Although L. W. did not try to ingratiate himself with ministers, one minister, after examining his Bibles and books, had written him a "letter of recommendation" that helped him in the community. A small-town newspaper editor ran an item on his Bible selling and L. W.'s buddy "cleaned up," but L. W. himself was less successful.

After L. W. and two others of the crew had delivered their books and before they returned to Nashville, they had taken off in the 1923 Ford touring car for the Toronto Fair and an excursion that took them to Niagara Falls, Montreal, into Maine, and to every capital in the New England states. They had returned through New York, crossing the Hudson and Peekskill, and traveled through Virginia before finally arriving home to Tennessee. Clearly, this lighthearted trip with his young friends had been a high point in the life of L. W., for he fairly sparkled as he recounted the experience after nearly a half century.

He had signed up for three months on the field, he said, and he had stuck it out. Though he had made little money, selling had been a positive experience, for he had learned to meet the public, and no doors had been slammed in his face. If he had failed to sell more, it was his own fault, because he admitted he just could not bring himself to "put the pressure on."

He told a couple of anecdotes to illustrate the kindness of many of the people he had encountered on the field. In one instance, a lady had cared for him a week when he became seriously ill from a bee sting. For years afterward he sent her a yearly Christmas card; then, a few years ago, the card was returned marked "Deceased." It was clear from his recital that L. W., despite his poor sales record, felt his youthful experience selling Bibles for Southwestern had been a high point of his life, and he had no regrets looking back over the experience.

J. K. was sixty-nine when interviewed in Nashville on 1 April 1980. He had recently retired from dentistry, a profession made possible by his book-selling in the 1930s. His samples had been similar to those of L. W., though he described a book not mentioned earlier, the *Comprehensive Analysis of the Bible*, which listed subjects and Bible verses relating to each. It sold in his time for $6.85, a substantial price. Being older than most, he had been made crew leader even during his first summer. Over a period of several summers he sold in Virginia, West Virginia, Pennsylvania, Maryland, Tennessee, Mississippi, and twice in Alabama, finding responses from the people much the same everywhere. His commission had been 40 percent on his own sales, 10 percent on books sold by those not in his immediate crew but under his general supervision. He did not remember precisely the amount of his earnings, but each summer he had netted several hundred dollars, not at all bad for the times. With this money, he had put himself through several years of college, then through dental school in Memphis, where in-state tuition at that time was $66 a quarter.

Like others, he had gone through sales training in Nashville, where, as he said, rudimentary elements of the Bible were taught along with sales techniques in order to familiarize the fledgling salesmen with their product.

R. W. H.: Would you characterize the instruction as what they used to call "high pressure" selling?

J. K.:   No, not at all, not at all. I mean it was the rural South, and, usually a lot of folks, if they had cars, they could drive, and if they didn't have cars, they'd just walk their territory, and usually, if you came to a house at dinnertime they'd ask you to have dinner, or if you were there at night, they'd ask you to spend the night with them. I don't guess there was ever anybody in our home [he grew up on a farm near Nashville] that they was not asked to break bread with us. At dinner, or what we called supper. We would ask them. There used to be an old pack peddler that'd come through here and he . . . would usually hit our house toward nightfall because he knew he would be asked to spend the night. We'd put his horse in the stable, and feed him corn and hay and he'd spend the night. He didn't owe us a dime. I mean it was just southern hospitality. That's really what you had on the book field. And people knew that you were just selling books, working your way through school, and they would feel like "Well, if I give him an order"—you didn't use that as a selling point, but it helped some because they would know, "Well, here's a boy working his way through school, so if I can buy something that I need, like a new Bible"—and you found them rather trusting.

Let me give you an example. I sold a man a Family Bible there in Chilton County, Alabama, and when I delivered it to him he was on his knees, picking cotton, and he said, "Aw, I hate to see you," says, "I sure wanted that Bible, but I haven't sold my cotton yet and I just can't take it." I says, "Well, I'll just leave it with you, it's quite all right, and I'll come back and collect before I go back to school." And one day I was driving in toward Clanton, and I was in an old touring car, Chevrolet, one I just bought to deliver and sell Bibles in, and I met this man in a two-horse wagon. He pulled over to the side of the road, and when I come by he flagged me down. He said, "Well, I sure am happy to see you." Said, "I want to pay you for my Bible." He took a check out and it was for six hundred and some odd dollars, and he owed me seven eighty-five. And I says, "Well, I don't have change for that." He says, "Oh, I'm sorry." Says, "I sure wanted to pay you for that Bible." He said, "I'll tell you what you do." Says, "The bank's closed, but you go in and go round to the alley and knock on the back door, and the manager'll be in there. He'll come out and open up. And you tell him to give you seven eighty-five and deposit the rest of this in my account." I looked at the man in amazement. I said, "Aw, you don't want me to do that." I says, "You've never seen me forty-five minutes in your lifetime." I said, "What's to keep me from just taking your check and taking off?" The man looked at me in amazement. He says, "Aw, you wouldn't do that!" Says, "Giddap, there!" [to his team] and just drove off. And sure 'nough, I took that check into Clanton, knocked on the bank door. The manager come out, and I told him the story and who I was and he went in and deposited it to his account and gave me a check for seven dollars and eighty-five cents. CAN YOU IMAGINE THAT HAPPENING TODAY?

When mealtime came, you were a guest, J. K. remembered, and you would not insult someone who asked you to eat by offering money. From time to time he was invited to eat with a black family, when he happened to be present at mealtime, and he accepted as with anyone else, though in those days it was unusual in the Deep South for blacks and whites to share the same meal table. He did not remember that the company suggested deducting a sum from a book, if you had sold one to a householder who had hosted you overnight, though it had been his policy to deduct a sum, usually two dollars. The company had told them always to offer to pay; Southwestern salesmen were not deadbeats. Here J. K. assumed the voice of the company official instructing novices on the field:

> Above all, if you are going out and saying you represent us, represent us in a nice way. Be a good salesman and an honest and fair salesman, so we'll be proud to say that you represent us, just like you're proud to say you represent us. Because we have a name. [Now in his own character] After all, this company dates back to the Civil War . . . and hires more young salesmen, I guess, than any other company in the continental United States. And lots of boys that are professional lawyers and doctors and dentists and ministers and school-teachers, educators worked their way through school because Southwestern Publishing Company gave them a job.

It has perhaps been observed that this picture of selling coming from J. K. is quite different from that presented in the article "High Pressure Selling in the Bible Belt," cited earlier, though the two salesmen were working during the same period and for the same company. Why the difference? There is, of course, the matter of individual temperament; two individuals will react differently to the same experience. There is the fact that "High Pressure" was published almost contemporaneously with the informant's experience of selling, whereas J. K. was interviewed more than forty years afterward, when time might have obscured details and mellowed memories. But there seem to be more cogent reasons even than these.

The author of "High Pressure" was a well-known popular writer of that day. The title of his article capitalized on the Mencken term "Bible Belt," then fairly recently and scornfully coined. The article was also published at a time when such works as *Tobacco Road* had depicted the South as the nation's number one economic problem and social embarrassment. The South had seized the consciousness of the nation as distinct and peculiar, much outside the mainstream of the national life. There was incentive, therefore, for the author to dramatize in a magazine of mass circulation certain of those aspects that made the region appear unique and uncouth. And what could be more dramatic, short of violence—which achieved its own notoriety—than selling Bibles for profit in an area where the hard sell confronted a rural society permeated with a history of hospitality toward guests, if not always toward strangers, and resting on a base of religious sentiment passed down from John Calvin, John Wesley, Francis Asbury, Peter Cartwright, Alexander Campbell, and reinforced by the preachers of the 1930s?

In addition, the young salesman hero of "High Pressure Selling" was obviously not under the stern necessity that J. K. was of making his own way through college; his own admission was that money earned selling Bibles supplemented assistance from his family. But J. K. was entirely on his own. He uttered not a word of criticism of the company or its sales policies; he clearly felt that Southwestern had made it possible for him to receive a professional education. With the drive and will that came from knowing that if he failed his hopes for a professional career were over, he had been a remarkably effective salesman. His lifelong sense of gratitude toward the company that had made a successful career possible for him is perfectly understandable.

The longest interview by far was conducted on 16 April 1979, with three young men./8/ J. C., born in Nashville and currently working for South Central Bell in that city, was twenty-seven at the time of the interview. B. F., also a native of Nashville, was twenty-four and in graduate school. M. E., now a professional salesman, had been responsible for recruiting the other two. J. C. sold in the summers of 1975 through 1978; B. F. in the summers of 1974 through 1976; while M. E. sold in the summers of 1972 through 1976. All three eventually became crew leaders, managing groups that varied in size from three to twenty. Since the time of their selling did not wholly coincide, their line was not identical, but the mainstay of each salesman had been the Family Bible—in the King James Version, of course. The company called this Bible, which had an extensive, though dated, study-aid apparatus, the "Home Religious Library." J. C. recalled that in his first summer the price had been $35.95, but by his last summer inflation had driven the price up to $42.95. In addition, J. C. had sold a Bible reference book, a set of children's books, and a two-volume medical set. He sold more of the Bible reference books, however, than anything else.

When asked about Sales Training School, M. E., who called it "a unique experience for students," described the training period as a cross between a psychology course and a seminar in sales technique. The main emphasis had been on learning to meet people and sustaining oneself emotionally in order to withstand the rejection that was often encountered in door-to-door selling.

B. F.:   When you first go into it, you're treated as if—it kind of scares you to death—We have rehearsals on getting in doors and whatever and going over talks—and they are pretty rough on you at first and by scaring you a little bit, by asking questions you can't answer, the students become intent on learning information; they open up a little more. And then . . . as the week progresses, by Thursday afternoon it's been only three or four days, you would have thought that you knew everything there is to know about selling door-to-door. They've instilled that much confidence in you, and if there's encouragement at the end of this week, that's really good, and there's one or two points you can work on, you're doing real well.

R. W. H.: In your training did you do any dramatizing, where some of you would be the salesperson and somebody the reluctant customer . . . ?

M. E.:   Very much so.

B. F.:   They had—one of the props on the stage where we met at the War Memorial Auditorium in Nashville, and they had a big door prop on the stage, and they'd have the sales manager greeted by "Mrs. Jones," and all the customers we'd be calling on would be referred to as "Mrs. Jones". . . and we'd act out the parts . . . and she's not going to let you in the door, and she'll answer negatively to some of your questions. Anyway, we had a door up there and practiced and showed people knocking on the door. Knock three times, not just once. Knock hard but not too hard. Don't do any melody knocks—da ta da da, like that, so and so forth, where everybody else could see it on the stage.

R. W. H.: Was this before they got their new quarters when they held classes in the War Memorial Auditorium?

M. E.:   This was even after they got the new quarters. What they had during the session, as schools got out and salespeople arrived in Nashville . . . not everybody met at the War Memorial. If it's a large group, they do, but they also worked at the different motels and some of the theaters, movie theaters at the end of the day. About 7,200 people were lined up to sell books that summer.

R. W. H.: I have the article here from *Time* magazine published in '73 and it says [reads], "The recruits, mostly clean-cut kids, memorize their spiel 'Hi Miz Jones, I'm Joe College, and I'm out here in your neighborhood calling on some of the church people.'" Is that authentic?

M. E.:   Pretty much.

R. W. H.: And then, this interested me, I'd forgotten it. "They're encouraged to [reads] 'charge' the front porch". . . I'll skip a few words . . ."starting the first call at exactly 7:59 A.M. . . ." What is the psychology of starting at 7:59 instead of, say, 7:30 or 8 o'clock?

M. E.:   The psychology behind it is that, basically, you're dealing with college students, again, who are very much unself-disciplined, as you know, being a teacher. They had trouble organizing their time . . . so Southwestern realizes that unless they're on a very, very tight schedule, carefully planned for them from the beginning, that college students are sometimes likely to kind of work at random when they feel like it and not when they don't.

The psychology is that there has to be, in order to make a living at selling books in the summertime, you have to call on so many people. Out of that "so many people" they know that a certain number will let you in the door. Out of those that let you in the door, a percentage will let you show. Out of the certain amount that you show, several of them will buy.

But if you don't work consistent hours, make the numbers work for you, then you'll never be a success at it. So it's very important that they start at 8 o'clock every morning and then finish every night at 9:30.

R. W. H.: It was that 7:59 rather than 8:00 that—

M. E.:   That's a carry-over from Lombardi's time. If you've read any of his books, when he said be at practice at 8 o'clock, he meant 7:45. So when they say 8:00, they mean 7:59. That's all it was.

R. W. H.: Did you in the training sessions, as seems suggested here, have songs that you sang, to pep you up? The one that's given here [reads from *Time* article], "Goodbye to *no* and *never* / Goodbye to doubt and fear. / It's a good thing to be a bookman / And to be of good cheer." Did they sing that when you were there?

J. C.:   Right.

M. E.:   It's a grand thing to be a bookman; / It's the best thing I know; / It's a grand thing to be a bookman, / Everywhere I go.

All: Goodbye to *never*, / Goodbye to fear. / It's a great, great thing to be a bookman, / And to be of good cheer.

J. C.:   They used to tell us to sing these songs between houses.

R. W. H.: Between houses?

J. C.:   They used to tell us, especially the first summer, to run between houses, so we could keep our minds off what we were doing. So they figured if we were walking between houses, to some extent then it would give us more time to think about the negative aspects of what was happening to us.

So the training was full of things to kind of keep your mind occupied with positive thoughts to keep you going during the day.

B. F.:   Everything was scheduled about the day. You got up at 6 o'clock, showered at 6:15, ate at 6:30 . . . as soon as you got in, you had to fill out that day's paperwork, see what you had made, and whatever, do your other work . . . into bed at 11 o'clock.

R. W. H.: And your manager took care of that . . .

B. F.:   Start from Sales School . . . start Sales School at 6:00, go to bed at 11 o'clock.

R. W. H.: Did you have a close where, by the time you got through talking, you had the pencil over in the hand of your prospective customer and the order book . . .?

B. F.:   Well, we had the order book . . . that was the close, was filling out the order on the book itself. And you were taught to fill out the order, just keep going, just as a part of the talk, you begin filling out the order, their names . . . you just kept writing till you got a negative response. And then if you did, then you'd make another close.

R. W. H.: Did you find selling in Pennsylvania quite different from selling in a southwestern state like Texas?

B. F.:   Yeah, it was a heck of a lot different. The sales were the same, the people were—just—whereas in Texas you'd have people who'd just welcome you . . . they'd sit and talk and just carry on a conversation but never buy—wouldn't even think of buying a book. They were just being nice and friendly. In the North, people didn't do that. If they wanted your product, then you could come in. If they wanted a book, you could demonstrate. They wouldn't invite you in just to be folksy.

M. E.:   It might be interesting to point out that the last three years that all of us sold, the number one teams sold in the state of New York. I think probably back when you sold . . . it was confined mostly to the South and Southwest states, but in more recent times they've found that there's a great market up North and also in the Northwest—been in California and Oregon and Washington, quite a bit, and they have revamped their selling techniques to fit those areas and done quite well . . . the methods they teach you should work up North, down South, out West, in a large city, in a small town, in the country. The same method is designed to work no matter where one is, so long as the method is applied correctly. That's why the schedule is so important.

All three men had done well financially. The lowest sum earned was $2,100 for J. C.'s first summer, and M. E. had cleared $20,000 his fifth summer, the largest amount earned.

The three men were a veritable mine of information. M. E., who had spent more time than the others with the company, seemed to have a thorough knowledge of every aspect of its operations in the 1970s. All three men agreed that getting a book deposit remained a problem, even in the more affluent 1970s. If he sensed a fair chance for delivery, the salesman would explain that since he went to considerable expense in having books shipped to him and could not risk failing to collect, the customer should write on the order his "Christian word" that he would take the book when delivered. Often such persons still would not accept the book when the salesman returned, having had second thoughts after cooling off from the hard sell. The customer could even be withdrawn, nervous, or hostile. Sometimes an errant customer would run out the back door, with the salesman close behind. In one case, upon the appearance of the salesman with the book, the customer darted out the back door, got into his car, and raced to a neighbor's house. The salesman followed in his own car, entered the house, searched throughout, and eventually found his customer hiding in the shower stall.

How did these salesmen, in retrospect, feel about their experience? M. E. felt that it had been the "most wonderful thing in the world" for him as a student to have been given the opportunity to meet people in this way. Since selling was his present occupation, he felt that he had gotten a basic background in understanding percentages of rejections and sales, how the "numbers" work, and that he had learned in a summer what it had taken many of his present colleagues several years to learn. B. F. agreed that it had been a positive experience. He could now speak with a farmer, a banker, a lawyer, with practically anyone, with more confidence. J. C. said that he could not have secured his present position with South Central Bell had he not worked for Southwestern, "because any sales-oriented company is going to look very favorably on somebody who's had two or three summers' experience with Southwestern, because they know Southwestern has an excellent training program. . . ."

When asked about black and female persons on the field, M. E. replied that the company had initially formed six or seven black divisions, selling a line of materials of special interest to black customers. Black salespersons were trained, along with black sales supervisors, and they did very well, selling chiefly to members of their own race in the cities. Saleswomen had originally been brought in, he said, to sell cookbooks, but, in line with national trends that saw women entering all areas of employment, women started selling successfully in all categories. Their training has been the same as that of men, though women have been instructed not to call on a house if only a man is present. They are also instructed not to be out working as late at night as men are expected to be.

M. J., a black student salesman, was twenty-two when interviewed in Cookeville, Tennessee, on 1 May 1980. Though born in South Carolina, he now calls Miami his home. He had just graduated from a state university in Tennessee, where he had been on a football scholarship. Although he had not been obliged to sell books in order to stay in college, he had found the activity in the summer of 1979 so remunerative in both money and experience that he was, when interviewed, busy recruiting a crew of ten students, all white, to sell books in the summer of 1980.

Initially he had been the only black member in a group of four. He had sold *The Layman's Bible Encyclopedia*, a Bible story collection for children, student handbooks, and other books designed for special appeal to black customers. His crew had been assigned to Wichita, Kansas, where he had sold mostly to black people but also to whites in mixed neighborhoods. He had experienced no particular difficulty in selling to white customers. From the beginning he had resolved to have the positive experience that he indeed succeeded in having. After a couple of initial days of frustration, he rapidly learned the tricks of his trade and started hitting a consistent $200 or $300 a day in sales, with a 43 percent commission. Occasionally, by working from 8:00 A.M. to 9:30 P.M., he had even sold $500 in a day. On weekends he had worked his "gravy list"—people who had not been at home during his regular hours.

He was asked if he considered the sales techniques he had been taught at Sales Training School to be "high pressure" selling. He did not consider them as such.

> M. J.:   You've got to be persistent, a little bit. But it's a way of being persistent without putting pressure, and I found that knowing names was a jewel of all success in selling. If you can know a lot of names—I was good at remembering names—that won the customers a lot of times. That gave me a chance to at least show my books. And if I got a chance to show, my chance of selling, a lot of the time, was at least 70 percent.

> R. W. H.: You say names—you mean people that this other prospect knew?

> M. J.:   Not necessarily knew. But you just call, like you might know Mary that lives down at the corner. And I used ladies' names with ladies and men's names with men. Because if I used a lady's name with a man, the men more than likely will say, "Aw, what does she know?"

In closing a sale, M. J. said it is very important to follow word for word the close learned in Sales School. If you kept on talking without trying to close, you could talk a customer right out of a sale.

> M. J.:   Every time I used to bring out my books, I always would take my order pad out with it at the same time. The reason for that is that you never want to show the books and then reach down in the case and bring out the order pad. At first, that'll scare people. First thing they'll say is, "Aw, hell, what I got to buy now?" So what I do is I take my order pad . . . I say, "Mary got 'em, Sheila got 'em, Dorothy got 'em, Sam got 'em." I go like that and I go into showing the book.

> R. W. H.: You knew they knew Dorothy and Sam?

> M. J.:   Well, no, not necessarily, but if I keep calling off another name, my chances of them knowing is a great deal better, whether they know 'em or not. And the big thing is this: if all them people got 'em, they must be pretty good. I say, "What do you think a set of these cost?". . . I say, "Mary said she guessed they cost about $80, Sheila guessed that they cost $90, and would you believe that Sue Ellen guessed that they cost $125?". . . They say, "Boy, that's some good books. A set like that has got to cost at least $90." I say, "Would you believe they only cost $43.90? . . . Mary, Sheila, Dorothy, and

Sue Ellen like the way I do business. I'm taking orders today and will deliver your books at the end of the summer. That way gives you the rest of the summer to save up and make the balance. Now, if you were to get a set of these, that would make it easier, wouldn't it?" They'll say, "Yeah." Then I say, "What I'll do is this: I'll drop you a card a week or ten days in advance and let you know the exact day I'll be by with your book. Now, if I drop you a card . . . there'll be someone home, won't there?" Likely, they'll say, "Yeah, yeah." I say, "Are you usually home during the day?" I answer an objection before it comes up. . . . I say, "If not, could you leave a note on your door? Maybe I could drop them to your neighbor next door." I say, "Like the way Mary, Dorothy, Sue Ellen like the way I do business, delivering the books myself, making sure they are in perfect condition." Okay. But I say, "In order for me to do this, I need to get your name and address. But first, let me ask you something: how do you get your mail—here or at the post office?" They say, "Naw, we get it here." I say, "What's that box 232?". . ."No, no, that's box 234.". . . I say, "Let's see—you don't plan on painting the house between now and then, do you?" They say, "Naw it's going to be white." So I say, "A white house. Will a green fence be always round the house when I come back?" They say, "Yeah, yeah, we don't plan on taking it up." So I go ahead, I get all that down, you know. . . . [Here the tape was accidentally erased, but it is clear the customer balks.] I say, "I'm sorry, Mrs. Jones," I say. "Sometimes I get so excited because Mary, Sue Ellen, Dorothy, and all them done got 'em. I just assumed everybody was going to get 'em."

M. J. was not being facetious when he asserted that he did not consider these sales techniques to be high pressure. High pressure or not, they have certainly been effective. His earnings in seven weeks in the summer of 1979 were $4,100. His opportunities for much larger commissions would come, he knew, when he had a crew of men under him in the field.

M. J. said that he sold mostly to women and, from time to time opportunities for amorous adventures presented themselves, but he resolutely stuck with his job of selling and cleared out before complications could arise. Evidently possible seduction is a situation salesmen do sometimes encounter; M. J. had heard stories told by others. It goes without saying that company policy would be to discourage rigorously any such entanglement. For though Southwestern is not church-related and is strictly a commercial enterprise, it is probably safe to say that its moral code is as rigorous as any Fundamentalist church would insist upon. Not only is illicit amorous activity questionable in itself; more importantly, it detracts from the central mission, piling up those sales.

M. J., who had only praise for Southwestern, showed a magazine issued by the company with photographs of top producers in sales for the preceding summer. A substantial number of these photographs were of blacks and women. He said that during the past summer three of the top salespersons had been women.

C. F. was one former Southwestern saleswoman who was kind enough to respond at length in writing to questions sent her./9/ Though a native of Kentucky, she was in June of 1980 an attorney practicing in Dallas. In 1971, 1972, and 1973 she sold in and near Macon, Georgia, in Philadelphia, and in Kansas City. Since Southwestern only initiated the use of women as salespersons in 1970, she had been the only woman in a crew of men in one or two of the territories she had worked. In 1971, she had netted $3,000; in 1972, $5,000; and in 1973, $1,000. The reason for the decline in her profits in the third summer, unusual with success-ful salespersons, was that she had been assigned a territory that had been canvassed with the same materials by a salesman the preceding summer. This carelessness in assigning territory evoked some sharp criticism from her. The company, she felt, had little investment in its salespeople; therefore, it did not take as much care as it should have done to avoid this serious duplication of effort. However, her sales had contributed substantially to paying for her law school studies, and she felt some loy-alty to Southwestern. Her evaluation of her experience was poignant:

> I believe that selling books was one of the most valuable experiences I have had during my life. I met people, went to places, and did things that I would not have done otherwise at an age when I could most appreciate the experiences. I matured.
>
> I gained self-assurance in dealing with people; I learned how to deal with unusual situations; I gained appreciation for what I was, where I came from and for my family, especially my mother and what she had done for my family. I learned about business. . . .
>
> I experienced the physical flavor of this country and felt the heartbeat of its people. Southwestern gave me the opportunity to view America "up-close and personally" and this is something I con-sider so important to my own growth that I believe it overrides the negative aspects of the Southwestern experience.

But there were negative aspects of selling, which she now sees from a lawyer's perspective. She points out an almost total lack of responsibil-ity in all matters that the company exhibits toward its salespeople. As she put it, "I believe in most business endeavors, employers are more sup-portive and have more invested in the success or failure of their employees than does Southwestern."

C. F.'s legal analysis of the salesperson's relationship with the company was instructive. She pointed out that Southwestern guards its position as an independent contractor dealing with other independent contractors (sales-people) in order to limit its legal responsibility for the personnel. With this arrangement a number of benefits accrue to the company. It does not have to deduct federal income tax from the salesperson's check, since he or she is regarded as self-employed. No contributions need be made to Social

Security. By avoiding Uncle Sam's paperwork, Southwestern saves over-head by not having to hire additional clerical personnel. Furthermore, the company also avoids responsibility for any injuries suffered on the field. An employer proper, under Workman's Compensation Insurance Coverage, has, of course, some responsibility for harm that befalls employees in the course of their duty.

When asked if she had experienced any particular advantages or dis-advantages as a female salesperson, C. F. replied that her sex may have made it easier to "get in the door." But she and her family had suffered some concern for her personal safety during the long, strenuous hours. Though C. F. candidly expressed her ambivalence toward certain com-pany policies, she strongly and positively affirmed the total experience as an important feature in her development of self-reliance and other habits of mind essential to her success as an attorney.

As evidenced by the interviews, many salespersons have reported favorably on their experiences selling Bibles. Some have even regarded the work as the outstanding opportunity of their lives. G. A., interviewed on 8 May 1980, felt differently and expressed himself unequivocally. A native of Memphis, G. A. is now forty and teaches English in a state university. He sold Bibles and books about 1960 for Southwestern, his main sales item having been a Family Bible, which sold at that time for about $30. He also sold *Nave's Topical Concordance*, a couple of dictio-naries, and a Bible encyclopedia. Like others, he had gone through the sales-training period.

> G. A.:   The tone of the meetings [sales training] was a combina-tion of a cheerleading session with a big game and a Fundamentalist revival service. One of our speakers was from Yale Divinity School and had just made some fantastic sum of money the previous sum-mer, selling. I also remember the climax of the week, which was a trip up to the top of the National Life Tower [where the company was then headquartered] to be interviewed by the big man—God at the top of His tower Himself . . . that was the climax of the week. He had a map of the United States on the wall behind him and a view of Nashville out the windows and on the wall were pins to show where the various crews were going that summer.
>
> R. W. H.: Would you say the instruction you got in this training period was what is sometimes characterized as high pressure selling?
>
> G. A.:   Yeah. The major focus of the training was, as I recall, how not to hear the word "No." How to get around objections.

G. A. sold in Pennsylvania Dutch country for three days, with a crew from a Tennessee church college, netting a $90 profit. He had looked forward to the travel experience as a "grand and glorious adven-ture," an opportunity to see a part of the country he did not know.

Although he did enjoy the trip and the people he met, all too quickly he experienced a crisis of conscience because he found himself selling to people he knew to be poor, who felt obligated to "buy a product because it was the Bible, a sacred object to them." This realization led him to quit after only three days of highly successful selling. Several years later G. A. served for a time as Director of Christian Education at the church in Nashville where some of the company officials were members. At that time he confronted them with his deeply felt criticism. He told them that "the sales techniques they taught were manipulative," that their appeal was to people's sense of duty and guilt to make them buy a product they might not actually need. He further informed them that their product was poorly designed, gaudy, and had outdated commentary. Their defense was that they were shifting emphasis away from the Family Bible and upgrading their products generally. He remembers the discussion as amicable, though one of the officials had been—it is not surprising—defensive, arguing that "the sales techniques are the same techniques generally used and accepted whatever the product might be." G. A. had no dramatic adventures to report, since his sales career had been so brief. What remained in his mind was the pseudo-inspirational tone of the training sessions, the long hours spent memorizing canned sales speeches from the small pamphlets distributed at sales training, and the final insight and disillusionment on the field.

Several parents of young men who have been on the book field were also interviewed, though their responses must be acknowledged to be impressionistic and random. The parents consulted in the limited sampling were generally critical of the lack of responsibility Southwestern seems to take for the young salespeople, some of them very green and naive. Yet these mothers and fathers also conceded that the adventure on the field was for most participants a memorable "coming-of-age" rite. Considering the difficulty many parents have today "launching" their offspring, the self-reliance gained on the field was applauded. Also, in view of the costs of higher education, both yesterday and today, it is the rare parent who is likely to object when a son or daughter nets several thousand dollars toward college expenses during a single summer.

Conclusions and Lingering Questions

After talking with a number of Bible salespersons, who represent experiences of a period of several decades, including representatives of two new but highly visible categories of salespeople, black and female, it is possible to state, in conclusion, several points. All the sophisticated techniques that have been successful in moving other commodities in this consumer-oriented society have been applied to the door-to-door selling of Bibles. While The Southwestern Company may appear to be folksy, with its veneer of piety, and seemingly anachronistic in its method of selling, it is a hard-boiled, amazingly shrewd, and highly efficient business enterprise. It is also, like any competently managed business, constantly changing. What could be said of Southwestern in the seventies will not necessarily apply throughout the eighties. To the most polished market-tested sales strategies are added those appeals to religious sentiment, overt or latent, that are a cultural heritage not only of the South but also of the entire nation, in that extended Bible Belt which is the contemporary United States. The door-to-door Bible salesperson is armed with sales talks that still capitalize on this sentiment, though crude appeals used in the past have been revised, modified, and even in some cases eliminated from the company literature. Salespersons still invoke the simple desire of most people to own a Bible, and they inflict guilt where one is not owned. Though there may be dust on the Bible, it still, we suspect, is to be found in most American homes. Once, homes throughout the South owned only two books, the Holy Bible and a home medical encyclopedia; today, while there may be many booklets, magazines, and *Reader's Digest* collections in homes throughout the United States, the Bible still holds the honored place.

While, according to recent reports, the company today stresses in its sales talks the virtue of its products rather than the salesperson's need to pay college expenses, one can be sure that many Americans, valuing the work ethic and respecting the young person who wishes to better himself or herself through higher education, look with special favor on the clean-cut, polite young student who appears at their door. In the few remaining remote rural territories, the salesman, or now woman, still provides a welcome break from the monotony of daily life; this salesperson is also frequently well rewarded, since a considerable number of farmers have today suddenly found themselves affluent, able to buy any book that strikes their fancy.

Once upon a time Bibles were sold door-to-door in southern rural regions, chiefly by southern white Protestant males. Now the salespeople who appear in towns and cities throughout the land are recruited from everywhere and include blacks, women, and Hispanics. The company has grown, changed with the times, and diversified. Still the selling of Bibles would appear to be what is associated in the popular mind with The Southwestern Company. It is the image of the youthful Bible salesman, sample case in hand, trudging down a dusty country road, that has become a part of American literature and folklore. This is the colporteur, American style.

Yet nagging questions remain. Should piety—even superstition—be manipulated in a commercial enterprise? Should overpriced and often unneeded Bibles be hardsold to persons who can sometimes ill afford them? Can gaudy editions of the Holy Bible, with outdated commentary, be ethically promoted by persons of discernment and conscience? Is it wise use of the energies of young people to put them on the field, often with few resources, to peddle materials of inconsistent quality?

When shoddy art work, garish pictures, and commentary first produced over a century ago and revised too little since are offered with the most advanced, scientifically tested sales techniques, it is hard to avoid the conclusion that a company is using salability as its chief criterion. Should not a company that recruits salespeople in part through an appeal to their desire to place the Holy Bible in more homes also take greater responsibility for presenting works of quality and making available a better selection of commentaries, Bible aids, and even Bible translations? In literary beauty as well as popular appeal, the King James Version is still unexcelled. Yet when a family is purchasing a second or even a third Bible, as is frequently the case in a Southwestern transaction, more attention should perhaps be given to the possibility of their acquiring a newer, more accurate, and more easily comprehended translation.

Many criticisms of Southwestern strategies are, of course, reservations about American capitalistic practices in the larger sense. But within the presumed security of their own homes, with appeals to their paternalistic concern for youth, is it ethically right to hardsell citizens with products that are sometimes inferior, almost always overpriced, and frequently superfluous? In this setting the beneficial competition of the American open marketplace, which has given us such outstanding editions as the Washburn College Bible, has not really been able to operate.

It would be unfair to evaluate hastily, either positively or negatively, the business of Bible peddling in the United States, particularly as it has been practiced by The Southwestern Company. The goal of a Bible in every household is far from unworthy, and once there were few established bookstores in the country, almost always located in metropolitan areas. Traveling salesmen, welcomed as couriers from the outside world, once provided a needed service. The Southwestern Company itself has always operated fully within the law; its officials have been respected Tennessee businessmen and political and civic leaders. Some have exemplified in their own careers the Horatio Alger myth of the poor boy who becomes wealthy through decency and hard work, according to the Puritan ethic. Thousands of successful business and professional people throughout the country witness to the self-reliance, confidence, and independence gained in youth through the selling experience, which also made possible financially the necessary training for their careers. It should not be forgotten that The Southwestern customers have never merely purchased a rather expensive Bible; they have always made an investment in American youth.

NOTES

/1/   A recent advertisement in a Nashville-published Christian denominational periodical noted that a local television personality, who is also a preacher, is available with his wife for banquet entertainment. Their edifying themes are Christian living and the free enterprise system!

/2/   It should be mentioned that the men in the film *Salesman* always started their work in a new territory by setting up a display at a local Catholic church, where they obtained the names of prospects. On their visits to these prospects they invariably invoked their common faith as Catholics. Although it did sell a Catholic Bible for many years, The Southwestern Company has always been predominantly Protestant in personnel and style.

/3/   Observations come from my own (Ralph W. Hyde's) experience selling for Southwestern in 1936.

/4/   This was also the summer that I, then a youth, was selling Bibles in Alabama. Several points meet.

/5/   I personally remember one middle-aged woman, possibly forty-five, who lived less than thirty miles from Montgomery, yet had never been there. The capital city of Alabama might as well have been on the moon as far as she was concerned.

/6/   "Cultured" hardly describes the sad, sallow people, perhaps suffering from pellagra (the diet of many was corn, corn, corn), I encountered in the back country of Alabama. These were the people whose photographs are seen in the now classic *You Have Seen Their Faces* (1937) by Erskine Caldwell and Margaret Bourke-White and in *Let Us Now Praise Famous Men* (1941) by James Agee and Walker Evans. As for the salesman's claim that his Bible was published much later, both Bibles would probably have been the King James Version, though the salesman's probably had a concordance, the prospect's probably not. About twelve years ago a salesman from Southwestern called on me. I had a look at Genesis 1 in his Bible sample. At the top in the middle column was the entry "Earth created 4004 B.C.," as it had been in my sample in 1936.

/7/   Although every informant gave me permission to use his or her name, initials only will be employed for identification in these interviews.

/8/   One young man was a former student of mine.

/9/   C. F. was also an undergraduate student of mine.

WORKS CONSULTED

Alexander, T. H.
1937   "High Pressure in the Bible Belt." *The Reader's Digest* 30: 37–41.

Brown, Joe David
1971   *Addie Pray*. New York: Simon and Schuster.

Dolan, J. R.
1964   *The Yankee Peddlers of Early America*. New York: Clarkson N. Potter.

Hilts, Len
1974   *Each Man His Mountain*. Printed in the United States of America: SCS Project.

The Maysles Brothers and Charlotte Zwerin
1969   *Salesman*. New York: New American Library.

Morley, Christopher
1955   *Parnassus on Wheels*. New York: J. B. Lippincott.

O'Connor, Flannery
1971   *The Complete Stories*. Garden City: Farrar, Straus and Giroux.

Owen, Guy
1965   *The Ballad of the Flim-Flam Man*. New York: Macmillan.
1972   *The Flim-Flam Man and the Apprentice Grifter*. New York: Crown.

Stone, Alma
1962   *The Bible Salesman*. Garden City: Doubleday.

Time
1973   "The Good Buck." 101 (June 25): 86.

Wright, Richardson
1967   *Hawkers and Walkers in Early America: Strolling Peddlers, Preachers, Lawyers, Players and Others to the Civil War*. New York: J. B. Lippincott.

York, Max
1969   "The Summer Has A Thousand Doors." *The Nashville Tennessean Magazine* (July 6): 13.

VII

The Bible as Literature
For American Children

Allene Stuart Phy

American children's literature started with adaptations of the immortal stories of the Bible, and the art of Bible storytelling remains popular even today, though the juvenile bookshelf now provides a wider variety of secular tales than ever before. For as long as the making of juvenile books has been regarded as an art, books based on the Bible have achieved recognition. In 1938, when the first Caldecott Medal was awarded for the most distinguished picture book for children published in the United States during the previous year, Dorothy P. Lathrop's *Animals of the Bible* was the winner. As recently as 1978 the coveted Caldecott was awarded Peter Spier for his humorous and imaginative visual retelling of the Noah's ark narrative. The history of children's literature is sprinkled with the titles of celebrated books based on the Bible. Yet the narration of Bible stories has varied in style from past to present, and a number of interesting issues emerge when attention is given to the Bible storybooks designed for American children.

Several questions suggest themselves. How have Bible stories traditionally been presented to children and how are they presented today? Are Bible stories viewed as exciting literature, as cultural heritage, as moral exempla, or as lessons on the path of salvation? Have Bible stories been presented with the sophistication, artistry, and beauty that has increasingly characterized other literature produced for the enjoyment of American children? Or, are these stories marketed chiefly for their pious appeal rather than merit of design and execution? Are Bible stories produced largely for those affiliated with religious denominations, or are they marketed as other attractive children's books would be, to a general North American audience? Are the same books designed for Jewish, Catholic, Protestant, and secular children, or are there several juvenile markets? Does the American "religion in general," vaguely benevolent, nondoctrinal, relativistic (which used to be most clearly associated with the name of Norman Vincent Peale) make its appearance in children's

books? Or has the revival of religious conservatism of the last few years
made itself strongly felt?

Are there attempts to bowdlerize the Bible in these books, in the
way other classical literature is sometimes "polished" for childhood sensibilities? What is done with biblical violence, references to God's wrath,
troublesomely complex theological concepts, alleged racism and sexism,
and the sexual adventuresomeness of esteemed biblical patriarchs? Does
anti-Semitic feeling ever creep into these stories, as it frequently has in
adult biblically derived narratives of former years? Are Bible stories
embellished in their retelling and, if so, how? Are these stories told in
informative, educational fashion, providing historical facts about the life
and times of biblical personalities and nations? Is there humor present in
the original biblical narratives, and, if this humor exists, how is it conveyed to children? Is the humor superimposed on the stories by writers
who believe children's books must be whimsical or funny, or does the
humor emerge from the Bible itself?

What principles of selectivity operate when editors and storytellers
make collections of children's Bible tales? Which episodes and personalities
appear most frequently in these narratives? Which are ignored or slighted?
Finally, how are the two central personalities of the Jewish and Christian
religions—Moses and Jesus—presented in these books for children? What
theological pronouncements, affirmations, or heresies, ancient and modern,
seem stated or implied?

Bible Stories of Earlier Times

Even before children's literature had separated itself from that of
adults, children had been deeply touched by a narrative poem that was
the first true "best seller" of the New World. An Englishman, Michael
Wigglesworth, transplanted in Massachusetts in the last part of the eighteenth century, produced a work of epic pretentions, "The Day of
Doom," which set the "five points" of Calvinism to doggerel. In 1876,
when Moses Coit Tyler published his definitive *History of American
Literature 1607-1765*, aged persons could still be found in New England, in rather large numbers, who were able to repeat by heart this
poem, which they had learned in childhood. Its pages were assigned as a
matter of course to little children to be committed to memory along
with their catechism, and Cotton Mather predicted that the poem would
be read in New England until The Day of Doom itself.

Tyler shared these observations on this curiously remarkable writing:

> This great poem which, with entire unconsciousness, attributes to the
> Divine Being a character the most execrable and loathsome to be met

with, perhaps, in any literature, Christian or pagan, had for a hundred years a popularity far exceeding that of any other work, in prose or verse, produced in America before the Revolution. The eighteen hundred copies of the first edition were sold within a single year; which implies the purchase of a copy of "The Day of Doom" by at least every thirty-fifth person then in New England, an example of the commercial success of a book never afterward equalled in this country. (294)

"The Day of Doom" captures the Calvinistic awe in the presence of a supreme being who can use the damnation of even newly born babes for his majesty and glory. The dead arise from their graves to be judged mercilessly in their total depravity. Babies who perished in infancy see themselves condemned everlastingly for Adam's sin, while Adam, redeemed among the elect, sits near the judgment seat of Christ. When the infants plead that their condemnation is unfair, their judge grants them one concession, "the easiest room in hell."

Doggerel, to be memorized by children, was placed on the lips of Jesus himself:

> Ye sinful wights and cursed sprites,
>   That work iniquity,
> Depart together, from me forever,
>   To endless misery;
> Your portion take in yonder lake
>   Where fire and brimstone flameth;
> Suffer the smart which your desert
>   As its due wages claimeth. (Tyler: 292)

Biblical narratives, retold with strong and definite theological interpretations, continued to be popular from colonial times into the present century. Remote from the centers of learning in New England, children of the hinterland frequently had access to only two books, the Bible and a home medical encyclopedia. Abraham Lincoln was not the only rural child, far from the American cities and cultural enclaves, to read the Bible by firelight, though the eloquence and wisdom of sacred scripture undoubtedly spoke more directly to his profound mind than to the minds of most. In the very last years of the nineteenth century and early into the twentieth, children of the South had access to another book, which retold Bible stories especially for children. This was the *Child's Bible Reader*, placed in thousands of southern homes by the earnest door-to-door salesmen of The Southwestern Company of Nashville, Tennessee. In hamlet and farm, this book was likely to be the solitary literary possession of a southern child, who would study its crude but potent illustrations for hours, learning by heart its stories.

Little editorial information was provided by the title page of *Child's Bible Reader*, but the book was entered according to Act of Congress in the year 1898 by W. E. Scull. The narratives and artwork crudely assembled in the book appear to have been in the public domain, with the stories attributed to Charlotte M. Yonge, "the noted author and missionaries' friend." "Aunt Charlotte" is described in the introduction as a maiden lady previously living in the East, where she has taught school and worked in Sunday school since young womanhood, assisting in the infant and primary departments of her home church. Aunt Charlotte, the reader is told, has just now traveled across country to visit her sister in a far western state, and it is here that she is telling her Bible stories to two nieces and a nephew. The stories can be read, the editor advises the reader, straight through or in groups of three short stories each Sunday—one after breakfast, one after dinner, and one after supper—as originally designed.

The precise relationship of the "Aunt Charlotte" who tells these stories to Charlotte Mary Yonge, the famous English children's writer, historian, and Church of England journal editor, is not made clear, though it is unlikely that any Bible Belt children of the early century were unduly perplexed. In a time and place where few books were available, *Child's Bible Reader* gripped the imagination. For almost three generations, the book remained a major tool of Sunday school teachers of every Protestant denomination throughout the South, and it is even rumored to have made its way into some Roman Catholic homes. No credit was given by the editor for the illustrations so generously sprinkled—often at odd places—throughout the book. Most were crude line drawings, though there were some full-page color plates, at least in some editions of the book. These were poorly reproduced—not unusual for the time—again uncredited, and seem largely to have been reproductions of the paintings of the masters or the German academicians. Their different styles and varying quality, as well as their anachronisms and questionable application to the text, probably also caused no great concern to children who had had little opportunity to develop discriminating tastes in books or art. For some incongruous reason a woodcut of the Church of the Holy Sepulcher appeared, in one edition at least, near a drawing of Ganesha, the Hindu elephant-headed god, who seemed mistakenly to have wandered in from another book, yet was still a tantalizing object of wonder. Depictions of the crucifixion and resurrection were particularly dramatic, even though Jesus changed size, shape, and features in each one./1/

The narratives themselves were designed for an interdenominational but definitely Fundamentalist audience. The New Testament was treated as a fulfillment of the Old, a typological storytelling approach that would begin to disappear as the twentieth century progressed. The women of the ancient Hebrews were described as "very beautiful," while children were invariably quaint and sweet. Although "the Jews" were identified as the opponents of Jesus, Aunt Charlotte made it quite clear that the Romans were the ones who crucified him. Pious messages and morals were drawn at every point, even when they had to be wrenched out of the original Bible texts. While Aunt Charlotte's narrative style was generally lively and straightforward, the problematic morality of some of the battle narratives of the Old Testament was glossed over, and the questions arising from the domestic conduct of patriarchs were totally ignored. Implied was the message that it is not for humans to question the ways of the Almighty. Inescapably, a certain blandness resulted from this polishing of lively Old Testament narratives. The youthful reader, for example, was left to wonder how the Cities of the Plain could possibly have been wicked enough to deserve their total destruction, but Aunt Charlotte made it quite clear that the works of the Lord are just.

Children of yesteryear delighted in the blue-tone illustration of little Jesus in Joseph's carpentry shop. Mary, a proud and beautiful young mother with elegant nimbus, spins gracefully on a nearby porch, watching her son, while pet doves hover about a ledge. Jesus himself is scantily clad in the manner of a Victorian child posing for his studio portrait; his halo is identical to that of his mother's. The carpentry tools he carries form the shape of a cross. Joseph, who significantly lacks a halo, is, for once, virile and youthful in appearance, an active man who works happily at his honorable trade./2/ In these old illustrations children saw Jesus, a child like themselves, maturing and increasing in wisdom and favor with God and man. They could not easily forget the image of the adult Jesus gently placed in his rock tomb, lovingly attended by the women who anoint his lifeless body. It was especially the woman with the beautiful hair who remained in memory, a haunting image from childhood.

Readers of *Child's Bible Reader* today have grandchildren or great-grandchildren who own scores of more artistic and sophisticated books. Yet it is not always the portrait of Jesus by the master artist that becomes the wonder-working icon among simple people. It is more often the crudely hewn folk image that becomes the object of veneration. Juvenile culture in many instances resembles folk culture. Few children today, who know the refined work of Brian Wildsmith or Celestino Piatti, experience the spell that was exerted by those curious blue-tone reproductions in the old storybook.

Throughout the last decades of the nineteenth century and well into the twentieth, Victorian sentimentality dominated children's books, whether they were Bible stories or purely secular narratives. A quintessential example was *Pictures and Rhymes to Bring Little Ones Happy*

Times, published in 1902. The book appears today as an odd collection of fairy tales, pious narratives, and crude verses, with, among other curious and strangely appealing selections, a Bible alphabet, containing a Bible reference and message for each letter of the alphabet. Alphabet books have always been a staple of children's literature, and Bible, history, and animal alphabets were especially common. Little distinguishes this one from many others, and the tone is quite clear from a few samples:

> C for Christ, so gentle,
>   meek, and mild,
> Who dearly loves each
>   little child.
> . . . .
> P for Good Physician, Christ,
>   the people did name,
> Who healed the sick, the
>   impotent and lame.
> . . . .
> U for Uz, where good
>   Job lived and died,
> Whose patience God
>   so sorely tried.
> . . . .
> Z for Zaccheus;
>   O may we all
> Obey like him the
>   Saviour's call./3/

At the beginning of the present century, Bible study was still regarded as an essential component of the education of the young in a good part of the country. A juvenile perception of biblical lore from this period has survived in the series of essays written about 1904 by Virginia Cary, a precocious ten-year-old girl growing up in Kentucky. Virginia was reared in a devout Episcopalian family, and many of her juvenile musings, later to be published by one of her descendants as *Oh Ye Jigs and Juleps* had to do with her childhood interpretations of the Bible.

At age ten she visualized heaven as a place where Peter or Moses, "or somebody" lines you up and passes out the crowns; later you grow wings. Contemplating the alternative to heaven she acknowledged that while she did not wish to go to perdition, at least interesting people would be there: Nero, Herod, Judas, and Jezebel would all be around. References to the Day of Doom had not disappeared from the Prayer Book Virginia knew, but the "Fearful Day of Judgment" no longer struck genuine terror in the child's heart. Little Virginia concluded that although she was doing her best to merit heaven, if she had to go to hell at least she hoped to go to the one for Episcopalians and not "the red hot blazing one the Baptists are going to have," which she had heard the preacher vividly describe on a visit to the Baptist church with one of her friends (Hudson: 53).

Virginia was already composing her own prayers, obviously derived from the phrases and cadences of the Psalms and the Book of Common Prayer: "O ye Sun and Moon, oh ye beans and roses / Oh ye jigs and juleps, Bless ye the Lord, Praise Him and Magnify Him forever. Amen" (Hudson: 37). She grew up, married and became Mrs. Hudson, was widowed early in life, and supported her family by operating a boarding house. Throughout her adult life, this Kentucky woman increased in knowledge and understanding of the scriptures and developed an eloquence, as subsequent adult writings bear out, acquired largely from her early exposure to the Bible and the Book of Common Prayer. Scores of her students remember her even today as a truly inspiring Sunday school teacher, to whom they owe a lifelong love for the Bible.

Favorite Bible Subjects

Most people, young and old, at all times and places, have read the Bible selectively. Certain human personalities from the ancient epic capture the imagination, while particular episodes seem to exert a constant fascination. Perceptions of biblical events and characters, of course, change with maturity and with continued reflection by those who make the Bible a part of their entire lives. What was just a lively story in kindergarten may later become a significant exemplum or an account of life in an intriguing historical period. The juvenile perception of Bible characters, events, and situations has been carefully if informally studied, and today publishers use more sophisticated marketing research and make a special effort to speak to the needs of children. Definite principles of selection have always operated and continue to do so when books of Bible stories are prepared for children from kindergarten through grade nine, the usual range for which juvenile literature considered as a separate category is produced.

Even the youngest children have their favorite tales; they wish to hear the adventures of Noah, Jonah, Samson, and David. They enjoy the parables of Jesus, simple but masterful narratives by any reckoning. Holiday times offer special opportunities to use Bible stories. Chanukah, Rosh Hashanah, Passover, Easter, and Christmas provide fine marketing possibilities for children's books, and each year new holiday books do appear.

But the stories children always prefer are well known and turn up most frequently in both Bible story collections and the books that retell and illustrate, often elaborately and masterfully, a single Bible episode. Jesus and Moses are by far the heroic personalities with whom children most identify. For younger children it is not difficult to single out the following additional Bible subjects as the most popular, though of course there will be differences, based on exposure and interest, between children living in Jewish homes and those living in Christian homes: (1) The nativities of Moses and Jesus. (2) Any narrative centering on a child, especially when the child is seen outwitting an adult. "The Christ Child in the Temple" is the supreme such story. The story of David, *le petit* of the traditional folk tale, the youngest son who performs feats of bravery and is chosen while older brothers are passed over, is also popular. (3) Baby Moses in the bullrushes resembles the foundling-hero of a Grimm Brothers tale, while Joseph is another persecuted, though arrogant, child who makes good, becoming the Horatio Alger-style hero in ancient Egypt. Children also enjoy the Gospel episode in which Jesus blesses little children and reprimands the adults who try to ignore them. (4) Any story concerned significantly, or even peripherally, with an animal: the ass of Balaam, the sheep of David, the animals attending the nativity, and so on. (5) Stories of exciting adventure: Moses's audiences with Pharaoh, Esther's perilous exploit in the ancient Persian court, the fall of Jericho, Jonah's journey in the belly of the whale, the Flood. (6) Descriptions of flamboyant personalities, such as Samson or Goliath (who may occasionally be more admired by children than David who slays him, though generally the appeal of the tale is that of seeing a bully get his comeuppance at the hands of a lad). Children also identify with small Zaccheus, like the sound of his name, and are amused by the vision of a grown man, however small, climbing a sycamore tree to see Jesus. (7) Sketches of lovable personalities and their noble deeds; Jesus, Moses, Samuel, David, Ruth, and Peter are high on the list.

Just as there are many Bible stories that children, the world's great ritualists, ask to hear over and over again, there are other Bible subjects that have been largely ignored, at least since the 1930s. Children are rarely introduced to the Apocalypse (Revelation), the life and letters of Paul, or the full epic of Joshua. The book of Joshua has been dismissed as too bloody for the nursery, presenting too many problems in "justifying the ways of God" to the human young. The epistles of Paul have often been discarded as too intellectual and too theological to be very clear or of much interest to young people. Paul, while the favorite of churchmen and theologians, has in fact never been a very prominent figure in popular piety and remains less familiar than Peter, who, with his obvious human failings, has appeared more approachable. Yet recent efforts have demonstrated that with a bit of imagination and narrative skill, the life and letters of Paul can be presented to older children as the adventure documents from the ancient world that indeed they are, providing, while relating the missionary journeys of the apostle, the opportunity to present a complex panorama of life in the rich national cultures of the first century. The Apocalypse, so long considered too bewildering and arcane for the young, has recently become a favorite of the youth drug culture and the secular survivalist movement, which does not add to its chances of penetrating the nursery.

The best books on the American juvenile market have increasingly demonstrated creative ways of presenting favorite tales from the scriptures. Children love animals, and juvenile books, based on both secular and sacred subject matter, are filled with them; frequently they are the idealized, romanticized, and anthropomorphic animals with whom young children are widely believed to identify. Noah's enormous menagerie has long inspired authors and illustrators of children's books, most of whom have relied on the richness of secular traditions that have grown up around the story as well as on the humor and power of the Bible narrative itself. The Duvoisin ark alphabet book and Lois Lenski's account of a miniature Mr. and Mrs. Noah's exploits are only two contemporary examples of the many attractive ways in which the story has been retold for children.

The first Noah's ark classic in American children's literature was the work of E. Boyd Smith, fondly remembered as one of the first master illustrators of juvenile books. He was born in St. John, New Brunswick, in 1860, was reared in Boston, and was educated in France. Issued by Houghton Mifflin in 1905, *The Story of Noah's Ark* was written and drawn with Boyd's already celebrated wit and style, remote from the sentimentality and stock piety then fashionable. The pictures, with their strong lines yet delicate colors, were reminiscent of the work of the great French juvenile illustrator, Boutet de Monvel, by whom Smith was doubtless influenced. This acclaimed "crossover volume" (a book that adults enjoy as much as children) presented a narrative of considerable humor and appropriate pathos, in some ways echoing medieval dramatizations of the tale. Noah is surrounded by ridicule when he starts his building project. One neighbor even demonstrates, with upturned hand, the impossibility of the sort of flood Noah predicts. The biblical phrasing of the text, solemn and cadenced, provides an inviting counterpoint to the liveliness of the pictures. Workers on the ark are always on the verge of striking for higher wages. When the bark is completed, dinosaurs try to climb aboard but are sadly left behind to become extinct, along with other lumbering mammoths and mastodons, who just do not move fast enough to reach the ark. Mrs. Noah protests the impossible domestic conditions on the craft, and everybody is stricken with the *mal de mer* when the flood finally begins.

Smith's career flourished, and he went on to illustrate remarkable scenes from American history and folklore. *The Story of Pocahontas and Captain John Smith*, his own nationalistic answer to Boutet de Monvel's classic *Jeanne d'Arc*, helped establish the iconography of the dark-complexioned national heroine, while other books glorified farm life and the railroads. But no other Boyd book achieved the distinction or height of artistry attained by *Noah's Ark*.

The Flood as a subject for children's stories maintains its undiminished popularity. Feminists, who have in recent years developed their own critical approach to juvenile literature, approvingly note that in the Noah's ark storybooks females appear with the same frequency as males and that all creatures survive the flood in monogamous pairs, even those that intend to live polygamously once they reach shore. This equal attention to the female is rare in juvenile books, and it seems to have taken biblical authority to achieve it here! (Stacey: 117).

Peter Spier, whose adaptation of the peerless old story won the Caldecott Award for 1978, is a famous Dutch-born American illustrator. His book employs as its text a classic Dutch poem by Jacobus Revius, and, as in Smith's earlier book, his spirited illustrations provide a contrast to the gravity of the text. The vivid and generous visual detail that has become Spier's signature greatly enhances his book. Noah is drawn as an earnest but temperamental patriarch, while his wife, constantly complaining and even fearful of the mice that come into the ark two by two, is the traditional comic shrew made familiar by medieval dramas. Noah has trouble getting the stubborn donkey into the ark in the first place, yet he has to shoo extra birds away. Tigers are delivered already packaged in their cages. Forlorn extra animals are left behind, and the floods are seen slowly covering them, as the ark sails. Meanwhile, inside the ark Noah has a terrific task feeding all his animals, providing for the tastes of all, and preventing some animals from making meals of others. There is constant activity in these close, not very sanitary, quarters, where both humans and animals reveal their quirks. Yet Noah obviously loves his animals, makes them as comfortable as possible, and proudly gathers eggs from his hens. The great whales, whom the Lord so proudly created and will not lightly destroy, have a better time of it, being allowed to swim alongside the craft, and Noah even does a little fishing from the deck of his vessel. When the dove finally returns with the olive branch, the message that the floods have receded, Noah and his wife embrace with happiness. The animals also rejoice, dancing as they leave the ark, for they too have been restored to the good graces of their creator, who has made his new covenant with them as well as with humanity. The cat, however, having had kittens, is content to stay inside the ark in an empty abandoned basket. Noah plants his vineyard, with the majestic rainbow of the promise over him, while the empty ark rests at a tilt on the mountain in the background. Children are, however, spared the revelation of his subsequent drunkenness and disgrace.

Spier produced a delightful book, possibly a masterpiece, which, like Smith's earlier interpretation, celebrates the beauty, diversity, and whimsy of creation. A moral is clearly implied, though not preached. All these strange and amusing species on which God, a deity with an obvious sense of humor, lavished such love, remind the child that this creation should be cherished and preserved. All these creatures wise and wonderful, great and small, bright and beautiful glorify God by their existence upon the face of the earth and enrich human life.

Noah's animals are not the only biblical beasts to have given children hours of entertainment. Several books about animals have been designed chiefly to please and incidentally to generate interest in the Bible. Others have sought to provide significant and sometimes useful zoological information as well.

Dorothy P. Lathrop's *Animals of the Bible*, that first Caldecott Medal winner, remains a distinguished, beautiful, and available book today. It is still in print, and every self-respecting library owns at least one copy. The art-nouveau pictures, though in black and white, are among the most attractive to be found in any picture book, for young or old. Texts from the King James Version of the Bible, generally brief, accompany the illustrations of animal faces, which are expressive, lively, and tenderly individualized. Most of the important Bible animals appear, from the lowly scapegoat driven into the wilderness and the hen who gathers her chicks under her wing, to the majestic lion which lies down with the lamb. The colt ridden by Jesus on Palm Sunday is strongly rendered, though the human figure astride is less impressively drawn. Dorothy P. Lathrop obviously was more charmed by animals than by people, even than by Jesus himself. What line from all the Bible, or any other literature, is more moving in its simplicity than the one that begins Psalm 42: "As the hart panteth after the water brooks, so panteth my soul after thee, O God!" That thirsty hart is sketched with delicate grace.

Living Animals of the Bible, written and drawn by Walter W. Ferguson, lacks the subtlety and poetry of the Lathrop book but is a more informative factual treatment of the subject. Illustrated profusely and attractively in full color, the Ferguson book provides an abundance of information about the animals of scripture. Hebrew, Latin, and English words for each animal are given, along with the Bible texts in which the animal is mentioned. The habits of each creature in the ancient Mediterranean world are then described. The book provides many hours of entertainment and instruction and is less a Bible storybook than a work of natural science, though it is produced with an artistry not evident in the usual science text or trade book. The author, originally a New Yorker, was well qualified for his task, having lived for many years in Israel, the scene of his research.

The prolific Isaac Asimov, when he is not promulgating his Laws of Robotics, writing satires and science fiction stories, or annotating Shakespeare, has occasionally turned his attention to children and the Bible. His book *Animals of the Bible*, with pictures by Howard Berelson, will not supplant the earlier books but is readable and attractive. While the text is slight and the charming pictures dominate the volume, Asimov does provide facts from the Bible and from natural science about the major animals (even mythological ones, such as the unicorn) that are mentioned in scripture.

A reading of the daily newspapers would give the impression that the creation narratives are the most controversial part of the Bible as far as juvenile instruction is concerned. Children's storybooks have usually delighted in accounts of creation, and illustrators have found the subject a challenge to their skills as well as another opportunity to display an assortment of the splendid animals they always enjoy drawing. Though creation in contemporary children's books is usually presented as straight narrative, without theological embellishments, attempts to employ typology, or efforts to rationalize or reconcile creation with science, some inventive variations have made their appearance.

Sekiya Miyoski is the author-illustrator of *The Oldest Story in the World*, an imaginative rendition of Genesis first published in Japan in 1964 and adapted by Barbara L. Jensh for American children, recommended for grades one through three. The classically simple, almost Zenlike retelling of creation conveys a sense of primordial awe and mystery. The voice of God says to the waters, "Move apart," and they, of course, comply. Patterns and designs in strong colors—including whimsical birds and fish floating in primeval sea and sky—suggest the infinite fecundity of creation. Movement and drama are conveyed by swirling, almost abstract patterns, as Adam and Eve name the various creatures. A few years before this book was published it might (like the notorious and marvelous *Rabbit's Wedding* by Garth Williams) have caused serious controversy: Adam is African in appearance, while Eve is obviously a Japanese maiden, and they are both unclothed children. Today the racial variety—and even the nudity—seem fitting and innocent.

Lisl Weil's *The Very First Story Ever Told* presents another variation, not without charm, which is a clear departure from the message
and tone of the original biblical narrative. Adam and Eve are Rousseauistic children, romping naked in Paradise, riding camels and whales, and
having a fine time playing all day with dancing bears and kangaroos. In
this retelling of "The Fall," which appears to eliminate both the anti-
feminism and the sentimentality frequently found in adaptations of the
narrative, even God's anger is softened. After breaking their promise to
the Good Lord, Adam and Eve realize that they have been naughty.
They leave the Garden with sheepish, downcast eyes, followed by their
faithful dog. They are obliged to fashion a tent for shelter and must even
eat spinach! Weil's "mock primitivistic" illustrations are in perfect harmony with her narration. Paradise is indeed the land of childhood
desire, where the lion and the lamb lie down together, and the child can
happily play in the viper's nest. Yet instead of the tragedy of the loss of
Paradise, the Fall becomes a parable of a child's maturing and assuming
responsibility for his own well-being. Weil has written and drawn an
entertaining, whimsical tale in its own right—with a very contemporary
message—though this is hardly the Bible story.

Bible Narratives in a Pluralistic Society

The recent creation and animal storybooks are almost equally
suited—or unsuited—to Jewish and Christian children. Yet there are
several concerns in our present pluralistic society that the publishing
industry, especially children's trade book publishers, must keep in
mind./4/ In a book designed to reach both the churched and secular
juvenile markets, terminology is important. "Christ," the confessional
term, is sometimes best avoided in favor of "Jesus" or "Jesus of Nazareth"
when reference is made to the founder of Christianity. Sometimes an
author, along with an illustrator, can avoid controversy and produce a
book about the child Jesus that totally avoids offense to either pious or
secular sensibilities. Since people rarely expect complex theological statements in children's books, it is often possible to write a straightforward
description of the life of a boy growing up in ancient Nazareth.

Other terms too must be used with care. "Old Testament" and "New
Testament" are the most commonly understood designations for the divisions that make up the Christian Bible, though "Hebrew Bible" and
"Greek Bible" may be more polite terms in the pluralistic context, confusing as they can be to children. The use of "B.C.," "A.D.," or "C.E.," and
"B.C.E." in dating can also cause offense, in the case of the former, or
confusion, with the latter. Words such as "myth" and "legend" must be

used with special care in books addressed to a broad public, since one person's myth may be regarded as another's history, and while the authors of books may have a Platonic or specialized literary understanding of such terms, the typical parents are not likely to be pleased when they see a cherished dogma referred to as "myth." To their minds a myth means a fantastic story that no rational person can believe. Designations such as "Jew," "Hebrew," "Israelite," and "Israeli" should also be used precisely, in view of historical accuracy, descriptive efficiency, and the possibility of confusion on the part of the child.

Librarians in public schools and community libraries often find it safest to purchase books of stories from the "Old Testament" since these may be common heritage for a larger number of children than narratives from the Gospels. Reviewers for *School Library Journal* and other significant publications addressed to teachers and librarians are very alert to these considerations. The Old Testament, many storytellers point out, is also the more literary of the divisions of the Bible, providing richer materials for children's story sessions.

Although Christians traditionally—and almost all Christian artists of the past—have read the "Old Testament" in light of the "New Testament" and found it filled with images, prophecies, and omens of the advent of Jesus, it is remembered by American publishers who address a wide audience that the Jewish people find their Bible quite complete and view Christian typology as strained at best, ludicrous at worst. Critical approaches to the Bible today, in this literalistic age, avoid typology for its ambiguity as well. Children's books well into the early twentieth century sometimes matter-of-factly employed the typological approach, but it is almost never found today, even in Bible stories designed specifically for specialized denominational audiences. The loss of the ability to enjoy literature allegorically or anagogically is a cultural impoverishment, one must concede, whatever the disappearance of the earlier approach may represent theologically or may contribute to the cause of Jewish–Christian rapprochement.

A further area of great potential offense is in the portrayal of the personality of the founder of Christianity. Christmas books are still probably the most popular in the juvenile market, and the infant Jesus figures prominently. A number of more recent books have thoughtfully attempted to describe what the childhood of Jesus must surely have been like as he grew up in ancient Nazareth. The best of these books, careful to show that Jesus and his family were practicing Jews, have presented Jesus as a significant historical figure within the Jewish tradition as well as the founder of Christianity. The Jewishness of the child Jesus, once largely ignored, has rightfully been acknowledged in most of these newer books, which are more historically accurate than ever before and reveal a strong sense of social responsibility on the part of authors and illustrators alike. Some of the artists who wrote and illustrated these books even traveled to the Holy Land, making detailed sketches of the cities and towns in which Jesus lived and conducted his ministry. Yet hastily assembled books still appear that, even while professing piety, show an unattractive, effeminate portrait of Jesus, quite at variance with the Gospels. William Blake and John Wesley, gifted though they were, probably deserve equal reproof for not resisting the temptation to rhyme "meek and mild" with references to he who "became a little child," but inferior art and sentimental piety have perpetuated this offensive image. The better books are replacing the stilted pious image with a more virile, intellectually curious Jesus. Books written for both secular and religious audiences seem to have been making the effort to present a truly attractive historical personality rather than the Little Lord Fauntleroy Savior inherited from Victorian sentimental religiosity./5/

Problems of Bible storytelling, especially in a religiously pluralistic society, are considerable. Difficulties presented to children include the often archaic language of favorite versions of the Bible, references to obscure and ancient customs, which must be explained, the recounting of violent acts, bloodletting, treachery, and the curious battle decrees of the deity reported in the Bible.

Bible Storytelling Techniques

Since the Bible is the most revered as well as most problematic book in Western society, many people, both religious and secular, have strong feelings about the way it should be presented to susceptible children. When should the Bible be allowed to speak for itself, and when is a paraphrase in order? What should be demanded of the storyteller, whose narratives derive from the text? Some bookmakers have discovered that the best policy is to let the Bible indeed speak for itself, in carefully selected and generally short passages. Dorothy P. Lathrop's *Animals of the Bible*, as previously observed, uses appropriate Bible texts, without commentary, as captions for the artist's illustrations. The King James Version was chosen for its overwhelming popularity, influence, and literary beauty. *Small Rain*, the appealing 1943 book of Jessie and Elizabeth Orton Jones, chooses brief passages of poetry from many sections of the Bible and illustrates them with contemporary childhood scenes. Ahead of their time, the Jones women drew, even in the forties, children of all races playing happily together. One little girl wearing glasses appears recurrently, giving a pleasing touch of realism to an otherwise idealized book. No words are added to the Bible passages; the visual commentary alone is sufficient for this book, which has been available for almost forty years, to present the poetry of sacred scripture.

The ancient art of storytelling has been experiencing renewed popularity during the last two decades, and even oral storytelling is increasingly recognized as a professional activity to be practiced in libraries, schools, and churches. Bible storytelling presents unique problems, but skilled practitioners and at least one true master of the art have emerged in recent years.

Even while they watch their language and choose their stories judiciously, what principles should guide Bible storytellers? The narrators must be lively, honest, and respectful of the material and the audience. A Bible episode cannot rely on pious appeal alone for its acceptance but must be a good story in its own right, well told. Of necessity, children may have developed a greater tolerance than adults for the didactic and the sentimental, to which they are so often exposed, but they do not really like sermons. They prefer to reach their own conclusions at the end of stories, with a bit of guidance at most.

The story should not be distorted; these Bible tales have survived because they have archetypal power and their own internal integrity, and they should not be lightly violated. They generally need not be "improved upon" either. In fact, any such attempt may be fatal. Care should be taken with interpretations. It is often best to permit the stories to make their own points, though it is useful and interesting if the storyteller can supply historical detail and explanations of references to obscure objects and habits. Sometimes children want to know why a particular story has enjoyed its special position in tradition. It may be helpful, for example, to inform children that the story of Esther traditionally explains the holiday of Purim. Gentile children may also enjoy learning how Purim is celebrated by their Jewish classmates.

The violence that is an inseparable part of a number of Bible stories should not be thoughtlessly expurgated. Children know the ferocious fairy tales of Charles Perrault and the Brothers Grimm, they often watch the evening news, and they cannot and probably should not be protected from a knowledge of the reality of violence in the world. It may be, as certain child psychologists, particularly Bruno Bettelheim, have suggested, that violence in children's stories serves a necessary therapeutic function, acts as a safety valve for aggressive feelings, and helps prepare for eventual adult life with its tensions and responsibilities.

While it is possible to colloquialize successfully, it is generally best to avoid a complete translation of these ancient stories into prosaic vernacular. Humor, when it does not belittle but shows admiration for the truth, beauty, and wit of the original story, is not out of order. In fact, the humor of the Bible, inherent in many of the stories especially loved by children, is all too often neglected rather than stressed.

Fortunately a recognized master of the storyteller's art has on occasion turned his attention to Bible narration for children. Isaac Bashevis Singer, a practitioner of the vanishing art of Yiddish storytelling, comes to his task with an international reputation as man of letters and the prestige of a Nobel Prize. In public statements Singer has repeatedly acknowledged his respect for the child as audience, suggesting, not totally with tongue in cheek, that the children's author has to be more skilled than the one who writes for adults, because children will not tolerate the fetishes and fads, the pornography and pessimism, which often pass for literature on the adult market.

An example of Bible narration at its best and the art of the true Yiddish storyteller is *The Wicked City*, which Singer published in 1972. In choosing to tell of the destruction of the ancient city of Sodom, the symbol still of unspeakable wickedness and a subject largely ignored in contemporary children's Bible storybooks, Singer demonstrated his originality. His remarkably vivid narrative should ideally be read aloud with a Yiddish accent; it is basically a told story committed to writing, and all the better for this, since children's books are as often as not read aloud. The charm and humor of Singer's style are evident from the beginning. Without violating the integrity of the biblical narrative or distorting its theme, Singer designs a series of embellishments. Like the tales of Charles Perrault, *The Wicked City* is sprinkled with double-entendre to be savored by the adults who are probably going to be reading the story to children. Several instances of special wit are noticeable; there is, for example, Singer's description of the most unkosher feast the Lot family prepares for their visiting relative, Abraham. They serve him "all the finest delicacies of Sodom," including a kid stewed in its mother's milk and other abominations to the Jews. The reader is informed that Lot is a lawyer by profession, and he has become very popular with the wicked Sodomites, who are always in trouble with the law. He and his family have adapted all too easily to the sinful pleasures of this City of the Plain, and it is with great reluctance that they are persuaded to leave their prosperous and "liberated" life there. Lot's wife cannot wrench herself away, but fatally looks back, and even the daughters carry away with them from the city the depraved philosophies they have acquired there. Whatever its deeper implications, Singer's redolent narrative is primarily the tale of a great disaster that justly befell a wicked city and of the few who were permitted to escape. Despite his humor, he has managed to convey the keen sense of unspeakable evil.

Illustrations are as important as texts to children, who often "read" pictures, and the visual beauty of juvenile books is one reason so many adults take secret pleasure in them, becoming closet collectors. Many remember nostalgically their fascination with a grandmother's illustrated Bible, where, along with the family records of births, marriages, and deaths, could be found pictures of Solomon preparing to chop the baby in half, David slaying a lion, Samson toppling the temple at Gaza, and Jesus driving the moneychangers from the Temple and again jumping skyward at his Ascension.

Illustrations designed for children differ in some significant ways from those in which adults delight. A richly detailed picture, justly admired by an adult, may appear too cluttered, too busy for the young child. It is generally acknowledged that the child's eye does not fully mature until about the age of seven. The rather simplistic drawings that children themselves make are not due solely to the limitations of technique; they really tend to see many objects similarly to the way they strive to draw them. Nevertheless, it should not be assumed that a great work of biblical art, an El Greco or a Rembrandt, will not necessarily be suitable for use in a child's book. Maturing children should not be deprived of the treasures of Western religious art, and it is not inappropriate to use them as illustrations in storybooks designed for older children.

Bible illustrations in juvenile books should be examples of attractive visual art, never careless expressions of ready-made, sentimental piety. The pictures should avoid grossly falsifying the historical period depicted. Even if the greatest of artists have almost always painted biblical personalities and settings anachronistically, in the detail of their own times, there is no point in unnecessarily cluttering the child's retentive mind with misinformation.

Fortunately some readily available Bible story collections have been provided with exceptionally appealing art work. The illustrations of *The Taizé Picture Bible*, with their lively colors and "enlightened primitivism," are the work of Brother Eric de Saussure of the Protestant Taizé monastic community in France. Other fine examples include the Brian Wildsmith and Janusz Grabianski illustrations for the Philip Turner and Norman Vincent Peale Bible story collections respectively. Though de Saussure, Wildsmith, and Gabrianski are European-born, their work is widely distributed in the United States. Turner, a British churchman, is a fine storyteller, and Peale's narratives, though less interesting than the Grabianski paintings accompanying them, are not the embarrassments his adult writings might lead one to fear.

Present Trends in Bible Storytelling

What can be expected of juvenile Bible storybooks in the near future? From a survey of the most recent volumes of leading publishers, a number of trends emerge. Women of the Bible are receiving more attention than ever before from both commercial publishers and the denominational presses, no doubt in response to pressures and complaints of the women's movement as well as the new awareness of the interests and needs of women within the churches. It is not surprising that the books from the more conservative religious presses still glorify the traditional roles of women, but others are more assertive. Little attention has as yet been given the stories of Judith and Susannah from the Apocrypha, though these rousing, entertaining narratives would seem especially to lend themselves to feminist messages, even if they may not be acknowledged by all as fully "biblical." Despite the distaste of Martin Luther, who labeled it "pagan depravity," the story of Esther has always been a favorite with children, who enjoy the "Never Never Land" milieu, the dramatic irony, and the last-minute reprieves of the tale. Today in the retelling, Vashti, the pagan queen who refused to expose herself to the leers of a drunken court, is admired almost as much as Esther, who saved the Jews. Jewish feminists have made certain Vashti receives her due, and today they sometimes honor her along with Esther when they celebrate the feast of Purim. The importance of the story to this holiday is certainly one reason for its popularity, though its narrative power is even more significant than its usefulness as a subject for holiday books. *The Story of Esther* by Ruth F. Brin, amusingly illustrated by H. Hechtkopf, is an especially engaging contemporary presentation of Esther's adventure, narrated in fairy-tale style and supplied with humorous visual embellishments, showing a clever woman gaining control of a silly king. Though this book was an Israeli import, its appeal on the American market makes it worthy of discussion.

An example of a religious denominational response to the demand for more attention to biblical women is an interesting and pleasant two-volume work, written, published, and sold by the Daughters of St. Paul, with Botticelli-style illustrations by Gregori. Volume one, *Women of the Bible*, surveys the women, virtuous and otherwise, of the Old Testament. The matriarchs of Israel, Miriam, Deborah, Ruth, and many others are commended for their devotion to God and duty, but it is curious that although Esther, Potiphar's wife, and Delilah are featured, Jezebel, the arch-bitch of the Bible and a great favorite with children, is missing, along with the intriguing and mysterious ancestress of Jesus Christ, Rahab, possibly because her profession would require too much explanation.

Volume two, *Women of the Gospel,* somewhat more enthusiastically surveys the New Testament women, both named and unnamed, centering, without surprise, on Mary the Mother of Jesus. The stories all lead to clear moral conclusions, and the series ends with the statement on "Woman's Sublime Mission" that was issued by Vatican II.

Tales from the Apocrypha, which would seem to offer such rich resources for children's storytellers, seem to have been largely neglected in recent years, with the exception of the Maccabean narratives, designed and marketed chiefly for Jewish holidays. The Apocrypha, which should be important at least to Roman Catholic children, is neglected by publishers in their efforts to reach the broadest American juvenile market. The tendency today is to avoid matters on which there is divisive opinion, even though there are many writers and artists who would enjoy exploring this neglected territory. The Chanukah books, which are the exceptions, deserve circulation beyond the Jewish juvenile audiences that now form their readership. Howard Greenfeld's retelling of the Maccabean story, in a book tastefully designed by Bea Feitler, can rarely be found outside Jewish libraries, and this is not solely because the illustrations are so restrained and are limited to emblematic motifs from established Jewish noniconographic traditions.

A notable exception to the general tendency to obscure the life and career of Paul for the juvenile market is *Paul and the World's Most Famous Letters*, the work of the well-known British theological thinker, Rosemary Haughton. Designed for ages ten and up, this sound work of responsible scholarship has hardly been a best seller. Though its dull photographic reproductions and somewhat patronizing narrative style (even the "cute" title) make it less than the ideal Pauline introduction, the book represents a serious effort by a significant writer to communicate important information to the young.

For the last half century Bible storybooks have been attempting, on the whole, to be more instructional and less devotional. Their narratives are more carefully placed within their historical settings and social contexts. Before publishing their now classic nativity book, Maud and Mishka Petersham, whose work dominated high-style children's books during the 1930s, made a trip to the Holy Land so that their locales, pastoral and idealistic though they turned out to be, nevertheless were authentic in detail. Other illustrator-writers have followed the lead of the Petershams. More scholarship and pride of craft than ever before are going into the making of children's Bible stories. Books about Moses' youth often suggest some of the splendor of ancient Egyptian society. When illustrators draw the child Jesus, he is now frequently shown wearing the ceremonial religious attire of a young Jew, and information about Jewish life in the first century is generously provided in the text of these books. Rosemary Haughton's book is an example of the extent of the research than now goes into many books designed for older children. But even in books for younger children, accuracy of detail is increasingly evident. Beverly Brodsky's picture book of Jonah, with her highly original and imaginative illustrations, demonstrates her knowledge of art styles and motifs of the ancient Near East. This expertise has certainly produced a major crossover book, equally suited to the nursery or the living room coffee table, not to mention both the art and juvenile stacks in the library.

There is also increased attention now being given to juvenile books of poetry and prayers, even while Bible storybooks in general become less devotional. *The Golden Treasury of Prayers for Boys and Girls*, selected by Esther Wilkin and illustrated by Eloise Wilkin, is still one of the outstanding bargains on the juvenile market, despite inflation. Not all the Golden Books, the inexpensive, mass-marketed series of which this is a part, are equal in quality; individual volumes are in fact frequently inferior items, yet the Wilkin collection can take its place beside Caldecott classics and other outstanding books on the nursery shelf. Brief selections from biblical poetry—from Daniel, Proverbs, Deuteronomy—are included beside texts from the Talmud, the Qur'an, and an assortment of interesting prayers and religious poems from many lands. The well-conceived illustrations reveal children of different religious traditions from around the world at prayer and with their families.

Children's prayer and service books are also occasionally published. Rabbi Abraham Klausner's *A Child's Prayer Book for the Holidays of Rosh Hashanah and Yom Kippur*, with the paintings of Shraga Weil and Nachum Gutman, is an adaptation for children of the Reformed Jewish liturgy, with its scriptures and Bible narratives. Though few children unassisted would find it engrossing, it is an attractive, dignified volume. Up to this point other juvenile liturgies have been, on the whole, gimmicky and unimpressive, but a substantial number are being published each year.

Another trend beginning to be discerned is the Bible storybook that is illustrated by children themselves. Professional reviewers greatly admire these books, though one suspects the volumes may find their way more frequently to adult coffee tables than to bookshelves in children's bedrooms. Probably influenced by the magnificent Israeli Expo exhibit of drawings of Jerusalem by children from around the world (an exhibit that toured the United States in the late seventies), Madeleine l'Engle, a Newbery Award winner/6/ and *grande dame* of juvenile letters, who has her office in New York's Cathedral of St. John the Divine, has published *Ladder of Angels*, a collection of Bible stories graced with sixty-five full-color illustrations by children of many nationalities. The book is advertised, not inaccurately, as a combination of "images only a child could visualize with the evocative meditations of a spiritually mature writer." The paintings were selected for inclusion after having been submitted in an international contest held in Jerusalem, under the sponsorship of Mayor Teddy Kollek. From the creation, in which God's two hands reach down from the clouds, bestowing upon the earth camels, giraffes, sea horses, and all manner of marvelous beasts—the work of eleven-year-old Gero Bennins of Münster, West Germany—to Nehemiah's arrival in Jerusalem—an anachronistic but imaginative interpretation by another West German, Isemhild Kuseten, age ten—major episodes from the Old Testament are simply narrated in an unusual book appropriate for both Jewish and Christian homes.

Juvenile books usually take about seven years before they begin to echo the theological and devotional preoccupations current in adult literature. A final trend that will probably be more evident in the juvenile field within the next few years is the transposing of characters and situations of Bible stories into modern times and places. Not too many such books have appeared yet, probably because publishers know their market; literalists that they are, all but the most sophisticated children tend to be confused by such literary and visual conceits. But one example is so outstanding that it deserves attention. William Kurelek is generally regarded as one of Canada's most illustrious artists. Fortunately for children, he has on several occasions designed books primarily for them, though these books have always become crossover objects delighting persons of all ages. Remembering how the great Renaissance painters, who were also illustrators of the Bible, had transplanted the Nativity to their native Tuscan countryside, Kurelek decided to explore images of Madonna and Child in the ethnically diverse, rich mosaic of Canadian society. The book that resulted, A Northern Nativity, is also the testament of a personal pilgrimage. A few years ago Kurelek, in a state of depression, traveled to Mexico and later to England, where he suffered an emotional breakdown and subsequently underwent a religious conversion that gave him new vitality and strength to continue his life and pursue his art. Upon his return home to Canada, Kurelek made this extraordinary collection of paintings. Subtitling his book Christmas Dreams of a Prairie Boy, he supplied a text of poetic prose to accompany his outstanding art work.

Throughout Canada, territorially the second largest nation in the world, Kurelek discovers and paints again and again the Christ Child and the radiant maternal face of the Madonna in diverse scenes: in an Eskimo igloo; in a cow shed near a field where Canadian cowboys are rounding up their beef cattle; in a deserted train boxcar; in the shack of an Indian family; in the stalled car a truckdriver befriends; in a mountain chateau; in a prairie farm cottage; in a forest across the river from Ottawa with the towers of the Houses of Parliament in the background; in a grain elevator; in a crowd at Niagara Falls; in the Salvation Army shelter of a city resembling Toronto, where a black family is being fed; in a horse buggy owned by Old Order Mennonites; and finally in the manger of a lumber camp stable. All over the bleak land of snow-covered winter Canada the light of Christ shines and the joy of his nativity is experienced.

Not all the successful new books are such coffee-table treasures of the printer's art. Children's books that bring together large collections of Bible stories, generally from both Testaments, are still much in demand. These books, usually less experimental than the volumes representing the trends, are highly regarded as substantial publications that provide hours of pleasure. In inflationary times, they are regarded as especially good purchases, while the single Bible story books, no matter how splendidly illustrated, sell for ten dollars or more today and often appear to be less than bargains.

The Wildsmith-Turner, Grabianski-Peale, and Taizé collections are found in most well-stocked public and school libraries. A more recent large collection, *Bible Stories for Children*, was solemnly offered by its publisher in 1980 as "one of the most important books Macmillan has ever published." It contains narratives by Geoffrey Horn and Arthur Cavanaugh and graceful, vividly colored, though conservative, illustrations by Arvis Stewart. An editorial board representing America's three largest religious groups—Jews, Catholics, and Protestants—carefully reviewed the material and presumably found it inoffensive. In these stories the biblical epic again unfolds from creation through the Ascension, though there is no mention of the Apocalypse or the founding of the primitive churches by the apostles. While the anthology is a welcome addition to the shelf of Bible storybooks, it does lack the distinctiveness of the Taizé and Wildsmith-Turner collections. The wisdom of using an editorial board of ministers of different denominations, apparently with censorship powers, is also questionable. This is, of course, the procedure that was earlier established in a string of bland radio, television, and film productions based on the Bible and designed primarily for adults.

It is perhaps fitting to conclude this survey-analysis by mentioning a very different contemporary retelling of selected Bible stories. *In the Beginning, A New Interpretation of the Old Testament* by Shirley Van Eyssen was issued as a "Here-and-There Book" in 1970 by Harlin Quist, publisher of a series of peculiar and visually innovative books designed, according to one critic, for children "of refined and somewhat decadent tastes." The dust jacket promises—and warns—that "here is an interpretation of the Old Testament which, while respecting the literature of the

Bible, avoids characterizing God as an avenging deity. Instead, the book echoes the sentiments of a familiar hymn: God is Love, God is Truth, God is Beauty." Though these words seem to threaten a bowdlerized, Pealeistic adaptation of the least problematic Bible stories, the narratives turn out to be courageously selected and retold with responsibility, authority, and liveliness. God comes through as a deity a child—or an adult—can not only understand but also sympathize with in his righteous indignation, his frequently unrequited love for his people, and his long-suffering patience with mischievous humanity. God is appropriately the central character of these selections from the Hebrew Bible, just as he is the central character of the Bible itself.

The concluding story in this book is a meaningful version of another old favorite, the tale of Jonah and his adventure in the monster's belly. The angry prophet, after his deliverance (the point at which many juvenile accounts, lamentably, leave off), is seen pouting under a withering vine, complaining that his dire prophecy against the Assyrians and their city of Nineveh has not been fulfilled, thus depriving him of his prophetic credibility. The Lord, who can never be trusted properly to execute his threatened vengeance, has heard the contrite prayers of the people and beasts of Nineveh and has spared them. More interested in his prophetic reputation than the salvation of Nineveh's inhabitants, Jonah continues to pout. But God has the last word in the narrative—and in this extraordinary book—a message in harmony with the Bible itself and important to the American child today and the spirit with which Bible stories are best told:

> You regret the loss of the vine, which I, in mercy, created for your survival. Yet you would have this great city destroyed, which was built by the toil of thousands. You say that Nineveh and its inhabitants must be shown no mercy, but you, Jonah, were glad indeed to receive My forgiveness. Know now, as all men shall one day discover, that God's mercy shall not be confined only to one man, but to all men of the earth.
> For God is Love, and Love belongs to the whole of humanity, if they will only stretch out their arms to receive it. (64)

In this manner, the book, further graced with some of the most tantalizingly dramatic illustrations in the entire range of juvenile literature, ends with a statement of the great overriding message of the Jewish and Christian scriptures.

Final Observations

In conclusion, it is hoped that this discussion has indicated some of the reasons why Bible stories can be as important to children today as they were in earlier periods of North American history, when their study was regarded more as a duty than as pleasure. Today books are more attractive, better edited, and more dazzlingly illustrated than ever before. Children's literature is one area of popular culture where the finest craft and highest artistic integrity are in evidence. These books are made for Jewish, Eastern Orthodox, Roman Catholic, Protestant, and secular children, and, whenever possible, publishers like to supply the same book to all these groups. Contemporary books not only attempt to present lively Bible narratives; they also try to promote racial harmony, ecology, kindness to animals, nonsexism, and other ethical messages as well. They are striving more and more to demonstrate the brotherhood and common religious aspirations of Jew and Christian. A large number of these publications also try to provide factual information about the ancient world and its civilizations. Some subjects and characters, as always, continue to be favorites of children and are neglected by Bible storytellers at their peril. Yet attempts are also made to broaden the child's knowledge and understanding of scriptural tradition by presenting more complicated and less familiar stories, poems, epistles, chronicles, and prophecies. Finally, it is not inappropriate to observe that the two great figures of the Bible and the Jewish and Christian religions—Moses and Jesus—are, as shown in their infancies and ministries, the lasting favorites of North American children.

NOTES

/1/   Although several editions of *Child's Bible Reader* were examined, comments are based on the edition cited.

/2/   Joseph has, of course, been rather badly treated in popular piety, folklore, and art. Generally he appears as a slow-moving, balding man, much older than his family.

/3/   This book not only acknowledged no author; it also dispensed with pagination.

/4/   Anyone who develops Bible books and materials to be presented to children in America's pluralistic society must become acquainted with the brilliant work of Thayer S. Warshaw, a former high school instructor of classics who pioneered the teaching of Bible literature in the public schools. For several years Professor Warshaw was associate director of the Indiana University Institute on Teaching the Bible in Secondary Education. My own debt to him is so great that I tend to forget where his ideas end and my own begin.

/5/   Some recommended books would include: Claire Huchet Bishop, *Yesha, Called Jesus* (New York: Farrar, Straus and Giroux, 1966), illustrated by Donald Bolognese; Norman Kotker, *The Holy Land in the Time of Jesus* (New York: Harper and Row, 1967); and Florence M. Taylor, *A Boy Once Lived in Nazareth* (New York: Henry Z. Walck, 1969), illustrated by Len Ebert.

/6/   The Newbery Award, given by the American Library Association, is the most prestigious prize in American juvenile literature. It is awarded annually to the author of the book judged to be the best of the previous year.

WORKS CONSULTED

Asimov, Isaac
1978   *Animals of the Bible*. Garden City: Doubleday.

Bettelheim, Bruno
1976   *The Uses of Enchantment: Meaning and Importance in Fairy Tales*. New York: Knopf.

Brin, Ruth F.
1976   *The Story of Esther*. Minneapolis: Lerner Publications.

Brodsky, Beverly
1977   *Jonah: An Old Testament Story*. New York: J. B. Lippincott.

Daughters of St. Paul
1970   *Women of the Bible: The Old Testament*. Boston: Daughters of St. Paul.
1975   *Women of the Gospel*. Boston: Daughters of St. Paul.

Duvoisin, Roger
1968   *A for the Ark*. New York: Lathrop, Lee and Shepard.

Eyssen, Shirley Van
1970   *In the Beginning: A New Interpretation of the Old Testament*. New York: Harlin Quist.

Ferguson, Walter W.
n.d.   *Living Animals of the Bible*. New York: Charles Scribner's Sons.

Greenfeld, Howard
1976   *Chanukah*. New York: Holt, Rinehart and Winston.

Haughton, Rosemary
1970   *Paul and the World's Most Famous Letters*. Nashville: Abingdon.

Horn, Geoffrey, and Arthur Cavanaugh
1980   *Bible Stories for Children*. New York: Macmillan.

Hudson, Virginia Cary
1964   *O Ye Jigs and Juleps!* New York: MacFadden Books.

Jones, Jessie Orton
1971   *Small Rain*. New York: Viking Press.

Klausner, Abraham J.
1974   *A Child's Prayer Book for the Holidays of Rosh Hashanah and Yom Kippur*. Yonkers, NY: Emanu-El Publications.

Kurelek, William
1976   *A Northern Nativity: Christmas Dreams of a Prairie Boy*. Montreal: Tundra Books.

Lathrop, Dorothy P.
1937   *Animals of the Bible*. Philadelphia: J. B. Lippincott.

L'Engle, Madeleine
1979   *Ladder of Angels*. New York: Seabury.

Lenski, Lois
1948   *Mr. and Mrs. Noah*. New York: Crowell.

Miyoski, Sekiya
1969   *The Oldest Story in the World*. Valley Forge, PA: Judson Press.

Peale, Norman Vincent, and Janusz Grabianski
1973   *Bible Stories*. New York: Franklin Watts.

Petersham, Maud, and Miska Petersham
1931   *The Christ Child*. Garden City: Doubleday.

de Saussure, Brother Eric, artist
1973   *The Taizé Picture Bible*. Philadelphia: Fortress.

Singer, Isaac Bashevis
1972   *The Wicked City*. New York: Farrar, Straus and Giroux.

Smith, E. Boyd
1905   *The Story of Noah's Ark*. Boston: Houghton Mifflin.

Spier, Peter
1977   *Noah's Ark*. Garden City: Doubleday.

Stacey, Judith, Susan Béreaud, and Joan Daniels, eds.
1974   *Sexism in American Education*. New York: Dell.

Turner, Philip, and Brian Wildsmith
1968   *Brian Wildsmith's Illustrated Bible Stories*. New York: Franklin Watts.

Tyler, Moses Coit
1962   *History of American Literature 1607–1765*. New York: Crowell-Collier.

Weil, Lisl
1976   *The Very First Story Every Told*. New York: Atheneum.

Wilkin, Esther, ed.
1975   *The Golden Treasury of Prayers for Boys and Girls*. New York: Golden Press.

World Bible House
1902   *Pictures and Rhymes to Bring Little Ones to Happy Times: A Collection of Catchy Rhymes and Amusing Stories for Our Little Ones. The Whole Appropriately Illustrated with Original Juvenile Drawings*. Philadelphia: World Bible House.

Yonge, Charlotte M.
1898   *Child's Bible Reader*. Nashville: The Southwestern Company.

VIII

Popular American Biblical Imagery: Sources and Manifestations

Ljubica D. Popovich

The North American continent, despite its long-established reverence for the printed word, has in the last half of the twentieth century, as a result of its spectacular technological progress, developed a culture that is primarily "pop" and visual. The majority of Americans under age forty have grown to adulthood without acquiring strong writing or reading skills and without a personally transmitted oral tradition. The visual mass media—primarily television, but to a lesser extent illustrated magazines and pictographic advertising posters—have become the prime instruments for transmitting information. Products are sold through pictorial advertising, whether food items displayed in a supermarket, late model automobiles freshly placed in a dealer's lot, or the religious philosophy of a guru or popular evangelist who preaches on television. Television has left millions visually predisposed rather than verbally oriented. When little is left to the individual's visual imagination because the media provides all the images—anonymous, commercial, ready-made— the popular iconography of a culture merits attention not primarily as a study of individual achievement but as a source of sociological data./1/

Even the Holy Bible, it has been discovered, must be presented visually if it is to maintain a hold on the minds, hearts, and imaginations of North Americans. Visual renderings of events and personalities from scripture become as important in this day of presumed literacy as they were for illiterate persons of early Christian and medieval times, who acquired part of their religious indoctrination from icons and stained-glass windows.

American popular religious art is so diverse and multiform that it is initially somewhat difficult to differentiate from that of other nations. Many European artistic traditions of past and present have flowed into the stream of American religious art. The impressive visual traditions of Judaism, Eastern Orthodoxy, Roman Catholicism, Lutheranism, Anglicanism, and other forms of Protestantism have made their contribution.

The iconoclasm of Calvinism has had its impact. Even the cults and sects, which have so flourished in the United States, have had their influence, notably the Shakers, with spirit drawings, the Mormons, with depictions of their elaborate angelology, and groups of black Christians, with their paintings of ebony Madonnas and Afro-Christs. When Americans think of biblical characters or visualize in the mind's eye biblical scenes, they owe something to distant Byzantium, much to the Italian Renaissance masters and the Dutch painters, and probably even more to the nineteenth-century European romantic and academic tradition, with its fascination for exotic animals and desert hues.

Use of the Masters

Yet Americans have made definite selections from the wealth of religious art inherited from the ages. It is profitable to examine the identifiable roots of this popular religious art, beginning with the great masters. The work of Leonardo da Vinci (1452–1519) appears to be overwhelmingly the most important single source of American copying. *The Last Supper*, which Leonardo painted in 1495–98 on the refectory wall of the Dominican convent of Santa Maria delle Grazie in Milan, may have given the entire Western world since the nineteenth century its definitive vision of that central Gospel event. Not only is this scene reproduced today on every conceivable object—lamps, lamp shades, arm chair throws, crystal goblets, bread trays, cake molds, and crocheted table spreads/2/—but it has even been satirized in a scene from Robert Altman's film *MASH*. Several recent catalogues of commercial houses that sell primarily secular curios reveal mutations of Leonardo's masterpiece in plaques that glow in the dark, on three-dimensional postcards, and in groupings of bisque figurines. Probably more than any other interpretation of a biblical event, Leonardo's *Last Supper* has captured the popular imagination; gaudily tinted reproductions can be purchased at cathedral bookstores, in variety stores, and even in roadside souvenir stands throughout the Bible Belt. The image, first created for a Roman Catholic religious order in Renaissance Milan, seems today to be thoroughly ecumenical in its appeal.

The religious revival of the romantic period formed a bridge for the wide entry into American culture of this truly great image, which captured the public's fancy first in engravings and later in various colored prints and "restorations." By the first half of the twentieth century, it was appearing on funeral home fans, postcards, the covers of Sunday school quarterlies, and in almost every other conceivable place. While many more recent artists, including Salvador Dali (1904–), have interpreted this biblical scene,/3/ not one has even remotely challenged Leonardo as the definitive visualizer of the event, as far as the general public is concerned. So omnipresent has Leonardo's image become that even Greek Orthodox churches in the United States—Holy Trinity in Nashville, Tennessee, for example—have sometimes departed from their own rich Byzantine iconographic traditions to include close variants of this *Last Supper* above their main altar doors.

An especially popular rendition of the image is to be found in the Upper Room Chapel in Nashville. The Upper Room, a central shrine of international Methodism, is also the world headquarters of the devotional publication by the same name, an organ of the United Methodist Church. In the main prayer chapel, visited daily by busloads of tourists who come to see the wonders of "Music City, U.S.A.," a curious adaptation of *The Last Supper* can be viewed. This three-dimensional reproduction, carved in limewood and walnut, was completed in 1953, having been executed by eighteen artisans who worked fourteen months under the direction of the Italian artist Ernest Pelligrini./4/ The tableau was made in Italy, then transported in pieces and reassembled in the United States. The figures were first coated with gesso and then painted in pale colors in an obvious attempt to suggest the faded qualities of Leonardo's now damaged work, currently being rescued from total loss by modern Italian restoration methods.

While the carved *Last Supper* in the Upper Room is technically impressive—and tour guides in the chapel delight in describing the intricate care taken in the reproduction and transportation of the work to the United States—as frequently occurs in popular art that feeds upon the creative genius of a master of a previous age, originality and freshness of vision got lost somewhere in the process of copying, remarkable though the technical features of the copy are.

Almost as popular as Leonardo's *Last Supper* is Michelangelo Buonarroti's (1475–1564) marble sculpture *Moses* (1513–1515), today to be seen in its original glory in the Church of St. Peter in Chains in Rome. This masterpiece seems largely to have determined the way both Jews and Christians today popularly visualize the lawgiver. Figurine reproductions of the work, of varying quality and in media ranging from fine Italian marble to plastic, are widely available. The statue was even, according to filmland gossip, one basis for the selection of an actor to play Moses in Cecil B. De Mille's film *The Ten Commandments*. Certainly actor Charlton Heston did bear a striking resemblance to Michelangelo's creation, and the 1956 film in which he starred is still shown regularly on American television at Passover–Easter time.

In Europe a break with the artistic traditions represented by Leonardo and Michelangelo came with the Protestant Reformation in the sixteenth century and even with the Counter Reformation within Catholicism itself. Many of the Protestant groups resulting from the revolt against Roman Catholic domination manifested strong iconoclastic tendencies, listing among their complaints against the parent church its extravagance in commissioning works of art, which in their very excellence presented the temptation to idolatry. Eventually a more earthy and realistic way of viewing central biblical characters and events emerged, calculated more to instruct than to beguile, though it proved impossible for even radical Protestants to erase totally from their imaginations the imprinting from the powerful images created by the artists of the Renaissance.

Occasionally individual images produced even during the centuries of religious conflict continued to speak to Catholics and Protestants alike. One ecumenical image of tremendous impact and ever-increasing popularity is Albrecht Dürer's (1471–1528) *Praying Hands*. Originally a detail from a large altar piece, the hands have become far better known than the full work from which they are taken. Like Leonardo's *Last Supper*, the hands have appeared in many variations and interpretations. Today they are widely used on greeting cards and are etched on the covers of Bibles. The hands, possibly the most widely dispersed of all visual religious images in America, are painted against backgrounds of varying colors. Sometimes a ray of light falls upon the hands; sometimes they are shown hovering over a Bible or clasped upon the Bible. The same hands, still obviously based on Dürer's work, are sometimes rearranged and viewed from various angles. They may be silvery, ghostly hands, while at other times they may appear robust and even peasant-like. Sometimes they are darkened in hue, to enhance their appeal in black American homes. Once again the catalogues of the supply houses and even secular companies suggest a multitude of ways this image in its two- or three-dimensional renderings can express piety in a home or on a person. Again, there are lamps, wall plaques, and bisque figurines, some of which glow in the dark. There are also pendants to be worn around the neck, in gold, silver, or base metal, as well as T-shirts, and more.

The popularity of the *Praying Hands* can hardly be surprising, for the hand has a long history in sacred art, and its use is by no means limited to the Christian tradition. A student of folklore and world religions would observe that the hand holds a magical place in the lore of India, from which probably comes palmistry. The Hand of Fatima is widely worn throughout the Islamic world for luck, and Middle Eastern Jews have their own form of the outstretched palm, called the Hand of the Cohan (Priest)./5/

Nineteenth- and Early Twentieth-Century Influences

Apart from selected works of the old masters, the most important influences upon the way Americans visualize biblical characters and events come from the nineteenth century. Gustave Doré (1832–1883) was an Alsatian who achieved success in England and subsequently in the United States. Doré's work, the influence of which has been traced down to both Cecil B. De Mille and Walt Disney, could always be identified by the fertility of imagination, the flamboyant dramatic sense, and the baroque power it manifested. Doré's Babylonian scenes, for example, have stamped on the imaginations of several generations the horror and excitement of the captivity, as well as the doomed splendor of the city of the hanging gardens. His interplay of light and darkness helped him create the drama with which his drawing teems. Combining a classical fascination with the human body and a romantic preoccupation with landscape, setting, and exotic foliage, his illustrations were always busy, cluttered with people, views, and architecture of all types. Many popular illustrators both of his own day and the present share these stylistic characteristics.

Doré appears to have done more archaeological research than most popular illustrators of his time. His Egyptian architecture, for example, though used as much to enhance the dramatic effects of his compositions as to provide an authentic setting for Bible narratives, was considered to have been remarkably accurate. It is well known that Egyptology as a study was well advanced in France and had been important since the Napoleonic Wars in Egypt. Obviously Doré as an artist cleverly utilized the knowledge that the scholars of his country would have made available.

Even in his own day Doré, despite his large following, was criticized as sometimes too common, too melodramatic, even grotesque. The same is said today about much contemporary "pop" art; Doré, thus, appears as a sort of godfather or prototype for the artist with popular appeal. But the excitement his works generated is easy to explain though difficult to duplicate by illustrators of less skill. He was certainly vastly more talented and daring than most other popular illustrators of his own day or of the present. His vision was theatrical, even operatic, while his interpretations of character were larger than life. And he did not always follow traditional iconography in representing Bible scenes; he felt free to innovate according to his inclinations. He preferred to illustrate those climactic moments from both Testaments and the Apocrypha that are most frequently recounted in Bible storybooks and in oral storytelling. From the beginning of his career Doré experienced immediate acceptance, and it was not long before his interpretations of many religious subjects became standard images for multitudes of people. While never recognized nor judged as a master of high art, Doré nevertheless displayed a unique vision and a distinctive stylistic signature. It is difficult to confuse a Doré creation with the work of any other illustrator, and to this day he remains a very popular illustrator of religious subjects. The American motion picture is possibly the greatest artistic heir of Doré.

Another strong visual influence, particularly in the latter half of the nineteenth century came, largely but not exclusively, from France. A collection of interpretative images of famous biblical female characters appeared and was widely acclaimed. These paintings of women, though dignified with recognizable biblical names, were highly idealized exercises in exotic voluptuousness on the part of the artists who painted them. Charles Landelle (1821–1908) painted a Rebecca who was the romantic conception of the exotic Arab woman, in graceful caftan and Moroccan-style jewelry, seen through the eyes of the French *colon*. The artist, who received many medals and honors for his paintings of biblical women, was further recognized when his *Rebecca* was purchased by the French government and later acquired by the Louvre. Landelle also painted a popular *Ruth*, seen holding her gleanings, barefooted in the alien corn but wearing a long flowing caftan over her richly endowed body. Her hair falls dark and loose about her pseudo-Semitic face, accentuating her large, ardent eyes.

W. A. Bouguereau (1825–1905), acclaimed in his own time and now enjoying a contemporary vogue, painted *Marie Madeleine* in profile, hands clasped above flowing dark garments, in an attempt to render deep spirituality. It is not surprising that Mary Magdalene was a favorite though sterotyped subject for these nineteenth-century lushly romantic and sensual paintings. Emile Auguste Carolus Duran (1837–1917) painted Mary Magdalene nude from the pelvis up, as an obvious reference to her earlier life and career, and none of the traditional signs of her later saintliness was included in his canvas. She was shown in profile, a pose derived from her posture at the foot of the cross in the crucifixion scenes of the old masters. Duran gave her full erect breasts and flowing hair equal emphasis. Frederick Sandys (1832–1904) painted the Magdalene with face rapt in contemplation, as if in love or experiencing the near-orgasmic ecstasy of the St. Teresa by Bernini (1645–1652). The Magdalene holds in her hand as her traditional attribute an unguent jar. Mary Magdalene appears to have been the favorite biblical woman of painters of this period, except, of course, for the ever-venerated Virgin Mary,/6/ who continued to be painted in traditions borrowed from the masters. Not only were the American films to perpetuate these visual images of biblical women; these interpretations also inspired numerous personal adornments. Rachel at the Well became a favorite scene in cameos and ornate buttons.

In addition to Doré and the Europeans who painted biblical women, four other artists of the nineteenth century and some of their individual works appear to have been germinal to much American popular religious art. These artists have contributed to an exceptionally large degree to the way Americans visualize Jesus and still demand that their popular artists depict him, in order to afford that instant recognition so essential to popular culture.

Holman Hunt (1827–1910), who was prominently associated with the British pre-Raphaelite movement in literature and art,/7/ painted *The Light of the World*, one of the interpretations of Jesus most frequently observed in reproduction on the walls of American homes. The work has been widely plagiarized, and there are various pop versions of the painting in which the figure of Jesus is shifted, rearranged, and shown from different angles. In the original, a stately, full-length standing Jesus is shown carrying an elaborate lantern and wearing a long-sleeved embroidered tunic, distantly reminiscent of a biblical high priest's robe. His right hand knocks at a door, in a visual paraphrase of the New Testament text (Rev 3:20–22) "Behold I stand at the door and knock." The figure of Jesus is surrounded by fantastic plants and foliage, while the flesh of his face is radiantly illuminated. The eyes of Jesus are large and passionate, under gently arched brows, while the face is pensive, sentimental, and somewhat effeminate. On the head is a combination royal crown and crown of thorns, with jewels intertwined with thorns. The image conveys a total impression of romantic melancholy and gentle wistfulness, and this probably accounts for the painting's appeal to the piety of its own time as well as ours.

Victorian England was certainly one of the major influences on the popular American artistic sensibility and piety, but two German academic painters exerted an even greater impact on American visual conceptions of New Testament subjects.

Bernhard Plockhorst (1825–1907), respected as a prolific painter, illustrator, and teacher, became truly famous for his historical and biblical scenes./8/ In the United States his work is still widely reproduced and imitated, often without attribution. *The Triumphal Entry into Jerusalem* and *The Good Shepherd* are probably his best known works, though his versions of *Christ Blessing the Children* and *Christ Taking Leave of His Mother* have also been widely disseminated. The inspiration of *The Good Shepherd*, the artist's best-known painting, is the Gospel of St. John (10:1–16). In Plockhorst's rendering, Jesus is a handsome, strong-featured, graceful, thoroughly noble figure, with a full beard and a splendid head of shoulder-length hair. The landscape against which he appears is non-Palestinian, but idyllic and pastoral, with rich vegetation and a distant meandering river. Jesus holds the traditional shepherd's staff, a wooden crook. He is barefooted, as he frequently is in Plock-horst's work, on a footpath of smooth stones. Quaint, romantic sheep look lovingly up at Jesus, while a tiny lamb, which he has presumably rescued, is cradled in his arm. A ram walks beside Jesus, leading the way along the stony path. Plockhorst was a thoughtful artist. The human figure of the Shepherd is truly monumental, with heavy, powerful feet, suggesting much walking. The hands, on the contrary, are small, convey-ing great sensitivity.

The reproductions of this painting are frequently found on living room walls in private homes. But *The Good Shepherd* is also popular in the nursery and reappears on all kinds of Sunday school materials designed for young children. It is safe to say that this is the face that multitudes of people visualize when they think of Jesus, and this image, though not the name of Plockhorst, seems to be more widely known among popular religious audiences in the United States than in the artist's native Germany.

The image of Jesus by Johann Heinrich Hofmann (1824–1911) is, if anything, even better known than that of Plockhorst. In fact, the images of the two artists are almost interchangeable in many people's minds./9/ Both artists followed similar traditions in depicting Jesus and yet reshaped these traditions, coming uncomfortably close, in the estimation of some, to presenting the Germanic type of Jesus who reigned so many years in the Oberamagau Passion Play before being discarded under accusations of anti-Semitism.

Hofmann settled in Dresden, becoming a professor at the Academy in 1870. From there his influence radiated throughout central Europe even before his work became so widely known in the English-speaking world. Like Plockhorst, he was a successful and multi-faceted artist, even though he too became best known as a painter of biblical subjects. Through these paintings he established himself as a dominant influence in popular religious art. His best-known works include *Christ Teaching from a Boat*, *Christ and the Adulteress*, and *Head of Christ*, which— with its limpid eyes, noble, regular features, and three-quarter profile— has become, through constant reproductions, one of the most familiar of all representations of the founder of Christianity. Hofmann's work, like that of Plockhorst, shows strong influence from the Renaissance but fil-tered through a Victorian European sensibility.

However, Hofmann's most venerated painting, found in hundreds of thousands of Roman Catholic and Protestant American homes alike, in a variety of reproductions and plagiarized adaptations, is his *Christ in Geth-semane*, which rivals Plockhorst's *The Good Shepherd* in popularity. In this work, it must be conceded, a highly trained, academically competent artist has presented in near definitive popular form a dramatic moment from the life of Jesus, producing a visual interpretation that has now become almost as well known as Leonardo's *Last Supper*. Jesus' isolation and agony in the garden are high pathos. The picture is impressive for its dynamic diagonal composition; Jesus in profile prays beside a huge rock, certainly consciously prefiguring the altars on which his sacrament will be offered in the centuries to follow. Luxurious robes flow about him, arranged in theatrical dishevelment. Over his shoulder the city of Jerusalem can be seen in the background, somewhat reminiscent, in the dramatic interplay of sky, clouds, and light, of El Greco's (1547–1614) *View of Toledo*. Three sleeping disciples can be seen in the background, having deserted the suffering Jesus in favor of slumber. The intertwined fingers of Jesus clearly suggest the spiritual and physical fear he is enduring, yet his face is calm, devoid of expression. It is the idealized face of the Plockhorst-Hofmann school, with those same regular features and handsome profile. Though Jesus is praying at nighttime, there are no stars in the sky. Yet Jesus has a nimbus, and a ray of light also falls upon him out of the otherwise dark heavens. He is soon to suffer the torment of the cross, and a barren, gnarled bush in the lower left corner of the picture makes allusion to the crown of thorns he is shortly to wear.

Hofmann's achievement was considerable in visually popularizing an event from the beginning of the Passion of Jesus. This scene, though known in Christian art as early as the fourth century, does not appear to have been emphasized until the advanced Middle Ages. While the Renaissance period found it an interesting, humanly appealing moment, it was the nineteenth century revival of this subject and, above all, Johann Heinrich Hofmann's rendition that made it one of the three or four best-remembered scenes from all the New Testament. It even started supplanting other moments in Jesus' Passion as a subject of popular contemplation. In Protestant homes where a crucifixion scene would have seemed too troubling, too crude, too gory, this moment near the end of the life of Jesus had enduring appeal, and reproductions of Hofmann's painting hung on many a wall. Furthermore, Protestant hymnals soon were filled with songs about meeting the Lord in gardens, reinforcing this image in the public's imagination.

The Hope of the World by Harold Copping (1863–1932) was another European painting of considerable influence and continued interest, though it never became as popular or as prototypical as the best-known works of Plockhorst and Hofmann. Copping was an English artist who enjoyed his greatest popularity in the United States in the 1930s, when his work was frequently copied and imitated. Americans found his interpretation of Jesus' blessing of the little children especially appealing, perhaps due to the strong sentimentality of the subject. Early Christian art had made little use of this Gospel episode, and its best-known previous rendition had probably been Rembrandt's "Hundred Guilder Print" (ca. 1648–1650). Copping's Jesus, however, resembles the Jesus of Plockhorst and Hofmann more than the Lord of Rembrandt. He is a powerful figure with a well-groomed beard and those familiar limpid eyes, clad in elegant robes that also cover his head. Several children, representing different races, are clustered around him, fashionably though ethnically garbed. A little Indian girl in sari sits on Jesus' knee, while a blond, blue-eyed, very British-looking child in a light frock stands by his shoulder. Jesus' arm is around this very blond little girl. A Chinese boy in pigtail is standing against Jesus' other knee, looking attentively up at him. The other arm of Jesus is around a small Polynesian girl, in grass skirt and beads, wearing flowers in her hair. Then, there is a fifth child, an unclothed black boy, seated at Jesus' feet, looking up at him. Only his back is seen in the picture, and he is clearly separated from the central grouping of children. He alone does not touch Jesus and gets no direct attention from either him or the other children, who appear to form a companionable but enclosed group. This separation of the black child from the rest of the group did not escape the notice of early commentators, who were so imbued with the racism of the time that they did not see anything amiss in what they acknowledged to be not only the visual but the psychological isolation of the black child.

Copping's figures of Jesus and the children were competently painted, though they were all stereotypes, lacking freshness of imagination or individual vision. A perpetuation of the nineteenth-century colonial mentality is readily apparent, and the painting seems to blare forth the message of Manifest Destiny or the White Man's Burden. However, one could hardly add the charge of sexism to that of racism, for three female children and two males, including the black boy, would seem to give females a slight edge in the picture. This may be no more than symmetry, however, since Jesus himself is the third male. Copping's painting was widely copied and employed in literature promoting missions and in missionary education. Today it is the most dated of all the popular works mentioned. While the subject is still popular, the exaggerated stereotypes and the neglect of the black child would no longer be countenanced and, even viewed in retrospect, appear offensive and embarrassing.

Favorite Biblical Subjects

Certain biblical subjects have always attracted more attention than others, even from the beginning of Christian art. Each age also seems to

choose from the many biblical narratives those that seem most pertinent
to the problems and preoccupations of the times. For obvious reasons,
because of the limited scope of its visual culture, which reflected the
constraints of the Third Commandment, Judaism did not develop the
elaborate pictorial art that Christianity, freely absorbing the visual traditions of the Greco-Roman world, produced. Yet certain subjects, characters, and events from the Hebrew scriptures formed a core of material to
be illustrated by early Christian artists, and these illustrations were justified on the basis of their didactic value. For centuries, these Old Testament events and figures were not necessarily contemplated for their own
importance but as prefigurations of events in the New Testament. They
were significant to the Christian concept of salvation.

Biblical typology, fostered by the early Church Fathers in their writings, played a major role in the iconographic programs of the early Christian and medieval periods. Today typology is seldom used in theological
exegesis, and therefore it is only natural that it is almost non-existent in
contemporary American popular art. Personalities and events from the Old
Testament (or Hebrew Bible) are savored visually for their own significance. Still, a certain selectivity continues. When Old Testament figures
and events are rendered by the popular artists, several factors determine
their choice. Most likely, their importance was underscored many centuries ago, and the artists are following a well-established repertory of
images. By representing traditional images or scenes, they are responding
directly to the market they address, a market that is visually very conservative. In the rare instances where the artist's personal predilections may
dictate the choice of a Bible subject, the acceptance by the mass audience is
less assured.

Creation, Jonah and the whale, and especially Noah's ark are favorite scenes for visual depiction. A revival of interest in the land of Egypt,
its culture, religion, and art, seems to be experienced in every American
generation, and it is not surprising that events in the Egyptian period of
the lives of Joseph and Moses are frequently selected for illustration. This
fascination with Egypt is by no means new. Joseph's life story was read
in the spirit of a novel throughout the Middle Ages, while the scenes
from his life, full of exciting events and places, were illustrated at least
from the sixth century on./10/ In recent years, the Horatio Alger quality
of Joseph's success story has made him a special favorite with Americans,
even those not bookish enough to have read the Thomas Mann novels
based on his exploits./11/

Abraham, Moses, and David were in the past among the most frequently represented heroes of the Old Testament. This continues to be so in
commercial religious art. Since this art has always had a large component

of pastoral romanticism, the representation of David as a shepherd boy is a special favorite, particularly in visual aid materials designed specifically for Sunday school instruction.

God the Father, though the central figure in scripture, was never incarnated and thus was seldom represented in art until the advanced Middle Ages. From the Renaissance on only exceptionally daring artists attempted to conceptualize visually that great and omnipotent power. Commercial artists dealing with popular images likewise generally have avoided depicting God the Father. Jesus, however, the incarnate son in Christian theology, and Moses, the lawgiver, remain the two central human personalities of the two great religions practiced by the majority of Americans, and they have been frequently represented visually. Because their images enjoy great popularity in religious art, they deserve special attention.

Moses, the powerful heroic figure, the lawgiver of the Hebrew scriptures, the prophet whom "the Lord knew face to face," was often represented in art. In popular iconography he has been given an easily recognizable face and physique. This central figure to Jewish and Christian traditions has been depicted in a manner which, despite Jewish iconoclastic inhibitions, has forged a real bond between the two religions; they enjoy a common visual image of Moses./12/

Michelangelo did not invent the horned Moses, though he definitively established the image. Whatever confusion may or may not have existed in translations of the Hebrew word for "horns" and "rays" when St. Jerome and others wrote of Moses descending the mountain with beams of light upon his countenance, horned helmets were certainly battle equipment of Nordic warriors, and earlier artists had painted Moses in such costume. The horned lawgiver with abundant Medusalike locks, an image later reinforced by its imitation in the American cinema, has continued to define Moses visually in the popular imagination. Even in children's storybooks Moses usually has tufts of hair that are hornlike in appearance.

In the great body of Christian art, the figure of Jesus is, understandably, the most important, whether in fine art or its popular derivative. In depicting the man Jesus, artists have always had to rely upon peculiar and questionable traditions./13/ The images currently popular in North America owe much to the Renaissance and much also to nineteenth-century romanticism and Victorian sentimentality. Needless to say, North American culture has added its own emphases. From secondary masters and, later, purely commercial craftsmen, our popular images of Jesus came into being, finding their way into both homes and churches. It is safe to say that the majority of producers of this work can be more accurately, yet without condescension, described as illustrators rather than fine artists.

Though the American public was initially inclined to use the creative energies of its artists for secular portraits glorifying prosperous sitters or for narrative representational art, biblical subjects continued to inspire the folk arts and, from time to time, even early commercial art. The firm of Nathaniel Currier (1813–1888) and James Merritt Ives (1824–1895) was responsible for expressing many religious themes in art. In the 1840s Currier created a lithograph, probably on commission, of the favorite Roman Catholic motif, the Bleeding Heart of Jesus. Students of the department of fine arts of Vanderbilt University today find this lithograph in the department's collection an interesting curiosity. When photography, which many regard as the ultimate popular visual art, came into wide use and developed some artistic claims, F. Holland Day (1864–1933), a colorfully eccentric and highly imaginative photographer, posed himself as Jesus for a series of extraordinarily realistic photographs of Passion scenes. These caused a sensation when placed on display in photographic galleries./14/ Yet the new society growing out of Puritan roots generally had little place for religiously motivated fine art. Despite its fear of being seduced by the beauty of high art, associated in many a Protestant mind with "Romanism," popular piety found itself starved without visual aids to devotion, immeasurably handicapped in the commission to teach the young. Popular conventions for representing Jesus, owing much to established traditions and something to new theological attitudes, inevitably made their appearance.

Today three dominant trends in representing Jesus can be most readily observed in popular art. First, there is the obvious survival of the nineteenth-century idealized image, showing the influence chiefly of Hunt, Plockhorst, and Hofmann. While the strong Victorian features are toned down somewhat today, the sentimentality and sweetness persist.

Second, attempts to portray Jesus as a more rugged, more decidedly human individual are evident. In these newer illustrations Jesus sometimes looks as if he could model for television commercials selling Levi shirts and Winston cigarettes. Today in the supply store catalogues, wall plaques are advertised in which Jesus is so Americanized that he could be Clint Eastwood's stand-in—he is rugged and powerful in appearance, though always immaculately scrubbed.

In the ancient Greek prototypes and antecedents of the earliest images of Christianity there were neither smiles nor tears, so the impassivity of Jesus' face in early Christian art could be easily understood, though this did not conform to biblical accounts of his personality. In Byzantine art Jesus never smiled, but in Gothic art his countenance started to brighten. Today in American popular art Jesus smiles and embraces freely. His smile extends indiscriminately to humans and animals, and the lamb he cradles receives the same smile as the child he blesses. It is interesting to note that in popular European stereotyped images of Americans, an easy smile is a readily identifiable mark. It follows that the smiling Jesus is a clear Americanization of his image.

But the Clint Eastwood Jesus has not completely replaced the sweet romantic figure so loved by the Victorians. It is significant that in recent movie versions of the life of Jesus the delicate, sensitive actor has been preferred generally over the more robust and rugged one. A desexualizing impulse might be one motivation behind such a choice. Whether sensitive or rugged, Jesus still can be identified by a nimbus, which is now more cleverly subdued in these still romantically tinged but seemingly more realistic pictures. Radiance is provided by the arrangements of clouds and sky about his head, and cloud formations may also be used as substitutions for the halo./15/

Finally, a third significant image of Jesus is making its appearance in popular religious illustrations; this is the ethnic Jesus. Attempts are made to show that Jesus was no Greek god, Byzantine Pantokrator, or Victorian choirmaster. He was a first-century Middle Eastern Jew, who spoke Aramaic, lived, and worshiped in the manner of his people. In order to achieve greater realism and respond to fitting Jewish criticism of Christian art, Jesus is frequently in the newer illustrations attired in a manner suggesting a first-century Jew and endowed with the strong features ancient art has associated with people from that part of the world. Jewish artists are sometimes even commissioned to make such drawings and popular illustrations.

Yet whatever the historical facts of the life of Jesus, the Christian doctrine of the Incarnation affirms the identification of "the Christ" with all humanity. Artists of many nations have as often as not depicted Jesus ethnically, providing him with the physical features of their own tribe or race. Contemporary American artists are frequently no different. "The black Jesus" was rather widely discussed during the civil rights movement, at the same time that theology schools started offering courses in black theology. The variety stores soon stocked throws and wall hangings in which a Hofmannesque Jesus suddenly acquired much darker skin. Gifted artists appeared to paint scenes from the life of the black Jesus, in works that sometimes transcended the visual boundaries between folk, popular-, and fine art. The work of Clementine Hunter (1882?–), an untutored but brilliantly endowed artist, is illustrative. Her *Nativity* (ca. 1970) and her *Crucifixion* (ca. 1975) are dramatic and poignant revelations of the meaning of the black Jesus.

While Jesus continues to be the most popular subject in American religious art, a final figure deserves mention because of the frequency of its appearance on all types of religious material. This is the Bible itself, often rendered as an open codex. It is not surprising to discover that especially among Protestants following Lutheran and Calvinistic traditions the Bible as a handsome visual object can become more attractive than "the graven images" seen in Catholic, Orthodox, and Episcopalian churches. On coffee tables in homes, and even in radiant display on church pulpits, an open Bible is frequently found, often in elegant binding and sometimes with the name of the owner, family, or church embossed in gold. It is obviously an art object in addition to sacred scripture placed within easy reach. This visual use of the Bible-object may be likened in part to the prominence given in traditional Jewish homes to the scrolls, the mezuzah, or other objects signifying reverence for the Word or the Law. Photographs or drawings of the Bible also freely appear, on greeting cards, devotional books, and religious instructional materials of all types.

Protestant iconoclastic sensibilities and bibliolatry, which make the Bible itself an icon, only partly account for this fascination with the open Bible./16/ The veneration of the Book was deeply embedded even in the pre-Christian folkmind. It was customary in ancient Egypt to bury with the dead richly illustrated scrolls, generally a "Book of the Dead," which gave an account of the life of the deceased. Thus equipped with illustrated records of their lives, these ancient Egyptians went to the final judgment of the god Osiris (Rossiter: 30, fig. 5; 50, fig. 35; 62, fig. 53; 83, fig. 3).

Since the early Middle Ages, every Christian church has treasured its Gospel book, and in art there were innumerable representations of Jesus holding the Gospel book, which might be a scroll but was more often a codex. Usually in paintings the book was closed, but occasionally it was opened, often to the Gospel according to St. John and the passage proclaiming "I am the light of the world." This visual fascination with the image of the Book thus provides another link between early and contemporary Christians and even between pagans and Christians. It is an achievement of modern Christianity and American democracy—owing much to the ancient Jewish emphasis on learning—that an object previously the expensive and exclusive treasure of a church or noble family is now the valued possession of many homes.

The Identifying Features of Popular Art

In American popular illustrations how are biblical persons and subjects recognized by the consumer? Rather simply. Children almost always are sweetly prettified in these illustrations; their blandness in recent years has been somewhat relieved by the careful addition to Bible scenes of children who suggest by their physical appearance, sometimes too stereotypically, various racial and ethnic types. Animals—sheep when tended by either David or Jesus as the Good Shepherd—are equally idealized, invariably clean and cuddly. Men frequently are darkly bearded and wear exotic head gear, the elaborateness of it depending upon the status of the individual involved. When Americans think of biblical characters or events, what they visualize in the mind's eye probably owes more to nineteenth-century exoticism than to the Bible itself. Biblical women are still sensuous and exotic creatures, generally conforming to notions of glamour drawn largely from the style of the nineteenth-century French Academicians. Mary, the mother of Jesus, is simply but gracefully attired in immaculate headdress. She is almost always young and generally pretty in a rather bland fashion. Mary Magdalene and the woman taken in adultery (usually suggested to be one and the same) are more elaborately dressed; their clothing tends to be dissheveled or at least in slight disarray. Esther, winner of the beauty contest in ancient Persia, is usually drawn in full exotic—if ethnically vague—garb. Ruth stands like a Rousseauistic peasant, barefoot and poignant amid her alien corn. "Vamps" of the Bible are easily recognized, not only by their black hair and eyes and sharp features but also by their powder, paint, and the extravagant tastelessness of their robes. Delilah and Jezebel are favorite subjects.

The flavor of distant lands is easily suggested in this art. Egypt is readily recognized by its background pyramids and palm trees, not to mention its lotus blossoms. The Holy Land, whether in secular or religious art, is drawn with square flat-roofed balconies, cyprus trees, and always camels. A strong ethnic flavor is usually suggested by the garments the characters wear. In the more carefully rendered scenes a near operatic-style decor rather than an archaeologically accurate reconstruction enhances the dramatic tension of the scene, if not its authenticity. This style of illustration is based in many instances directly on Doré and more indirectly on the Renaissance masters. An overall tendency is to glamorize the participants of an event and to heighten each scene dramatically. In popular art realistic renderings of Bible subjects and the Holy Land itself are difficult to find. Though photographs have become increasingly common as illustrations, these too represent the romantic tourist-poster school of photography in most instances. The Holy Land materializes like a vision from the Arabian Nights, a never-never land where it is not surprising that miracles are everyday occurrences.

Human gestures in these illustrations tend also to be stylized and ceremonial. They stem from a long tradition of visually expressed body language, easily identified and understood. Thus, the uplifted hand suggests benediction, be it by Jesus or by Jacob when he blesses his sons. The waved hand indicates denial. Grief and despair are expressed chiefly through exaggerated gestures, movements, and body postures; the face may be covered, the body clutched, or the cloak may be gathered around the human figure. Women still pull their hair when they are expressing anguish or bereavement, just as they have done through the centuries in real life as well as in art. In all these mannerisms and gestures the contemporary illustrator is beholden to both distant traditions of Greek theatrical expression and folkloric rituals (Popovich: 105–6, fig. 12).

In popular art analytic pleasure is generally thin, while the emotional response is strong. Individual style and artistic statement are subordinated to a popular, easily recognized formula. This art does not strive to expand experience but rather to reflect a piety that already exists in the viewer. The monotonous reiteration of established patterns and conventions, which may be likened to the familiar refrains of popular music, soothes and reassures but rarely poses intellectual challenges or expands and explores visual possibilities. Problems are not posed; therefore no new solutions are offered. Favorite, familiar scenes are rarely reinterpreted in any inventive way, either visual or theological, though small changes may show accommodations to the specific taste of the time. For example, coloristic tonality in these illustrations may oscillate, just as it does in interior design, between pastels, neutrals, or warm, earthy hues.

In the better examples of this commercial art, realistic, reassuring features, which remind one of the Norman Rockwell style, appear. The Holy Family seems to resemble, despite their halos and the classical flowing robes they wear, a middle-American father, mother, and child. This skill at realistic detail and the ability to create scenes bathed in nostalgic warmth represent the epitome of competence in American popular art.

The majority of those artists we generally term "serious" have been intensely involved in creating subjective styles, often formal, abstract, and iconoclastic. In recent years, however, the human figure has become once more the subject of serious painting, either under the guise of photo-realism, super-realism, or another such label. This still leaves to the illustrators the very lucrative commercial market of popular religious art. Only occasionally will recognized masters accept commissions from ecclesiastical sponsors or religious organizations to create special works of art to appeal to discriminating tastes and refined religious sensibilities.

Only occasionally, for their own purposes, whatever they may be, do these serious artists turn to religious subjects and express through them their personal insights. Georges Rouault (1871–1958)/17/ and Salvador Dali (1904–)/18/ have been among these rare contemporary artists. But popular visual art as a whole, when it expresses, reflects, or touches biblical themes and materials, cannot be assumed to be the personal expression of the individual creator. A popular artist is beaming his work at a particular market, armed with an advance knowledge provided by market research, which has carefully investigated this market. Usually the products aimed at the popular audience are fittingly anonymous, and rarely will they be controversial.

Serious Artistic Statements for the Masses

Religious art in the United States and Canada has flourished and continues to do so among the "primitive" artists, who are usually self-taught and who do not primarily seek popular appeal or commercial markets. These individual creative efforts, interesting as they are, do not belong within the scope of this study. Other artists, often highly trained, may be basically commercial yet not devoid of original ideas, genuine creativity, and the desire to communicate meaningfully. There are instances in which folk, popular, and possibly even "serious" art overlap, and it is appropriate to examine a few briefly. Some of the most interesting examples can be observed in the Whitney Museum of American Art in New York. Thomas Hart Benton (1885–1975) expressed a popular theme in *The Lord is My Shepherd* (1926), a genre scene in which a couple are shown at table while the words of the beloved psalm are inscribed on a painted plaque hanging on the wall./19/ More interesting and definitely more "American" is John Steuart Curry's (1897–1946) *Baptism in Kansas* (1928), where, surrounded by a watching crowd, a woman is submerged by a preacher in a wooden barn tub. A special biblical quality is added to the scene by a dove that hovers above and by rays descending downward to illuminate the event./20/ Peter Blume (b. 1906) turned to religious subjects on a number of occasions, giving his topics unique iconographic interpretations. Thus *Light of the World* (1932) is a street scene that includes a family gazing at a globe of light that obviously has spiritual significance for them. In his *Man of Sorrow* (1951), the wood of the cross is intertwined with bright ribbons./21/ Siegfried Reichart (b. 1925) gave his *Crucifixion* (1953) a completely cubistic interpretation, a true innovation in popular religious art designed primarily for illustrative purposes./22/ Philip Evergood (1901–1973) in his painting *The New Lazarus* (1927–1954) created a political allegory by introducing Nazi officers among the images of Lazarus, the Pietà, and Christ on the cross./23/ In her *Lady Madonna* (1972), Audrey Flack (b. 1931) tried to emulate with oil paint the highly glossed details seen in shiny photographs, while her image itself is reminiscent of Latin Catholic representations of the Madonna and Child, though here both figures were dressed up in their Sunday best./24/

The subject of Jesus' entry into Jerusalem has had a special appeal for American painters, possibly in part because Americans have always loved parades. Two characteristically American versions of this scene are appropriate to examine. *Christ's Entry into Garland, Texas* (1975) was executed by David Bates in mixed media, with paper cutouts projected in relief against a background and then painted. Bates's work, now in a private collection, renders the event as a procession through a small Texas town. Featured prominently in the parade are a police escort on motorcycles and other attendants on horseback. A sign proclaiming "Welcome to Garland" hangs from two flagpoles. Obviously inspired by a small-town parade, Bates's work has considerable complexity. One must search through rows of waving people, all dressed in festive finery, to find the crucial figure: on the main float, behind the motorcycle police and in front of a float carrying a marching band, three crosses can be discerned. From one of these crosses hangs the bloody body of Jesus, clad in a short loincloth. On the float can also be seen the inscribed words "Wave for love of Jesus." *Christ's Entry into Garland, Texas* contains, besides the elements of narrative illustration, an amount of serious social commentary, even satire. Bates seems to be saying that celebrations and parades are much more important to participants than the events that may be commemorated. Bates has certainly made no attempt to illustrate literally the Gospel event his work recalls (Matt 21:1–11; Mark 11:9–10; Luke 19:29–40; John 12:12–19). The Christ who enters the city of Garland is a suffering figure, not a triumphant one. The work does imply a number of opinions about the cause of Christ's sufferings, however, and the relationship of religion to small-town American society. Bates has obviously embodied a very personal vision in this strongly felt statement./25/

The painting of the same subject by Roger Brown (b. 1948) transfers the viewer from small-town USA to an American metropolis. In Brown's work, *The Entry of Christ into Chicago in 1976* (1976), the road of procession is a canyon made in the street by the surrounding skyscrapers of the city. Within lighted windows the night life of the city can be seen from the street, with music, dancing, and convivial socializing. On the street a lone woman holding a palm branch is greeting Christ, who is arriving on a truck. Like Bates, Brown has transposed a biblical narrative into a contemporary environment of the United States and implied a strong social commentary. Christ has indeed come to Chicago, but who cares? Life goes on as usual in this city of millions of anonymous people./26/

While popular art is usually viewed as a commercial enterprise not produced to express an individual artist's vision, these examples demonstrate that a popular audience may sometimes be addressed in powerful visual terms. Religious work can be designed to satisfy popular taste and yet make a strong sincere statement as well.

The religious work of Andreas (Andy) Albert (b. 1958) uses popular imagery while making powerful personal statements. Albert, a totally self-taught artist, accepted a commission a few years ago from Larkin Hix of Green Briar, Tennessee. Albert was to paint a scene modeled on a Paul Aaron composition that had been reproduced on a postcard Mr. Hix had received in the mail and had greatly admired. It was understood that Albert's work was to be donated by Mr. Hix to the Riverside Baptist Church, 1600 Riverside Drive, in Nashville, Tennessee, where it would be hung as a baptistry painting./27/

The young artist accepted this commission to copy a prototype, very much in the spirit that medieval artists agreed to reproduce prototypes, thus perpetuating well-established iconographic traditions. In both cases, that of the medieval artist and that of Albert, plagiarism was far from mind. The motivation was to pay tribute to the original. Yet like his artistic ancestors in the past, Albert could not resist adding his own ideas and interpretations. In Aaron's original, a jet-age Christ, somewhat resembling Superman in profile, is shown colorfully flying over what appears to be an American village. Below, from the village churchyard, souls reunited with bodies are seen emerging from their graves, many already flying to meet Christ in the air.

While the charge Albert received was to reproduce a work that the donor, his patron, fancied, the older work became merely the starting point and source of inspiration. Albert created a new work of art which, though paying tribute to Aaron's painting, became an individual artistic and religious statement. As a result, Albert has done for a Tennessee village (now the scene begins to take on specific detail) what Britain's acclaimed artist Stanley Spencer did for his native village in his painting *The Resurrection, Cookham*./28/

Albert introduced many changes in his work, which he entitled *Auferstehung* ("resurrection" in his native German) after its completion in 1980 (plate 3). His most radical modification came in the representation of Christ himself. While the placement of Christ in the painting is approximately the same as in Aaron's original, instead of rendering him in profile, Albert shows him in a frontal, full-figured view. His long hair and traditional beard are illuminated by an elaborate nimbus that frames his head, highly reminiscent of the nimbi that the evangelists wear in the Carolingian manuscripts of the ninth century. Within the nimbus design, the artist has intertwined almost cryptically, in free interpretation, some of the Greek letters that form the name of Christ. The arms of Christ are extended to receive and embrace the rising souls, while on his hands can still be discerned the nail wounds from the crucifixion.

While the rest of the sky is occupied by tiny curlicues of clouds, patiently and carefully executed in the manner often characteristic of self-taught artists, the middle ground is occupied by a sprawling village, set in a winter landscape. Each wooden house is carefully differentiated and separated by trees denuded of foliage. Into this scene of winter desolation, of lonely souls waiting for Christ, the Second Advent bursts. Two buildings, slightly off the formal center of the composition, attract the eye of the viewer. A steepled village church is clearly important, yet next to it to the right is a village store with a front sign proclaiming "Since 1909 Andy's Grocery." This is one of several ways in which the artist has included himself personally in his painting. An old blue pickup truck parked at the side of the building contrasts vividly with the copper-colored sign.

In the foreground of the painting, adjacent to the church, the village cemetery is represented, enclosed by a stone fence. It is in this area that the main action of the canvas takes place. Souls are seen responding to the sound of the final though unseen trumpet, rejoining their scattered bodies and rising from their tombs. While some of the graves are open, others grimly remain permanently shut. Upon inspection it is seen that the tombstones are inscribed with the names of real people, friends and relatives of the young artist. His own name is included as well. Among the faithful elect rising from their graves, the artist himself can be seen in a small self-portrait, which becomes Albert's signature. It is obvious that in and through his work, this gifted and unpretentious artist has expressed firmly held beliefs.

Far from plagiarizing Aaron's work, Albert has honored his model by making it witty, while at the same time imaginative, personal, and poignant. Commissioned to make a copy of the work of another painter—almost in spite of himself, or because of his own irrepressible artistic ego—he created a vibrant new painting, a work uniquely his own, even while adhering to the basic plan and theme of the senior artist, as requested by his patron. Andreas Albert's work is an example in popular art of a practice that can be readily observed in famous artists of all periods. One artist's statement serves as an inspiration for other state-ments, which develop and expand the original idea. Picasso was inspired by African masks, El Greco by Byzantine icons. While paying tribute to earlier masters, the artist transcends them in his own experience, as *Auferstehung* shows through its unaffected interpretation of two popular religious beliefs, the rapture and the resurrection.

To be considered finally is another kind of religious art, created by those and for those who have "found Jesus." This is an almost spontane-ous art aimed specifically at the younger generation, new converts to the ancient faith. Although this art is commonly found where youths congre-gate, only that produced where transient groups are temporarily formed, such as ocean beaches, will be briefly examined. Even though they are perhaps corny and sentimental, these works are fully contemporary in being frequently super-realistic as well as "self-destructible," and they are therefore deserving of some attention. Around 1980 murals of various subjects started replacing the frequently profane graffiti on the retaining sea wall of the Bolsa Chica State Beach in Huntington Beach, California. As recently as late March of 1982, a large red heart with white highlights could be seen. A bright yellow ribbon ran through the heart, bearing the inscription "Eternal Life thru Jesus."/29/ Similar ideas are repeated on the East Coast in, for example, chalk drawings by Randy Hoffman executed on the boards of the Ocean City, Maryland, boardwalk and popularized through reproduction on postcards./30/ Hoffman chose to draw a facial image of Jesus, bearing the message "Jesus Gave Us a Prayer." He further selected other episodes from the life of Jesus, the prayer in the garden and the Ascension into heaven, and accompanied each scene with an inscription he deemed appropriate. These images heavily rely on the style of nineteenth-century works of art that have already been discussed. The influence of Heinrich Hofmann is dominant, though these contemporary works offer changes in detail. Among other notable religious subjects painted by Randy Hoffman, there is an open Bible, containing several symbolic images—an apple, a snake, a chalice, and a cross—along with a series of meaningful captions, such as "Men's sin" and "Men's forgiveness."

Belonging to the new category of "self-destruct artistic statement" was Mark Altman's sand sculpture, *The Crucifixion*. Jesus on the cross, with his adoring disciples surrounding him, found a place alongside the familiar sand castles of other summer vacationers on the beach of Ocean City, Maryland. Although executed in such a temporary medium as fast-drying sand, Altman's skilled sculpture, as documented and preserved by the camera, conveyed a religious pathos that moved one observer to suggest comparisons to religious art of the Gothic period./31/

The Americanization of the Bible

These recent examples of religious art for the masses not only throw some light on new trends in iconography and upon the relationship between artist and audience, but they may also assist in our understanding of popular art and the sociological forces shaping it.

While popular art is not necessarily distinguished by the presence or absence of quality, rarely does this work stretch the imagination of those who enjoy or employ it. Though an influential popular artist may establish for an entire generation or even longer the ways in which people visualize certain characters and scenes, it is more likely that the popular artist is employing iconographic traditions already known and widely accepted by his audience. Highly imaginative or individualistic visual interpretations of biblical scenes are in fact likely to be rejected. All artists who earn their living by pleasing the masses learn that they must frequently restrain their individual creative impulses. As Christian bookstores report, the imaginative biblical illustrations of Brother Saussure of the Taizé community have sometimes been passed over, especially by children, in favor of the more stereotyped and anonymous interpretations common in the bulk of religious publications.

Illustrations tend to follow rather literally the narrative line of the stories to which they relate and seem generally oblivious to religious doctrine. The bulk of this visual material is also of little help in reconstructing the history and culture of biblical periods. One is left merely with the impression that the Holy Land is hot and arid, except at Christmas time, when there are "cold, winter nights." Biblical characters viewed in these illustrations are not industrious American Puritans; little work seems to be done apart from making an occasional plowshare, catching a few fish, and keeping well-behaved sheep.

While this art generally does not attempt to penetrate below surfaces, there are nevertheless some moral, ethical, and social values implied. Some of the newer material does seem to impart a mild ecological message, because the consumer is constantly reminded that creation is good as well as picturesque; it teaches compassion for animals, because, after all, both David, the favorite king, and Jesus, the savior, loved them, the Bible seems to say; and it promotes better race relations. While there are few if any innovative features, there is, as noted, more recent stress on the historical character of Jesus and some attempt to enlighten the viewer on Jewish customs. In the more recent paintings of Jesus blessing the children of the world, the black child no longer must sit merely at the feet of Jesus, careful not to touch the children of other races.

These visual images seem to reinforce while at the same time they reflect the piety in our pluralistic society. Films, television, and popular books generally attempt to appeal to the widest possible audience. This is the undisguised aim of commercial art. For example, Jews and Christians probably do not differ much in the way they visualize Moses; they both tend to see Michelangelo's image or Heston's face and physique.

The bland "religion in general" described by American religious sociologists also can be seen reflected in many of these mass-marketed materials, though the demands of the expanding market in an ethnically and religiously pluralistic society have resulted in a departure from some of the old stereotypes. The increased sensitivity of a pluralistic society has meant an added attention to Bible scenes where black persons may conceivably appear,/32/ and an attempt to show Jesus more and more against settings and in attire that reflect a Jewish milieu. Yet a major factor in the popular rendering of biblical subjects has been the commercial need to appeal to the broadest possible audience, often by avoiding the specific or the unusual.

Despite the different American religious traditions—chiefly Jewish, Eastern Orthodox, Roman Catholic, Anglican, Lutheran, Calvinist, and other Protestant, some of them with ancient and splendid visual styles all their own and some of them with iconoclastic instincts—there is less denominational variation in art preferences than might at first be expected. When a popular artist paints Jesus, this figure, because of clearly recognized if only vaguely codified conventions, can generally be identified by a Protestant, a Roman Catholic, or any other American, regardless of religious affiliation, or lack of one. With rare exceptions the work is nondenominational. Much of this art can be used equally by Jews and Christians. Since they are designed for the American masses, the broad general base of religious America, these illustrations remain conservative and familiar. They are meant neither to jar nor to offend.

The Old Testament, whose heroes are clearly identified by easily recognizable attributes, appears more for its own sake than for its presumed relationship to the Christian salvation story, even in conservative Christian study aids. Previously, as observed, the Old Testament was handled in art in two ways—as straight narrative and as the foreshadowing of events of the New Testament. Today it is almost exclusively illustrated according to the former way. We are living in a very literalistic age, and there is little inclination to try to comprehend systems of typology—even if the church leaders were promoting them, which they are not. Furthermore, Jewish sensibilities in a pluralistic society are justly acknowledged by treating narratives from Jewish scripture as self-contained.

The iconoclastic traditions have been especially significant in the United States, and the compromises that have been made from time to time, in attempts to follow the Third Commandment, deserve a study all their own. Calvinistic Christianity, so potent a lingering force in all North America, fearful of the seductive charms of visual art, distrustful of images, and revering "the Book," has made, as has been seen, its own contribution. Most groups, regardless of their interpretation of the Third Commandment or the austerity of their origins, have found it expedient to make compromises when it comes to instructing the young. Images have almost always been used for didactic purposes, yet this art among Reformed Protestants tended to be of a rather Spartan nature, so that it avoided the danger of lulling the mind away from "the Word." The ancient Orthodox Christians avoided or prohibited "graven images," fearing that they might cause idolatry, but they found a place of honor in their worship for the two-dimensional icon portraits of the saints, some of which then took on miracle-working powers in popular belief. In the same way, many American audiences have avoided the well-recognized masterpieces of art, or any art that might have higher aspirations, in favor of less sophisticated visual instructional material believed to be less beguiling.

Yet some interesting patterns can be discerned emerging in this pluralistic society. The examples we have examined certainly demonstrate anew that our popular culture is an Americanizing, unifying influence, helping to bring together peoples of different ethnic traditions and religious histories, thus providing all with some meeting ground. Today Jews and Christians throughout the country, for better or worse, see Heston's face when they think of Moses. And, in total contrast to the sternness of Byzantine depictions of Christ Pantokrator, Jesus frequently smiles in American paintings and illustrations. This facial expression, this smile, above everything else, seems to make the image of Jesus not only more popular and more approachable but also more American. Popular culture presents a reminder too that North Americans, like every other people who have ever lived and loved the scriptures of the Jewish and Christian religions, have contributed their unique insights and have, despite their heavy dependence upon European image makers, even asserted their right to proclaim a "more American" Moses and Jesus.

NOTES

/1/   Research for this article started in 1977 and is ongoing. While concentration was on popular religious imagery in the Nashville, Tennessee, area, examples were examined from as far away as the East and West Coasts, as well as from the great collections of American art, such as the Whitney Museum in New York City. Material was carefully examined in the following locations in and around Nashville: The Twentieth Century Christian Bookstore, Koinonia Book Shop, Cokesbury Bookstore, Baptist Bookstore, Adventist Bookstore (Madison, Tennessee), Methodist Publishing House, The Jewish Community Centre Library, the Temple Library, Ziebart's Bookstore, Mills Bookstore, George Peabody College Bookstore, Vanderbilt University Bookstore, and the library and bookstore of the University of the South (Sewanee, Tennessee). Without the library holdings of the Vanderbilt University Library, this research could not have been completed. A number of churches were also visited. At every location, people were consistently helpful, freely giving their time in conversation and consultation. Heartfelt thanks are extended to the directors and personnel of all the institutions mentioned.

/2/   See further Bessie M. Lindsey, *Lore of Our Lord Pictured in Glass* (Published by author, 1948).

/3/   Conroy Maddox's book is very instructive and interesting; see pl. 54, *The Sacrament of the Last Supper* (1955), Chester Dale Collection, National Gallery of Art, Washington, DC.

/4/   Full information may be obtained from The Upper Room, 1908 Grand Avenue, Nashville, Tennessee, 37202.

/5/   Ancient traditional Jewish art, generally iconoclastic to one degree or another, sometimes used an outstretched hand as a substitution for the more elaborate and forbidden representations of God. Usually the hand of the Lord could be seen coming out of a cloud, thus demonstrating visually a familiar biblical synecdoche, "the right hand of God." This was one of the Jewish symbols most readily and immediately accepted into early Christian art (Weitzmann: 62, 372, no. 341). The hand of the Lord was used to symbolize divine power, the commanding creative force that brought order out of chaos and light out of darkness. God communicated with his creation, according to the Bible, by stretching forth his hand. The hand also was sometimes used to represent the divine voice, which could hardly be conveyed visually without some such substitution.

In the Christian art that followed both in the Byzantine East and the Latin West, the hand gesture remained in use when important episodes from the New Testament were illustrated. Now Jesus, who was frequently substituted for God the Father when Christian artists depicted Old Testament scenes with God's presence, extended his hand in blessing, lifted it in command, or raised it in condemnation. Borrowed from the visual conventions of classical antiquity, in which the hand gesture belonged to an emperor or an orator, the language of Jesus' hand was conventionalized and easily understood by the beholder. Much of the ancient language of the hand appears to have survived the subsequent centuries and can still be found in religious art.

/6/   Due to the enormity, complexity, and great popularity of the subject matter, the Virgin and the Madonna and Child are topics that cannot be encompassed in this brief survey article but must remain themes to be examined at a later date.

/7/   The Pre-Raphaelite Brotherhood was formed in 1848 by a group of English artists and writers who wished to revive the style and spirit of the Italian artists before the time of Raphael.

/8/   Biographical information about Plockhorst is most readily available in the standard reference work, Thieme-Becker, *Allgemeines Lexikon* (Leipzig, 1955, 2nd ed.), V.VI, pp. 26–27.

/9/   For more information see Thieme-Becker, *Allgemeines Lexikon* V.XXIX, p. 400.

/10/   Illustrating the extent and popularity of the representation of Jonah and the whale is a rendering even in cast iron in the form of a vividly colored coin bank. This bank was especially popular with American children of earlier times and is now available in antique reproduction. An example of an original was examined in the private collection of Herbert Peck of Nashville, Tennessee.

For representations of the Joseph story in different materials see Weitzmann: 460–67, nos. 412–18.

/11/   Thomas Mann (1875–1955) wrote his Joseph series of novels from 1933 to 1944. The novels form a highly detailed, densely thematic tetralogy.

/12/   Representations of Moses that were established most likely in the milieu of the Hellenized Alexandrian Jews have persisted through centuries. Among the most ancient preserved examples is the representation of Moses from the famous synagogue at Dura Europos, a Roman outpost on the Euphrates River. This ensemble of paintings from about A.D. 250 features Moses prominently. Images of the lawgiver are also to be found in the frescoes of the early Christian catacombs in Rome, and they are carved on sarcophagi of the same period.

One of the best-known later representations of Moses is still to be seen in the Church of St. Vitale in Ravenna, dating from the second quarter of the sixth century, the period of Emperor Justinian. In that church Moses appears in several episodes: he is seen against rocky landscapes, surrounded by burning bushes—young, beardless, and clad in traditional classical garments. Moses would not, however, be readily identified by those who know him only in the post-Michelangelo visual tradition, and the Ravenna guides have to tell most tourists that this is he. Moses is seen untying his sandals, because he is indeed on holy ground, and his head turns to behold the fearsome theophany. God is symbolized in the traditional Jewish manner, by a hand emerging in blessing from the clouds.

Equally famous is the mosaic image of the bearded Moses from the monastery church of St. Catherine of Mount Sinai, the traditional site where Moses was given the tablets of the Law by the Lord. The mosaic, executed in the sixth decade of the sixth century, represents a middle-aged Moses, clad in classical-type garments, with short, dark hair and a rounded dark beard. He is removing his sandals before the burning bush, while the hand of God is seen emerging from a segment of sky in order to pass down the rectangular tablet of the Law. See further Volbach; Karpp; von Simson; and Forsyth and Weitzmann.

/13/   At the end of the fourth-century Christological disputes that shook the Church to its foundation, the images of Jesus we now know had begun to take shape. To create physical images, Christian artists could not rely upon Jewish traditions, which were predominantly nonfigurative, and the canonical Gospels were silent on the matter of Jesus' appearance. Although the theologians invented legends of miraculous iconic images of Jesus "not made by human hands," and spoke of the Veil of Veronica, which became a favorite pious story in the West, and the miraculously preserved portrait of Jesus belonging to King Abgar, a favorite legend of the Byzantine East, artists themselves adapted well-known Greco-Roman images as their prototypes. From these classical models several basic ways of representing Jesus emerged. One of them was as the beardless youth, based chiefly on pagan renderings of young deities and other heroic figures, such as Apollo, Hermes, or Orpheus. Pagan pastoral representational traditions combined with the Bible's own verbal pastoral imagery and resulted in the iconographic type of Jesus as the Good Shepherd, which is still popular today.

Another way of representing Jesus was borrowed from the iconography of mature pagan divinities such as Zeus. Regular features, a powerful physique, and luxurious hair and beard were the chief characteristics of this type. Both iconographic traditions existed concurrently in the Eastern and Western Christian churches at least from the fourth century.

These standard iconic representations were zealously guarded as the "true portraits" within the faith, and artists strictly conformed to these visual traditions until the late Middle Ages. It is only from the Renaissance on that artists have been allowed to take personal liberties in the way they have interpreted Jesus.

The Reformation witnessed a new iconoclasm, with a wide disfavor cast upon visual representations and a renewed stress on the biblical Word. Certainly this did not prevent one of the most brilliant artists of all those who ever dealt with religious subjects, Rembrandt van Rijn (1606–1669), from arising out of Dutch Lutheranism.

With the French Revolution in a powerful part of Catholic Christendom, a further almost fatal blow was dealt religious art and therefore Christian iconography as well. The advent of neoclassicism at the end of the eighteenth century and its sustained popularity were a disaster for religious art. The most capable artists concentrated their talents in other areas, serving nonecclesiastical patrons whose interests were in personal portraits or mythological subjects rather than Bible topics and themes. The task of representing biblical subjects generally fell—with a few notable exceptions—to the illustrators, who were often commercial artists willing to compromise artistic integrity for commissions. From this situation came changes that helped determine the form and direction that popular religious art takes even today. See further Volbach; Whitting.

/14/   See further Jussim: 120, 127, 128.

/15/   Radiances, which continue to surround in some form or another, the head of Jesus and other holy personages, even in the more realistic representations of today, are of ancient Eastern origin. They appear to have been brought initially from India into the Hellenistic artistic world as a visual convention and were probably first associated in the West with Alexander the Great when he was represented pictorially. Alexander, other rulers of the Hellenistic period, and later the Roman emperors, when portrayed in art, have these radiances, which then continued to be painted around the heads of Byzantine and early Christian rulers. Just as the Roman pagan divinities were given radiances, the Christian saints, and especially Jesus, when they were first painted, were fittingly provided with visual glow. From early times a complex symbolism grew up around the use of light in painting. Lumination is associated with divine wisdom and inspiration. According to the scriptures, light emanates from God, who "maketh the light to shine in darkness," and Jesus himself announced, "I am the Light of the World."

/16/   The open Bible as an iconographic subject is found in many instances; for example, the open Bible together with a spray of flowers is found on sympathy cards (Baptist Bookstore, Nashville); the Bible is the cover illustration for Edgar J. Goodspeed's *How Came the Bible?* (Nashville: Abingdon, 1976).

/17/   In the Courthion volume close to 150 entries address religious subjects; see further Dyrness: 124–96.

/18/ For a number of visionary religious scenes painted by Dali, see Descharnes: fig. 139, plates 42, 43, and 45; fig. 144, plates 47 and 48.

/19/ The Whitney Museum of American Art, no. 31.000.

/20/ The Whitney Museum of American Art, no. 31.159.

/21/ The Whitney Museum of American Art, nos. 33.5 and 51.5 respectively.

/22/ The Whitney Museum of American Art, no. 55.2.

/23/ The Whitney Museum of American Art, no. 54.60.

/24/ The Whitney Museum of American Art, no. 72.42.

/25/ This information was obtained during a personal interview with the artist, David Bates, in the spring of 1980. He was also kind enough to lend the illustration of *Christ's Entry into Garland, Texas* for further study.

/26/ The Whitney Museum of American Art, no. 77.56.

/27/ All the information about Andreas Albert was obtained in a personal interview with the artist, 8 June 1980, in Nashville, Tennessee, at which time the painting was also examined. Mr. Albert was born in Charlottenburg, West Germany, 22 August 1958, but has lived in the United States for the last thirteen years and has made this country his permanent home.

/28/ In 1980 a giant retrospective show of the work of Stanley Spencer (1891–1959) was mounted at the Royal Academy of Arts in London. He was generally acknowledged at that time as an eccentric but true genius. *The Resurrection, Cookham* was painted 1924–1926.

/29/ Professor Howard M. Warner has communicated this information, together with a photograph of the site.

/30/ Photograph by R. C. Pulling, published by HPS Inc., Dover, Delaware.

/31/ Photograph also by R. C. Pulling, published by HPS Inc., Dover, Delaware.

/32/ Possibly some of the more interesting Christian images today are being created by black artists, who seem to be less burdened by Western visual traditions, or intimidated by them. Thus they are able to produce fresh ethnic images that, although tied to the Bible text, exhibit a new spirit. See, for example, Louis B. Reynold and Robert H. Pierson, *Bible Answers for Today's Questions* (Nashville: Southern Publishing Company, 1973). This book was illustrated by John Brown, a black artist who was trained at the Harris School of Art. Ten illustrations included in this volume have strong ethnic overtones. The vibrant, deeply saturated colors stand out from the popular decorative tones generally used for such illustrations. A further example is the joint work of two artists, Allan Rohan Crite and Susan Gillian Thompson, currently (April 1982) exhibiting at the Carl Van Vechton Gallery, Fisk University, Nashville, Tennessee. Among their works can be singled out an especially powerful and graceful image of the black Madonna and Child.

WORKS CONSULTED

Courthion, Pierre
n.d.   *Georges Rouault*. New York: Harry N. Abrams.

Descharnes, Robert
1976   *Salvador Dali*. New York: Harry N. Abrams.

Doré, Gustave
1974   *The Doré Bible Illustrations*. New York: Dover Books.

Dyrness, William A.
1971   *Rouault: A Vision of Suffering and Salvation*. Grand Rapids: Eerdmans.

Forsyth, George H., and Kurt Weitzmann
n.d.   *The Monastery of Saint Catherine at Mount Sinai: The Church and the Fortress of Justinian*. Ann Arbor: University of Michigan Press.

Jussim, Estelle
1981   *Slave to Beauty: The Eccentric Life and Controversial Career of F. Holland Day, Photographer, Publisher and Aesthete*. Boston: David R. Godine.

Karpp, Heinrich
1966   *Die Frühchristlichen und Mittelalterlichen Mosaiken in Santa Maria Maggiore zu Rom*. Baden-Baden: Bruno Grimm.

Maddox, Conroy
1979   *Dali*. New York: Crown.

Popovich, Ljubica D.
1976   "Some Folkloric Elements in Medieval Art in the Territories of Servia and Macedonia." *Balkanistica* 3: 105–6.

Rossiter, Evelyn
1979   *The Book of the Dead: Papyri of Ani, Hunefer, Anhai*. New York: Crescent Books.

Simson, Otto George von
1948   *Sacred Fortress: Byzantine Art and Stagecraft*. Chicago: University of Chicago Press.

Volbach, Wolfgang Fritz
1961   *Early Christian Art*. New York: Harry N. Abrams.

Weitzmann, Kurt, ed.
1978   *Age of Spirituality: Late Antique and Early Christian Art*. Princeton: Princeton University Press.

Whitting, P. D.
1973   *Byzantine Coins*. New York: G. P. Putnam's Sons.

Mater Dolorosa.
N° 9? DES SEPT DOULEURS + VIERGE DE DOLORES.
Die schmerzhafte Mutter.

Plate 1

Mater Dolorosa of the Seven Sorrows, by Nathaniel Currier (1813–1888)

Lithograph from the Vanderbilt University Art Collection, reproduced by permission of Dr. F. Hamilton Hazlehurst, Chairman of the Art Department. Photograph by Herbert J. Peck, Jr., Photographer, Vanderbilt University. This lithograph appears to have been a purely commercial work employing familiar motifs and breaking no new ground. The sorrowful mother, portrayed in popular fashion, is blank and vaguely pretty. Despite the suffering thirty-three-year-old son in her arms, she is also youthful, as was expected in renderings of a pure virgin—at least since the time of Michelangelo. The Holy Land is conventionally represented; there are palm trees and flat-roofed buildings with balconies. The devotions to the Sacred Heart and the Mater Dolorosa, represented in the lithograph, are Roman Catholic practices, but early prints similar to Currier's were passed along in many families and, consequently, hung on some Protestant walls as well.

Plate 2

Early American Angel

Watercolor from the collection of Herbert J. Peck, Jr., used by permission. Photograph by Herbert J. Peck, Jr., Photographer, Vanderbilt University. The date and artist of this watercolor are unknown. The painting combines religious and patriotic piety in a manner that became familiar in popular American art. A joyful image, appropriate to holiday times, it celebrates Americanism and Christianity, probably in that order. The angel is easily identified, being winged and feminine in appearance, according to the lore of the time. Since a horn is being sounded, an attempt is probably being made to represent the archangel Gabriel. The American flag of the period and the cross are almost united, and reds, whites, and blues dominate the work.

Plate 3

Auferstehung, by Andreas Albert

Used by permission of the artist, Andreas Albert, of Nashville, Tennessee. The quiet of a small Tennessee village, which seems to have more dead than living citizens, is interrupted by the Second Coming and the Rapture. The dead fly forth from their graves to meet Jesus in the air. Detailed scrutiny reveals the names of friends and family of the artist on the tombstones, and a self-portrait is also included. The contrast is especially dramatic between the peacefulness of the snow-covered village (an unusual winter for Tennessee), with its tranquil houses, store, barn, and church, and the tumultuous sky with the sudden appearance of the Lord of Glory in swirling clouds.

Plate 4

Last Supper, by Arthur L. Britt

From the permanent collection of the Art Department of Alabama State University, reproduced here by permission of Dr. Callie B. Warren, Chairperson. Photograph by Lucian Smith, Photographer, Alabama State University. Arthur L. Britt's *Last Supper*, though a sophisticated rendering of the scene so celebrated in art, communicates clearly to a broad American public. The pathos of the moment is conveyed by the colors and patterns made by the figures clustered around the table. While there are echoes of Leonardo, Rouault, and a rich tradition of Western Christian art, this is a highly original statement. A bit of realism is added with the overflowing garbage pail under the table. This touch is reminiscent of Rembrandt, who even when painting mysteries of faith liked to present some prosaic detail to remind the viewer that human life continues much as usual. From the painting one discerns that the Incarnate God does not merely experience the grand moments of agony and exaltation; he shares the dirt and grime of human existence. The apostles are painted in differing hues and seem to represent the races of humanity. Jesus could be black, or any color, merely obscured by shadow. Arthur Britt was, until his untimely death in the summer of 1982, the chairman of the Art Department of Alabama State University and was nationally recognized as an educator. He was interested in communicating the black experience and the universal themes of all art beyond the circles of the academician and the connoisseur.

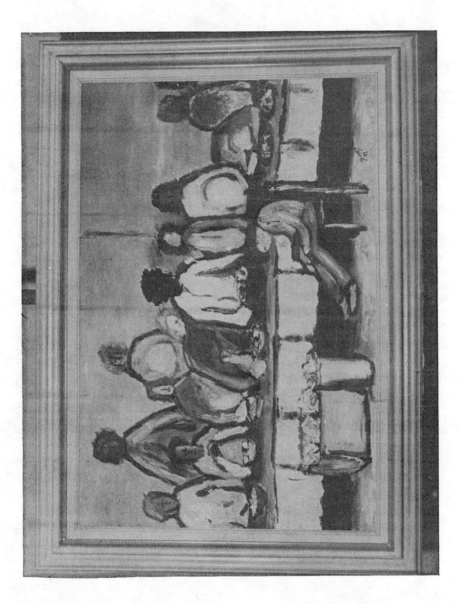

Plate 5

Crucifixion, by Robert Baynes

From the permanent collection of the Art Department of Alabama State University, reproduced by permission of Dr. Callie B. Warren, Chairperson. Photograph by Lucian Smith, Photographer, Alabama State University. Robert Baynes was a student artist at Alabama State University (class of 1981) when he painted this crucifixion. It is clear that Baynes has conceived a very American representation of Jesus, for it is impossible to determine the race of the figure on the cross. Jesus could be black, white, or even Oriental. He could be Mexican-American or Polish-American. It is appropriate that an American artist has painted this very American Jesus, suggesting in the visage the racial mosaic of the society. Two angels hover near the cross: one has caucasian features, while the other has an African face. Beside Jesus, one thief is black, and the other is white. The artist does not intend any statement about the "Good Thief" here but wishes to share his belief that Jesus died for the sins of all humanity. The mood of the picture is sad, dramatic, yet ultimately triumphant. The raised arms of the figure at the lower right of the cross, the pose of the angels, and even the uplifted palms of the suffering Jesus suggest this triumph.

Plate 6

The Light, by Ricky Nelson Callaway

Used by permission of the artist. Photograph by Lucian Smith, Photographer, Alabama State University. Ricky Callaway won national attention when he was still a student at Alabama State University (class of 1984). Although he does not use his art to preach an ideology, he has frequently found his images in his own background, Alabama's black society. His finest paintings have reflected life in the neighborhoods in which he has lived. He has been especially admired for his use of color and his ability to convey many moods through the interplay of light and shadow. But his themes are those of all serious artists, and he consciously seeks to leave his viewers with a sense of tranquillity. Above all, he wishes to communicate his vision—without esoteric quirks—to an audience of nonspecialists. At this point the serious artist becomes the popular artist. *The Light* presents a black Jesus, peaceful and triumphant even on the cross, dying for the sins of all humanity.

SELECTED BIBLIOGRAPHY
FOR FURTHER READINGS IN THE BIBLE
AND AMERICAN POPULAR CULTURE

Anderson, Robert, and Gail North. *Gospel Music Encyclopedia*. New York: Sterling, 1979.

Armstrong, Ben. *The Electric Church*. Nashville: Thomas Nelson, 1979.

Barrows, Cliff, ed. *Crusader Hymns and Hymn Stories*. Minneapolis: The Billy Graham Evangelistic Association, 1967.

Boles, John B. *The Great Revival 1787–1805: The Origins of the Southern Evangelical Mind*. Lexington: University Press of Kentucky, 1976.

Boles, John B. *Religion in Antebellum Kentucky*. Lexington: University Press of Kentucky, 1976.

Butler, Ivan. *Religion in the Cinema*. New York: A. S. Barnes, 1969.

Conway, Flo, and Jim Siegelman. *Snapping: America's Epidemic of Sudden Personality Change*. New York: Dell, 1978.

Cox, Harvey. *The Seduction of the Spirit: The Use and Misuse of People's Religion*. New York: Simon and Schuster, 1973.

Dickinson, Eleanor, and Barbara Benziger. *Revival*. New York: Harper & Row, 1974.

Doré, Gustave. *The Doré Bible Illustrations*. Introduction by Millicent Rose. New York: Dover Publications, 1974.

Dubuisson, Odile. *Children, Crayons and Christ: Understanding the Religious Art of Children*. Paramus, NJ: Newman Press, 1969.

Enroth, Ronald M., Edward E. Ericson, Jr., and C. Breckinridge Peters. *The Jesus People: Old-Time Religion in the Age of Aquarius*. Grand Rapids: Eerdmans, 1972.

Falwell, Jerry, with Ed Dobson and Ed Hindson. *The Fundamentalist Phenomenon: The Resurgence of Conservative Christianity*. Garden City: Doubleday, 1981.

Gallup, George, Jr., with William Proctor. *Adventures in Immortality: A Look Beyond the Threshold of Death*. New York: McGraw-Hill, 1982.

Goldman, Ronald. *Religious Thinking from Childhood to Adolescence*. New York: Seabury, 1968.

Hadden, Jeffrey K., and Charles E. Swann. *Prime Time Preachers: The Rising Power of Televangelism*. Introduction by T. George Harris. Reading, MA: Addison-Wesley, 1981.

Hamilton, Charles V. *The Black Preacher in America*. New York: William Morrow, 1972.

Hayes, John H. *Son of God to Super Star*. Nashville: Abingdon, 1976.

Kampf, Avram. *Contemporary Synagogue Art, Developments in the United States, 1954–1965*. New York: Union of American Hebrew Congregations, 1966.

Kelley, Dean M. *Why Conservative Churches are Growing*. New York: Harper & Row, 1972.

Marty, Martin E. *A Nation of Behavers*. Chicago: University of Chicago Press, 1976.

Marx, Herbert L., Jr., ed. *Religion in America*. New York: H. W. Wilson, 1977.

McInnes, V. Ambrose, O.P. *Taste and See, Louisiana Renaissance: Religion and the Arts*. New Orleans: V. Ambrose McInnis, Tulane University, 1977.

Menendez, Albert J. *Religion at the Polls*. Philadelphia: Westminster, 1977.

Meyer, Donald. *Positive Thinkers: Religion as Pop Psychology from Mary Baker Eddy to Oral Roberts*. New York: Pantheon Books, 1980.

Moore, Albert C. *Iconography of Religions, An Introduction*. Philadelphia: Fortress, 1977.

Morris, James. *The Preacher*. New York: St. Martin's Press, 1973.

Neuburg, Victor E. *Popular Literature, A History and Guide*. New York: Penguin Books, 1977.

Noonan, D. P. *The Passion of Fulton Sheen*. New York: Dodd, Mead, 1972.

Norton, Herman A. *Religion in Tennessee 1777–1945*, Knoxville: University of Tennessee Press, 1981.

Orr, J. Edwin. *The Inside Story of the Hollywood Christian Group*. Grand Rapids: Zondervan, 1955.

Owens, Virginia Stem. *The Total Image: Or, Selling Jesus in the Modern Age*. Grand Rapids: Eerdmans, 1980.

Quebedeaux, Richard. *By What Authority: The Rise of Personality Cults in American Christianity*. New York: Harper & Row, 1982.

Samarin, William J. *Tongues of Men and Angels: The Religious Language of Pentecostalism*. New York: Macmillan, 1972.

Schorsch, Anita, and Martin Grief. *The Morning Stars Sang: The Bible in Popular and Folk Art*. New York: Universe Books, 1978.

Sholes, Jerry. *Give Me That Prime Time Religion*. New York: Hawthorn Books, 1979.

Sire, James W. *Scripture Twisting: 20 Ways the Cults Misread the Bible*. Downers Grove, IL: InterVarsity Press, 1980.

Steinfels, Peter. *The Neoconservatives*. New York: Simon and Schuster, 1979.

Tamke, Susan A. *Make a Joyful Noise Unto the Lord: Hymns as a Reflection of Victorian Social Attitudes*. Athens: Ohio University Press, 1978.

Tangerman, E. J. *Carving Religious Motifs in Wood*. New York: Sterling, 1980.

Ward, Hiley H. *The Far-Out Saints of the Jesus Communes*. New York: Association Press, 1972.

Weisberger, Bernard A. *They Gathered at the River*. Boston: Little, Brown, 1958.

Whitman, Alan. *Christian Occasions*. New York: Doubleday, 1978.

Whittle, Donald. *Christianity and the Arts*. Philadelphia: Fortress, 1966.

Wills, Garry. *Bare Ruined Choirs: Doubt, Prophecy, and Radical Religion*. Garden City: Doubleday, 1972.

INDEX

Aaron, Paul, 212, 213
Abrahams, Roger, 89
Adams, Joey, 26, 29
Addie Pray, 137
Addison, Joseph, 38
Agnew, Spiro, 110
Alamo, Tony and Susan, 8, 130
Albert, Andreas, 212, 226–27
Alcoa Quartet, 89
"All in the Family," 30
Allen, Asa A., 105
Allen, Joseph, 45
Allen Quartette, 90
"Allen Revival Hour," 106
Altman, Mark, 214
Altman, Robert, 194
"Amazing Grace," 4
American Anglican Church, 6
American Civil Liberties Union, 3
American Weekly, 68
The Americanization of Dixie, 5
Anderson, Marian, 21
Andover Theological Seminary, 50
"Andy Capp," 36–37
Angels, 224–25
Angley, Ernest, 18, 121, 122, 123
Animals of the Bible, 165, 175, 176, 179
The Apostle, 54
d'Arc, Jeanne, 174
Armstrong, April Oursler, 65, 67
Armstrong, Ben, 7
Armstrong, Garner Ted, 105, 106
Arthur, Kay, 6
Arthur, Timothy Shay, 46
Asbury, Francis, 151
Asch, Sholem, 51, 53–54, 78
Asimov, Isaac, 176

Assemblies of God, 144
Association of Gospel Clowns of America, 8
Atkins, James, 89
Atlantic, 50
Auferstehung, 212–14, 226–27
Augustine, 134
Autry, Gene, 95
Ayer, William Ward, 106

Back to B.C., 34
Bailes Brothers, 98
Bailes, Walter, 98
Bakker, Jim, 8, 108, 114, 115, 121, 130, 133
Bakker, Tammy, 115, 117
The Ballad of the Flim-Flam Man, 137
Balsley, Phil, 99
Baptism in Kansas, 210
Baptists, 144
Barnhouse, Donald Grey, 106
Bates, David, 211
Baynes, Robert, 230–31
Baucom, Luther, 91
Beckett, St. Thomas á, 71
Behold the Man, 74
Benchley, Robert, 26, 28
Benet, Stephen Vincent, 137
Ben-Hur, A Tale of the Christ, 48, 56, 57, 59, 65
Bennins, Gero, 186
Benton, Thomas Hart, 210
Berelson, Howard, 176
Best sellers, 41–43
Bettelheim, Bruno, 180
Beyond the Gates, 50
"B-I-B-L-E," 96, 97

Bible
  and American popular culture,
    1–24
  and children's literature, 165–92
  and country music, 85–102
  and electronic church, 103–36
  favorite personalities of, 171–77
  and fiction, 41–84, 137–38
  and films, 13–15, 32
  and humor, 25–40
  and illustrations, 182
  as icon, 207
  merchandising, 137–65
  and musicals, 15–16
  parodies, 27–29
  and popular art, 193–233
  translations, 20, 95, 162
"Bible Belt," 1–5
"Bible Lessons," 98
"The Bible on the Table and the Flag
    Upon the Wall," 95
The Bible Salesman, 137
"The Bible's True," 94
Bierce, Ambrose, 39
The Big Fisherman, 58
Billboard, 95
Bishop, Jim, 64, 67–69
Black Heritage Bible, 20–21
Black religion, 20–22, 228–33
Blake, William, 39, 179
Blechman, R. O., 32
Bles, John B., 2, 3, 6
"Blessed Assurance," 4
Bliss, Phillips, 87
Blue Sky Boys, 97
The Blue Sky Boys and Wade Mainer,
    98
Bob Jones University, 15
Bode, Carl, 58
"Boner's Ark," 33, 38
Book of Common Prayer, 122, 171
Boone, Pat, 9, 75
"The Born Loser," 36
Boucher, Anthony, 74
Bouguereau, W. A., 198
Bradbury, Ray, 73
Bradford, Roark, 27
Brennan, Paul, 138

The Broadman Hymnal, 89
Brown's Ferry Four, 98
Brown, Joe David, 137
Brown, R. R., 106
Brown, Roger, 211
Brin, Ruth F., 183
Britt, Arthur L., 228–29
Brodsky, Beverly, 185
"Broom-Hilda," 36, 38
Brother Al, 105
"Brush the Dust from that Old Bible,"
    99
Bryan, William Jennings, 110
Bryant, Anita, 128
Bulwer-Lytton, Edward G., 62
Bunker, Archie, 3
Burns, George, 32
Burns, Jewell Tillman, 89
Burpo, C. W., 105, 118
Butler, Don, 5

Caldecott Medal, 165
Caldwell, Erskine, 59
Caldwell, Taylor, 44, 56, 60–64
Callaway, Ricky Nelson, 232–33
Calvary Episcopal Church, 105
Calvin, John, 151
Calvinism, 4, 50, 166–67, 194
"The Camp Meeting Hour," 108
Campbell, Alexander, 151
Camus, Albert, 20, 71
Candid Reminiscences, 52
Captain Kyd: Or the Wizard of the
    Sea, 46
Captain Stormfield's Visit to Heaven,
    50
Carnegie, Dale, 43
Carson, Johnny, 7, 18, 89, 114, 134
Carter, Jimmy, 5, 108, 109, 123
Carter, Wilf, 98
Cartwright, Peter, 151
Cash, Johnny, 14
Cassidy, David, 15
Catholics, 4, 16, 65–69, 166, 184, 205,
    216
Catholic World, 67
Cavanaugh, Arthur, 187
Cayce, Edgar, 62

Celebration in the Bedroom, 13
Cerf, Bennet, 26–27
Chassidism, 17
Chicago Sunday Tribune, 61
Child's Bible Reader, 167–69
A *Child's Prayer Book for the Holidays of Rosh Hoshanah and Yom Kippur*, 185
"The Chinese Situation," 28
Christ's Entry into Garland, Texas, 211
"Christ figures," 41–42
Christ in Gethsemane, 200–201
Christian Science, 17
Church of Jesus Christ of Latter-day Saints, 133, 194
Churches of Christ, 144
Civil War, 2
Clarke, Sir Kenneth, 19
Clement, Frank, 2
Clower, Jerry, 30
Clurman, Harold, 138
Coffin, William Sloane, 38
Colan, Gene, 37–38
Colson, Charles, 123
Comic strips, 32–39
Connelly, Mark, 27
Cooper, James Fenimore, 137
Copas, Cowboy, 96
Copeland Ministry, 8
Copping, Harold, 201–2
Cotton Patch Bible, 20
Coughlin, Charles E., 105
"Cowboy's Deck of Cards," 96
Critic, 50
Crouch, André, 10
Crouch, Jan, 124
Crouch, Pat, 126
Crouch, Paul, 122, 124
The Crown and the Cross, 60
Culpepper, O. B., 90
Currier, Nathaniel, 205, 223
Curry, John Steward, 210

Daily Guide to Miracles, 124
Dalhart, Vernon, 94
Dali, Salvador, 194, 210
Daughters of St. Paul, 183

Davis, Karl, 93, 98
Dawson, Virginia Douglas, 58
The Day Christ Died, 64–67, 69
The Day Christ Was Born, 64, 69
Day, Clarence, 25
Day, F. Holland, 205
"The Day of Doom," 166, 167
The Day Lincoln Was Shot, 67
Dealey, Ted, 27
Dear and Glorious Physician, 60–62
Death in the Afternoon, 28
"Death of God," 69–73
"Death in the Rumble Seat," 28
Death of a Salesman, 138
"The Death of Stephen Dowling Botts," 27
"The Deck of Cards," 95
Delmore Brothers, 98
De Mille, Cecil B., 14, 13, 41, 195, 197
Dennis and the Bible Kids: The Girls, 35
"Dennis the Menace," 35
Denton, Jeremiah, 2
Denver, John, 32
Detweiler, Robert, 64
DeVoto, Bernard, 57
DeWitt, Lew, 99
Dillow, Joseph C., 13
Disney, Walt, 197
Disraeli, Benjamin, 62
"D-I-V-O-R-C-E," 97
Donahue, Phil, 7, 114
"Doonesbury," 38
Doré, Gustave, 193–98
Dostoevsky, Feodor Mikhailovich, 71, 72
Douglas, Lloyd C., 42, 53, 56–58, 64, 66
Duran, Emile Auguste Carolus, 198
Durer, Albrecht, 196
"Dust on the Bible," 98, 100
Duvoisin, Roger, 173
Dyke, Henry van, 62
Dylan, Bob, 11

Early American Angel, 224–25
Eastern Orthodoxy, 17, 216
Eastwood, Clint, 205, 206

Ebony, 69
Edith the Good, 30
Edwards, Jonathan, 43
"Eek and Meek," 37
Egerton, John, 5
Eikerenkoetter, Frederick B., 105, 121
Einstein, Albert, 5
Eisenhower, Dwight D., 67
Electronic religion, 6–8, 104–36
Elfstrom, Robert, 14
Eliot, George, 62
Eliot, T. S., 28
Eminent Victorians, 28
An Encyclopedia of American Humor, 26
Encyclopedia of Humor, 26
l'Engle, Madeleine, 185
The Entry of Christ into Chicago in 1976, 211
Episcopal Church, 13, 16
Episcopalians, 4, 16, 45–47, 52–55, 70–71, 216
Eschatology, 130–32
Evergood, Philip, 210
Evolution, 94–95
Eyssen, Shirley van, 187–88

Faith healing, 17–18
Falwell, Jerry, 8, 108, 115, 118, 129, 130–33
"Family Bible," 99
Farmer, Philip José, 73
Faulkner, William, 26
Feitler, Bea, 184
Fellowship of Christian Magicians, 8
Feltman, Melbourne I., 138
Ferguson, Walter W., 175
Fiddler on the Roof, 31
"Fifty One Beers," 97
"Fireside Songs," 91
"Firing Line," 134
Firth and Hall, 86
Fisk Jubilee Singers, 21
Fiske, E. B., 72
Flack, Audrey, 211
The Flim-Flam Man and the Apprentice Grifter, 137
Flynt, Larry, 12

Ford, Gerald, 108
Foster, Hannah, 43
"Four Books in the Bible," 98
Freberg, Stan, 29
Fromm, Eric, 72
Fuller, Charles E., 106–7

The Galileans, 60
Gallup, George, 109
Gallup Polls, 1, 22
The Garden of Allah, 42
Gardner, Brother Dave, 30
Gardner, Erle Stanley, 43, 59
Garfield, James A., 49
The Gates Between, 50
The Gates Wide Open, 50
Gems No. 2, 50
"The Gentleman Soldier's Prayer Book," 96
Gerber, Steve, 37–38
Ghandi, Mahatma, 51
Gibbs, Wolcott, 28
Glossolalia, 16–17
Glosson, Lonnie, 98
Glynn, Elinor, 43
God, Man, and Archie Bunker, 30
Godspell, 16
The Golden Treasury of Prayers for Boys and Girls, 185
The Golden Turkey Award, 14
"Good Country People," 138
"Good News from the Vatican," 74
The Good Shepherd, 199–200
Gortner, Marjoe, 10
The Gospel According to Peanuts, 33
Gospel Praise, 89
The Gospel Road, 14
Grabianski, Janusz, 182, 187
Graham, Billy, 5, 66, 105, 107, 108, 118, 130–33
Grand Ole Opry, 2, 14, 88, 91, 95, 98
Grandpa Jones, 98
Graves, J. R., 139
Gray, Claude, 99
The Greatest Faith Ever Known, 65
The Greatest Story Ever Told, 14, 64–67
El Greco, Domenicos, 182, 210, 214

The Green Pastures, 27, 31
Gregori, 183
Greenfeld, Howard, 184
Griffin, Merv, 7
Grimm Brothers, 180
Guthrie, Woody, 11
Gutman, Nachum, 185

Hackett, Alice P., 41
Hadden, Jerome, 111
Hagin, Kenneth, 127
Haliburton, Thomas Chandler, 137
Halley's Bible Handbook, 118
Hamilton, William, 71–72
Hargis, Billy James, 105
Harris, Joel Chandler, 35
Harris, Phil, 96
Hart, James D., 41, 50
Hart, Johnny, 34
Haughton, Rosemary, 184, 185
"Have a Little Faith," 99
Hawthorne, Nathaniel, 44
Hayes, Roland, 21
Hebrew Christians, 8
Hechtkopf, H., 183
"Hee-Haw," 122
Heldebrand, E. T., 89
Heller, Joseph, 71
Hemingway, Ernest, 28
Heston, Charlton, 195, 216
"Hillbilly Deck of Cards," 96
History of American Literature 1607–1765, 166
Hix, Larkin, 212
Hoffman, Oswald, 107
Hoffman, Randy, 214
Hofmann, Johann Heinrich, 200–201, 205
Holy Bible—Old Testament (recording), 99
Holy Bible—New Testament (recording), 99
Hoover, J. Edgar, 65
The Hope of the World, 201–2
Hopkins, Doc, 93
"Hour of Power," 108, 133
How to be Happy in the Non-Electric Church, 112

Horn, Geoffrey, 187
How Shall We Then Live?, 20
"Howard the Duck," 37
Hudson, Virginia Cary, 170–71
Humbard, Rex, 7, 108, 118, 119, 120, 123, 132
Hunt, Holman, 199, 205
Hunter, Clementine, 206
Hunter, Jeffrey, 14
Husky, Ferlin, 96
Hustler, 12
Hutchinson, J. J., 87
Hutchison Family, 86, 90
Hyde, Ralph, 4

"I'm F-R-E-E from S-I-N," 96
"I'm S-A-V-E-D," 96
"I'm Using My Bible as a Roadmap," 97, 100
"I Believe This Dear Old Bible," 93
"I Believe that Good Old Bible," 93
I, Judas, 62–64
In the Beginning, A New Interpretation of the Old Testament, 187–88
Inge, W. R., 25
Ingraham, Joseph Holt, 45–48, 54, 60
"In the Garden," 4
Inherit the Wind, 110
Ionesco, Eugéne, 71
Irving, Washington, 137
Israeli, Exo, 185
Ives, James Merritt, 205

Jackson, Mahalia, 10
Jagger, Mick, 10, 15
Jensh, Barbara L., 176
Jesus
  in art, 199–202, 204–7, 210–14, 217, 223, 226, 233
  in children's books, 167, 177–79
  in film, 13–15
  in fiction, 41–78
Jesus Christs, 71–73
Jesus Christ Superstar, 15, 16, 31, 38
Jesus on Mars, 73
Jewish faith, 6, 53–54, 166, 177–78, 183, 185, 189, 216

Jewison, Norman, 15
Jews for Jesus, 6
Johnny Got His Gun, 14
Johns Hopkins Hospital, 59
Johnson, Merle Allison, 111–12
Jones, Clarence W., 106
Jones, Jessie and Elizabeth Orton, 179
Jones, Sam P., 88
Jonestown, 18
Joplin, Janis, 12
Judas, My Brother, 69–71
Julian: Or, Scenes in Judea, 44–45
Jung, Carl, 51
The Jungle, 51

Karl and Harty, 93, 96, 97
Kartsonakis, Dino, 10
Kazantzakis, Nikos, 71
Kazin, Alfred, 53
Kelly, Walt, 35, 37
Kennedy, John F., 110
Kennedy, Robert, 110
Ketchum, Hank, 35
Kilworth, Garry, 74
Kincaid, Bradley, 99
Kinchlow, Ben, 127
King James Version, Holy Bible, 25, 26, 27, 29, 95, 122, 145, 175, 179
The King of Kings, 13, 14
King, Martin Luther, Jr., 21, 110
Kingsmill, Hugh, 28
Kirkpatrick, William J., 89
Klausner, Abraham, 185
Kolleck, Teddy, 186
Krishna, 18
Kuhlman, Kathryn, 17, 105, 106
Kurelek, William, 186
Kuseten, Isemhild, 186

Ladder of Angels, 185
Lafitte, the Pirate of the Gulf, 46
Landelle, Charles, 198
Langguth, A. J., 71–73, 75
The Last Supper, 194–95, 201
The Late, Great Planet Earth, 130
Lathrop, Dorothy P., 165, 175, 179
Lauder, Sir Harry, 26
Lawrence, D. H., 72

Lazarus, Mel, 36
Leading Light, 91
Lear, Norman, 30
Leggett, Craig, 35
Lennon, John, 15
Lenski, Lois, 173
Leo XIII, Pope, 49
"Let's Go Back to the Bible," 98
"Let's Go to Golgotha," 74
Lewis, C. S., 19, 73, 74, 122
Lewis, Jerry, 116
Liberty Baptist College, 115, 129
Liebman, Joshua, 66, 75
The Life of Brian, 32
"Life's Railway to Heaven," 88
The Light, 232–33
The Light of the World, 199
Lindsay, John, 15
Lindsey, Hal, 130, 131
Liptzin, Sol, 53
Living Animals of the Bible, 175
Lloyd, James, 67
Long, W. P., 91
Los Angeles *Times*, 140
Luther, Martin, 103, 134, 183
"The Lutheran Hour," 106
Lutherans, 17, 56, 216

Macon, Uncle Dave, 94, 95
Maier, Walter A., 106
Malcolm, Donald, 68
"Mama's Bible," 91
"The Man," 73
The Man Born to be King, 76
The Man Who Dared to be God, 54–55
Mann, Thomas, 51
Mansfield, Jayne, 68
Manson, Charles, 15, 125
Marie Madeleine, 198
Marty, Martin, 111
"Married by the Bible, Divorced by the Law," 98
Marsh, Spencer, 30
Marshall, Catherine, 75
Martindale, Wink, 96
Mary, 54

MASH, 194
Master of the Magicians, 50
Masters Family, 95
Masters, Johnny, 95
Mater Dolorosa of the Seven Sorrows,
    223
Mather, Cotton, 166
McCann, Hazel, 58
McCravy, Frank and James, 91
Macdonald, Dwight, 28
McGhee, John, 90
MacLeod, Odeli, 98
Medved, Harry and Michael, 14
Mencken, H. L., 3, 4, 52, 150
The Mental Radio, 51
Methodists, 17, 144
Michelangelo Buonarroti, 20, 195, 204,
    216
Mid-American Bible Company, 138
Miller, Arthur, 138
Miyoski, Sekiya, 176
"Momma," 36
Monroe, Bill, 97
Moody, Dwight, 87
Monty Python, 32
de Monvel, Boutet, 173
Moody Bible Institute, 105
Moody, Ruby, 91
Moorecock, Michael, 74
Moral Majority, 129
Morley, Christopher, 137
Morris, George P., 87
Morris, Mrs. W. T., 90
Morrison, Toni, 21
Moses
    in art, 195, 203–4
    in children's books, 166, 172
    in films, 41
    and satire, 29, 31–32
"Mother's Bible," 90–92, 97, 100
"Mother's Book," 90
"Mother's Torn and Faded Bible," 91
Mott, Frank Luther, 41, 42
Mountbatten, Lord Louis, 28
Mull, J. Bazzell, 91
"My Mother's Bible," 86–89
"My Mother's Old Bible is True," 91
Myers, Paul, 106

Myers, Russell, 36
Myrick, David, 95

Nation, 50
The Nazarene, 53–54
Neeley, Ted, 15
Nelson, Willie, 99
New Gospel Voices, 90
The New Lazarus, 210
New Republic, 68, 71
A New Song, 9
Newsweek, 15
New York Times, 68
New York Times Book Review, 72
Niebuhr, Reinhold, 68
Nietzsche, Friedrich, 71
Nixon, Richard, 110
A Northern Nativity, 186
Norwood, Robert, 54–56

Oberamagau Passion Play, 200
O'Brien, John A., 65
O'Connor, Flannery, 138
O'Day, Molly, 98
Oh God!, 32
Oh Ye Jigs and Juleps, 170–71
"Old Familiar Tunes," 89
"Old Fashioned Revival Hour," 107
"Old-Time Gospel Hour," 108
"Old Time Power," 88, 89
"The Old Time Religion," 88
The Oldest Story in the World, 176
Ol' Man Adam and His Chillun, 27
Omarr, Sydney, 62
Oral Roberts University, 116
Our Lady, 52
Our Recorded Songs Number 3, 91
Oursler, Fulton, 61, 64–67
Out of the Silent Planet, 73
Owen, Guy, 137
Ozark Folksongs, 93

"PTL Club," 10, 108, 114, 115, 128
Paramount Quartet, 89
Parnassus on Wheels, 137
*Parodies—An Anthology from Chau-
    cer to Beerbohm, and After*, 28
Pascal, Blaise, 71
The Passover Plot, 70

Paul and the World's Most Famous Letters, 184

Peale, Norman Vincent, 61, 65, 66, 75, 165, 182, 187

"Peanuts," 33

Pensees, 71

Pentecostals, 16–17

Perrault, Charles, 180, 181

A Personal Jesus, 52

Petersham, Maud and Mishka, 184

Phelps, Elizabeth Stuart, 50

Piatti, Celestino, 169

Picasso, Pablo, 214

Pickett, L. L., 90

Pictures and Rhymes to Bring Little Ones Happy Times, 169–70

Pilcher, Diana, 121

Pius XII, Pope, 67

Plato, 43

Plockhorst, Bernhard, 199–200, 205

"Pogo," 35, 37

Popular Art, identifying features, 207–10

Popular Culture, identifying features, 1

Porges, Arthur, 74

"Praying Hands," 196

Presbyterians, 59, 144

Presley, Elvis, 10, 12

Presley, Vernon, 12

Prewitt, Cheryl, 127

The Prince of the House of David: Or, Three Years in the Holy City, 46–48, 54

The Profits of Religion, 52

Puritan suspicion of literature, 43–44

Rabbit's Wedding, 176

Rader, Paul, 105

Radio Evangelism, 104–7

Randolph, Vance, 93

Rapture, 226–27, 212–13

Rather, Dan, 127

Ray, Nicholas, 14

"Read the Bible," 96

"Read Romans Ten and Nine," 98

The Reader's Digest, 64, 65, 66

Reback, Marcus, 61, 62

Rector, Johnny, 98

"The Red Deck of Cards," 96

Red River Dave, 96

Reichart, Siegfried, 210

Reid, Don and Harold, 99, 100

Rembrandt van Rijn, 182, 202

Reno, Don, 92, 97, 100

Reno and Smiley, 97

"The Rescuer," 74

The Resurrection, Cookham, 212

Revised Standard Version, Holy Bible, 29

Revius, Jacobus, 174

Richardson, Samuel, 45

Riddle, Almeda, 89

Ritter, Tex, 96

Riverside Presbyterian Church, 59

The Road to Bithynia, 59

The Robe, 56–58, 65

Roberts, Oral, 10, 17, 105, 107, 108, 114, 115, 116, 118, 124, 126, 127, 128, 130, 133

Roberts, Richard, 115, 116, 118, 119

Robertson, Pat, 108, 114, 115, 116, 129

Robison, Carson, 94

Robison, James, 115, 129

Rogers, Dale Evans, 61, 75

"Rooftop O'Toole," 37

Rouault, Georges, 210

Rubinstein, Arthur, 10

Russell, Bertrand, 51

Russell, Henry, 87

Ryan, Tom K., 35

Ryman, Tom, 88

Sacred Heart Devotion, 223

St. Bartholomew's Episcopal Church, 54

St. John the Divine, Cathedral of, 185

St. Peter in Chains, Church of, 195

Salvadori, Henry, 49

Sandys, Frederick, 198

Sankey, Ira D., 87, 88

Sansom, Art, 36

Sartre, Jean Paul, 20

de Saussure, Brother Eric, 182

Save America to Save the World, 129

Savonarola, Girolano, 62

Sayers, Dorothy L., 76–77

Schaeffer, Francis A., 19–20
Schneider, Howie, 37
Schonfield, Hugh J., 70
School Library Journal, 178
Schuller, Robert, 112, 115, 116, 118, 119, 122, 125, 133, 198
Schultz, Charles, 33
Science Fiction, 73–74
Scientology, 18
Scopes, John T., 93, 94, 110
Scull, W. E., 168
Sears-Roebuck, 49
The Secret of the Cells, 46
"Seven Beers with the Wrong Woman," 97
"700 Club," 10, 108, 114, 115–16, 124, 127
Severeid, Eric, 110
Seweil, E. G., 89
Sex for Christians, 13
Shea, George Beverly, 10
Shedd, Charles and Martha, 13
Sheen, Fulton J., 61, 66, 75
The Sheik, 42
Short, Robert L., 33
Shore, Dinah, 114
Showalter, A. J., 89
Silverberg, Robert, 74
"Simple Gifts," 32
"Since I've Used My Bible for a Road-map," 97
Sinclair, Upton, 51–53, 54, 60, 75
Singer, Isaac Bashevis, 53, 181
"Sixty Minutes," 134
The Skin of Our Teeth, 31
Slaughter, Frank G., 44, 56, 59–61, 64
Small Rain, 179
Smede, Lewis B., 13
Smiley, Red, 92
Smith, E. Boyd, 173–74
Snow, Hank, 91, 98
Snyder, Tom, 7
"The Soldier's Bible," 96
Solomon on Sex, 13
Song and Story, 89
The Southwestern Company, 20, 139–63, 167
Sovine, Red, 96

Spencer, Stanley, 212
Spelling songs, 96–97
Spier, Peter, 165, 174
Springfield Republican, 53
Stamps, Frank, 91
Stamps-Baxter, 90, 91
Starns, Neva, 98
Statler Brothers, 99, 100
Stearn, Jess, 62–64
Stevens, Brenda, 124
Stevens, George, 14
Stewart, Arvis, 187
Stone, Alma, 137
Stoppard, Tom, 71
Story, Carl, 98
The Story of Esther, 183
The Story of Noah's Ark, 173–74
The Story of Pocahontas and Captain John Smith, 174
Stowe, Harriet Beecher, 50, 61
Strachey, Lytton, 28
Sutherland, Donald, 14
Swagerty, Mr. and Mrs. J. Douglas, 90
Swaggart, Donnie, 115
Swaggart, Jimmy, 108, 115, 117, 122, 124, 125
von Sydow, Max, 14

Tagore, Rabindranath, 51
Taizé Picture Bible, 182, 187
Tales of Uncle Remus, 35
Tame, LaVerne, 90
Taylor, Hartford, 93
"Tears in my Beer," 97
The Ten Commandments, 195
Ten Nights in a Bar-Room, 46
The Tennessee Baptist, 139
Tennyson, Alfred Lord, 21
Teresa, Mother, 134
The Terminal Generation, 130
"There's a Page in the Bible," 98
They Call Me Carpenter, 52–53
"They've Made a New Bible," 95
Thomas Nelson Company, 139
Thompson, Dwight, 117, 119, 126, 131
Three Weeks, 42
Tillman, Charlie, 87, 88, 89, 90
Time, 14

Tin Pan Alley, 86
Tobacco Road, 31, 150
The Tobacco Tags, 91
Tolkien, J. R. R., 73
Trinity Broadcasting Network, 131
Tripp, Laverne, 124
Trudeau, Gary, 38
Truehitt, Pee Wee, 98
"Tumbleweeds," 35
Turner, Philip, 182, 187
Twain, Mark, 27, 39, 50
Tyler, Moses Coit, 166
Tyler, T. Texas, 95, 96
Typology, 178, 203–10

Uncle Tom's Cabin, 50
Unification Church, 18
Unitarians, 44–45
University of Notre Dame, 65
Up the Line, 74
Upon This Rock, 60
The Upper Room, 195
Ussher, Bishop James, 142
Vanderbilt, Amy, 43
Vatican II, 4, 8, 184
Vaughan, James D., 90
Vereen, Ben, 15
The Very First Story Ever Told, 177
Vidal, Gore, 11
"The Viet Nam Deck of Cards," 96
View of Toledo, 201
da Vinci, Leonardo, 194, 201

Wagenknecht, Edward, 61
Wallace, George, 5
Wallace, Lew, 48–49, 57, 60
Wally Fowler's Oak Ridge Quartet, 95
Ward, Elizabeth Stuart Phelps, 50–51, 61, 76
Ward, Herbert D., 50
Ware, William, 44–45, 60

Warner, H. B., 13, 14
Warshaw, Thayer S., 189
Washburn College Bible, 162
Weil, Lisl, 177
Weil, Shraga, 185
Welling, Frank, 90
Wesley, John, 151, 179
"What a Friend We Have in Jesus," 88
What Happened?, 10
Wheat Street Female Quartet, 89
"When I Get to the End of the Way," 88
"When I Laid My Bible Down," 97
Whitehead, A. N., 39
The Wicked City, 181
Wigglesworth, Michael, 166
Wilder, Thornton, 31
Wildsmith, Brian, 168, 182, 187
Wilkin, Eloise, 185
Wilkin, Esther, 185
Williams, Garth, 176
Williams, M. B., 88
Wilson, Betty Douglas, 58
Wilson, Flip, 30
Wilson, Tom, 36
Within the Gates, 50
Women of the Bible, 183–84
Wood, George, 50
"Woodman, Spare That Tree," 87
World Convention of Christian Workers, 87
Wynette, Tammy, 97

Yerby, Frank, 42, 69–71, 75, 77, 78
Yonge, Charlotte M., 168
Young, Brigham, 43
Young People's Hymnal No. 2, 89
Youngman, Henny, 29

"Ziggy," 36
"Zoonies," 35

DATE DUE

DEMCO 38-297